SOUL SNATCHERS:

The Mechanics of Cults

Also by Jean-Marie Abgrall

Les Charlatans de la santé
Paris: Payot, 1998
English translation: *Medical Charlatans,*
due in 2000 from Algora Publishing

Les Sectes de l'apocalypse : gourous de l'an 2000
Paris: Calmann Lévy, 1999

SOUL SNATCHERS

The Mechanics of Cults

Jean-Marie Abgrall

Translated by Alice Seberry

Algora Publishing
New York

Algora Publishing, New York
© 2000 by Algora Publishing
All rights reserved. Published 2000
Printed in the United States of America
ISBN: 1-892941-04-X
Editors@algora.com

Originally published as *La mécanique des sectes,* © Éditions
Payot & Rivages, 1996.

Library.of Congress Cataloging-in-Publication Data 99-42485

Abgrall, Jean-Marie.
   [Mécanique des sectes. English]
   Soul Snatchers: The Mechanics of Cults / Jean-Marie Abgrall:
   translated by Alice Seberry.
      p. cm.
   Includes bibliographical references.
   ISBN 1-892941-04-X (alk. paper)
    1. Cults—Psychology. 2. Sects—Psychology. I. Title.
BP603.A3613 1999
291.9—dc21   99-42485

Algora Publishing
wishes to express its appreciation
for the assistance given by
the Government of France
through the Ministry of Culture
in support of the preparation of this translation

New York
www.algora.com

TABLE OF CONTENTS

suasion, 136.

7. CONDITIONING 127

8. PSYCHIC CONDITIONING 145

9. PHYSICAL CONDITIONING 185

INDIVIDUAL PATHOLOGIES

Depressive Phenomena, 274.—Generalized Anxiety and Atypical Anxiety Disorders, 274.—Neurotic Behavior, 277. —Psychotic Disorders, 279.

13. TREATING THE PATHOLOGIES

Prevention, 283.—Tracking, 287.— "Extracting" from the Cult, 289. — Therapy, 292. — The Emergency and Recovery Phases, 292.—Treating the State of Depression, 293.—Treating the Psychotic States, 294.—Treating the Neurotic States, 295.—Looking Back at the Manipulation, 296.—Getting Information, 298.—Synthesizing the Information, 272. — Interpreting the Information, 300.—Distinguishing the Pathologies, 301.—Reintegrating Reality, 302.—Regaining Autonomy of Thought and Direct Experience of Emotions, 304. — Reintegrating the Cult Member into Society, 305.—Problems the Family Encounters, 308.

FOREWORD

The 1990's witnessed a spectacular and terrifying resurgence of cults.

On March 20, 1995, ten people died and four thousand others required emergency treatment after a Sarin gas attack in a Tokyo subway. Investigations immediately confirmed that the Aum Shinri-kyo cult was involved. Their guru, Shoko Asahara, instigated the incident by a radio broadcast from Vladivostok, using his own radio facilities. In that picturesque Russian city he has several thousand followers, in addition to the five thousand listed in Japan. In his radio speech, Shoko Asahara called upon the faithful to commit collective suicide. "You needn't grieve, as death approaches," he said. The poison gas attack is merely a prelude to the "higher level of bliss" recommended by the guru.

Founded in the late Eighties, this cult claims to have a following in Japan of ten thousand, rather than the five thousand estimated by others. It has a strong presence in Russia, where it has benefited from connections with the upper echelons of the State and Army. It is also suspected of having close connections with the Japanese Yakusa and the Russian Mafia. Its guru, who says he found enlightenment during his stay in India, venerates Shiva, the Hindu God of destruction. He asserted that a holocaust would devastate the Earth in 1997. The cult seems to anticipate a time of cataclysm. In its various centers, particularly in the Kami-kuishiki Monastery close to Mount Fuji, investigators seized tons of chemicals that the sect intended to use in manufacturing poisonous gases. In addition, an attack helicopter and weapons of Russian origin were seized.

In December 1995, not far from the village of St. Pierre de Cheren-nes, the police discovered sixteen bodies burnt to ashes, laid out in an arrangement that suggested a symbolic reference to the sun. This discovery revealed to the world that the Order of the Solar Temple, believed to be defunct since October 1994, was still performing the dance of death that it had begun in Switzerland and Canada: in October 1994, several groups of similarly incinerated corpses had been found in burnt buildings occupied by the Order of the Solar Temple. In this case as well, collective death had been recommended by the cult for several years as the path leading to supreme knowledge.

In April 1993, the sect of Mount Carmel, near Waco, Texas, made headlines. Gathering around their guru David Koresh, the Davidians, "Marines of the Lord," barricaded themselves inside their temple. They were armed to the teeth and succeeded in defying the FBI for seven long weeks. The toll: eighty-six dead, men, women and children — just four days after the Master had proclaimed that an avenging God would punish his enemies.

In the prior twenty years there were many other incidents, equally horrible. In 1969, the film world was shocked by the death of the famous actress Sharon Tate. She was brutally murdered in an appalling attack led by Charles Manson, the self-styled Prophet of Satan and disciple of Szandor Vey, author of a cult handbook, *The Satanic Bible*.

November, 1974: the Los Angeles police attacked the headquarters of Donald De Freeze's Symbionese Liberation Front, attempting to release hostages. Six people were killed.

November 1978: television viewers the world over were horrified by images of carnage in Guyana. 931 people died by collective poisoning, not necessarily voluntary, under the direction of their guru, Jim Jones, a former Protestant pastor who proclaimed that he was God.

May 13, 1985: the police attacked an "anti-technology" group called "Move." Eleven people were killed and the property damage was estimated at ten million dollars.

1986: seven young women followers of the Japanese cult Michi No Tomo Kyokai ("Church of the Friends of the Truth") committed suicide after the death of their female guru.

Closer to home, in Missouri, on January 5,1990, seven former disciples of Jeffery Lundgren, Pastor of the Church of Latter Day Saints, were arrested for the murder of five people in connection with human sacrifice during the sect's rituals.

August 1992: Three federal agents were murdered by Randy Weavers, defender of the "Aryan race" and herald of the end of the world; two other people were killed in the course of an eleven day siege of his hideout in Idaho.

These events all have something in common. In every case, individuals who are cut off from the outside world are convinced that the Apocalypse is coming. Gathering around a charismatic but dubious figure to whom they have devoted their lives, they come to believe they are a "chosen" people — while developing a paranoia and a group sense of megalomania that lead them to deny both reality and the laws of society. Admittedly, not all sects come to such a dramatic end. Many go on their merry way, weaving their webs, consolidating their networks, their power and their wealth. Slave-holders by nature, they scorn the most elementary human rights.

Having run into this breed repeatedly, I wanted to see what makes them tick. This book is a clinical analysis of the cult phenomenon. It is like Ariadne's thread, intended for those who need to deal with cult manipulation. I have set myself three goals: to examine cult psychodynamics; to describe some of the elements of this specific psychopathology; and to penetrate the fog of obscurity that surrounds it. This book also attempts to be a reference guide for those who encounter cults in their family, their workplace, or society, and who do not know how to handle the situation.

I wanted to observe the minutest detail, down to the merest technicality. However, I also included some of the raw material found in sectarian writings and practices, without which any interpretation would be invalid. I hope my readers will be able, directly or by analogy, to arrive at their own answers to the questions raised about the various individual cults studied in these pages.

To conduct such a study is difficult, as the very meanings of the words "cult" and "sect" are not clear. The confusion surrounding the phenomenon is based in this lack of any precise definition. There is no legal, sociological, criminological or, unfortunately, psychiatric definition of these words. To discuss sectarian manipulation, it is necessary to define the framework of the observation. Cults and sects derive their strength from the legal right of religious freedom and, even more, from the legal right of freedom of thought. If the borderline between fundamentalism and sectarianism is difficult to establish, if the doctrines of certain so called "churches" are suspect; the real problem lies not in the intentions but the consequences. The person entering a sect is no longer free to act. He is continuously involved in an ever-spiraling dependence on the organization, which controls him completely. I therefore choose the framework of criminology and medical-legal psychiatry, although at times, due to the uniqueness of the subject, I will use a vocabulary found more often in esoteric or initiatory societies than in the Faculty of Medicine or Sociology. In my opinion, the criminal character of cults lies within the scope of "crimes and offences against private individuals," as defined in Act II of the [French] Penal Code.

Cults have existed since dawn of human existence, and their history gives some elementary answers as to how they work. However, today we are witnessing an absolutely unprecedented resurgence of mysticism. Malraux was first to announce this revival. In fact, the bankruptcy of the great ideological systems and the media explosion have given rise to these groups' renewed activity. Indeed, modern man's concerns are addressed far better and today's technologies are exploited more fully by these groups than by traditional religions.

A "follower" is a person who weds himself to the doctrines of the cult, is effectively submissive to the guru and gradually cuts himself from the rest of the world. The "creation of dependency" requires a specific sociological organization with a set of rules that lead to the phenomena of regression and of identity transfer, which combine to dissolve the individual into the group. Cults are microcosms having their own laws of operation and their own organization, language, and code, all of which combine to establish a unique dynamics. The interface between the cult microcosm and the social macrocosm is mental manipulation, which utilizes the latest methods and techniques of persuasion, communication and marketing. If the feeling of self-fulfillment, even ecstasy, is the alleged goal of this manipulation, the true result is the creation of individual and community pathologies that require specific forms of therapy.

Like drug addiction, the cult phenomenon touches every social stratum and plants its roots deep in the inner workings of the individual. It is hard to prevent, since it offers Utopia in place of social reality. The tools available to those fighting against cults are not yet well-suited to effectively combat their criminal character. May this book shed some new light on hitherto unanswered questions.

1.

CULTS AND MENTAL MANIPULATION

Sects and Errors are synonymous. If you are a peripatetic and I am a Platonist, then we are both wrong, for you combat Plato only because his illusions offend you, and I dislike Aristotle only because it seems to me that he doesn't know what he's talking about.

Voltaire, *Philosophical Dictionary*

"He Who Has Attained the Goal"

Originally, the word "sect" indicated a small group that wanted to secede from its social origins, or the disciples of a heretical Master.[1] However, its meaning does not end there; it covers a wide range of realities. In this maze, etymology leaves faint tracks. The word "sect" comes from the Latin "sequi," "to follow." The disciple of a sect follows a path in order to become an adept, someone who has achieved the goal (*adeptus*: having attained). He "follows" a Master; and at the same time he cuts himself off from the rest of humanity and becomes a "sectarian," or a person who is isolated.

Sects are not a new phenomenon. Plato and Aristotle had their devoted followers who clashed in philosophical duels. Jesus of Nazareth was an initiate of a sect, the Essenes.

It is a common error to confuse a sect with a secret or initiatory organization, whether involuntarily or in connection with an ecclesiastical or dogmatic choice. However, no common point exists between Scientology, Freemasonry, the (Chinese) Triad, Soka Gakkai, alchemy, White

Fraternity, or the New Acropolis. Sects tend to exploit the voluntary confusion that comes with naïvety. When accused of being charlatans, sects take advantage of people's willful naïvety. They go through the roof if they are compared to the Triad (a true Chinese Mafia); they plead a vague relationship with Freemasonry, which is generally respected (and, for the most part, respectable — save for the hazards of Lodge P2).

Many sects and cults claim that they are legitimate churches, which adds to the complexity of the problem. True, sects are scarcely defined outside of the theological sphere. This confusion arises from the peculiar history of the sociology of sects. Max Weber was the first to define the sect as something in opposition to the Church. Thereafter, Troeltsch, Niebuhr and Wach made efforts to refine the definition, but they did manage to break the Manichean dichotomy that is manifest in the Church/sect definition.

Cults are constantly playing on this ambiguity. They present themselves as a new religious movement, and reduce the level of the debate to a single dimension, religious freedom. French society has been secularity since 1905 (the law of separation of Church and State), proclaiming that the State shall not intrude into the realm of faith; however, the only people who have really looked into sects are representatives of the Churches, and a few academic who are convinced of the religiosity of the cult phenomenon.

Cults understand perfectly well that their interest lies in maintaining this confusion. They pay for some of their official endorsements and they discretely encourage university or public studies relating to new religious movements. In this they are abetted by certain old religious groups that would like to re-open the question of the lay society and who, to that end, push for the acceptance of some of their cult-like offshoots as independent religious movements.

However, the mosaic of cults that we see today is spreading the word about topics quite unrelated to religion. Gnostic movements predominate in Europe and pseudo-science feeds numerous ideologies. The notions of past lives, extraterrestrial civilizations, extra-sensory powers and so on rarely tie in with religious subtexts; rather, they belong to the realm of irrational thinking.

Thus, it is a fundamental requirement that we define this phenomenon within a framework that excludes religion as a frame of reference. Some elements of the definition must be borrowed from criminology, and ethno-psychiatry which brings in laic ethical terms. Unless we postulate this secularity, we will only engender confusion between religious or philosophical minorities and manipulative cult structures. Furthermore, we must abjure any value judgments as to the mystical or mythical content of the doctrine, which in these cults merely serves as the social alibi for a phenomenon whose practices are entirely asocial and, in some cases, antisocial.

Whereas religion is a phenomenon that coexists with society as a whole, the cult represents the opposite — it is a parasite on society. Certain groups may indeed be considered cult, although their message is in line with traditional religion. We must analyze their structures and their modes of operation. Then, while avoiding a semantic debate, we must distinguish the concept of the cult and the coercive cult.

A cult may be more- or less-highly developed; it is a group gathered around a leader or an ideology, religious or non-religious. It functions according to a secret method that is closed to outsiders, but the free will and the identity of the follower is left intact. Coercive cults, which we will call "CC's" for convenience, are more constraining and result in a loss of freedom on the part of followers. The boundary between the two is elusive, since the survival of any cult depends on strict discipline; the evolution toward coercion is ineluctable. And the key tool of coercion is mind control, on which cults have no monopoly: marketing and politics, for example, are rife with examples of mental manipulation. Furthermore, within normal religious or political movements, truly coercive organizations may exist that deserve the label of "cult."

Sects, Cults and Religions

Some religions and some political movements practice a kind of veneration of the leader. However, the ultimate goal is (generally) neither self-enrichment, nor mastery over other people. The "spiritual leader" is only a tool of the political or religious ideology, the instrument of a plan that can transcend the person himself. If he enjoys a special status, then it is merely in recognition of his abilities and does not confer on him a superhuman quality.

Some religions ascribe to their leaders a divine power, the best-known example being the Dalai Lama. In this case, there are no secret practices (except for certain rituals reserved for senior religious monks) much less mental handling of the followers, if one discounts the large crowds at festivals and public events. Religion presupposes freedom of thought without physical or mental constraint. In most cases, Churches aspire to be an integral part of society, even to be a dominant element (as in any State religion). If there are occasional constraints, for instance during initiatory rites, they are consciously accepted by everyone in the society. By contrast, the sect (and the cult) is defined in terms of a countervailing power, of opposition to the usual community models. The sect favors a separation from the community. Here, the rituals that cause social constraints are meant to exclude the member of the sect from the community and not to integrate him with it. When a religious practice relies on constraints, when it preaches isolation from the general cultural context, it becomes marginalized, it creates a neo-Church, an apostasy or a deviant group: a cult.

In reality, no practice is truly religious if it does not respect the legal context of the society in which it operates. Any practice that sets a group outside of the law can be the first step down a slippery slope toward an exclusionary cult-like dynamics.

Initiatory Secret Societies

Cults can sometimes be confused with secret initiatory societies, but they are organized differently. Secret societies of the traditional initiatory type are usually quite flexible. Their management may be collegial or solitary, but the leader (chief, priest, etc.) is elected by the ensemble. If he is self-appointed, he can be deposed and replaced. In addition, each member takes part in general planning; no one is manipulated, no one is manipulating — there is no manipulation.

Persuasion and Marketing

The last type of dynamics that we should exclude from our field of study is that of politics and marketing. Although manipulation is rampant in these fields, the acknowledged goal of profit and power is so obvious and the support base so widespread and fluid, the projection throughout society so broad, that it surpasses the concept of sectarianism. With one caveat: it sometimes happens that the group's dynamics turn coercive, as in the case of Lodge P2 (the initiatory society that devolved into criminal activity) and Amway[2] (the door-to-door sales organization that tends more and more toward cult-like activity) and, more recently, various pyramid marketing organizations.

Subjugation and Dependence

Drug addiction and cult membership are striking in their similarities. As a drug addict is dependent on legal or illegal drugs, the follower is dependent on a system of thought propagated by the sect. Drug addiction is defined by WHO as having three components: habitual use, dependence, and ever-increasing doses.

Addiction is defined as the habitual consumption of a product. In the case of the initiate, there is a progressive use of rituals and a way of using language that gradually become habit-forming. As with drugs, the teachings of the sect are administered bit-by-bit so that the initiate does not become overwhelmed and reject it (*cf.* "overdosing" which, in this context, would refer to a sudden awareness of the risks being taken). Each stage in assimilating the doctrines corresponds to a step towards dependence, when the natural defenses will be submerged under the parasitic thought processes.

Dependence, the second stage in this process of submission, consists in the progressive destruction of the subject's usual frame of reference. This allows for a substitute set of norms to be suggested that will set the subject apart from his former environment. The loss of his frame of reference creates a painful existential void that begs to be filled — that is, it impels the initiate to come up with anew model for behavior. Coincidentally, sporadic interruptions of the teaching or temporarily being apart from the new social group made up by these initiates is depressing, due to the lack of something that has become valuable; this feeling transforms itself into a real psychological need in the rebel disciple.

The dependence is twofold. First there is ideological dependence, subjection to the cult's thought; then there is sociological dependence, stemming from the membership in a new groups, which becomes a protective refuge, a substitute family where complicity takes over, unifying the disciples while cutting them off from society even more. Here you can see a very real similarity to groups of drug-users.

The third phase is the progressive increase in the constraints applied and the submission that results, with no chance of exit. At this stage the initiate is dependent on the cult, cut off from society at large, and psychologically and physically bound by obligations that deprive him of his free will and of all social and economic freedom. This process is in every respect parallel to that of addiction and drug dependency; in the same way, it leads to the complete subjection of the individual. However, while selling narcotics is illegal, as of today no law prohibits propagating such ideologies (except for Nazism, anti-Semitism, and racism).

Medical and Legal Aspects

The cult phenomenon is a typical case for criminology. It sits halfway between law and legal medicine, right at the heart of forensic psychiatry. CC's commit criminal actions against people and property, and sometimes they foment grander schemes that threaten state security. Here, then, is my proposition:

A coercive cult (CC) is a closed group, based on mental manipulation, organized around a master (guru) and an ideology.

It aims to establish a qualitative difference between the initiates of the structure and non-initiates, and its objective, overt or covert, is the enrichment of the group or of a part of the group.

It is established and developed by the exploitation of those who are manipulated, by those who do the manipulating.

Its effect on the individual is likely to entail physical and psychic disorders, which may or may not be reversible.

Brainwashing

Mental manipulation — or psychic conditioning, or brainwashing — is the basis for cult indoctrination.

History shows valuable examples of this. After the Korean War, the mental state of Americans who had been long-term prisoners seemed to indicate that certain techniques, deemed infallible, made it possible to "empty" a brain of its previous content, to "wash" it and to rebuild the subject's mind according to a different model. Journalist Edward Hunter explained that the goal of this brainwashing — it is he who popularized the term — was to "radically change a mind, so that the individual becomes a live puppet, a human robot, without the atrocity being visible on the exterior, the objective being to create a tool in flesh and blood, furnished with new beliefs and new thought processes inserted into a captive body."

The sad context of the Korean War, the sense of failure and guile felt in the United States, not to mention the need to vilify the enemy, no doubt contributed to the success of this version of the story. Although the term "brainwashing" is well-designed for (dare I mention) influencing people's perceptions. Nonetheless, despite the millions of dollars spent to de-condition the American prisoners and to condition Koreans and, after them, Vietnamese, no clear recipe has been developed — neither by psychiatrists nor by the secret services that were working in concert.

Cults could very easily have similar techniques at their disposal.

That is why they apply, through trial and error, programs of mental conditioning. However, a perfect program does not exist. Today's brainwashing techniques do not always succeed in creating the perfect robot, even if they prove to be sufficiently effective and dangerous to warrant study and censure. These "imperfect" techniques I shall now attempt to describe.

2.

CULTS — PAST AND PRESENT

From Antiquity to the 20th Century

From Antiquity to the 20th Century

Sects have existed in the social and religious field for nearly 2000 years. Sometimes reduced to a few members (Omphalopsists, or navel worshippers), sometimes burlesque (worshippers of the onion, or the Angel Cyclamen), they have also played philosophical roles (the Platonists, Peripatetics, Jansenists) and political roles (Golden Dawn, the Illuminati of Bavaria), with sometimes macabre or dramatic episodes (the castrati of Russia, the SS Black Order).[1] Their history is worth following for, while their techniques have evolved, today's sects revisit traditional topics whose origin sometimes goes back to the pre-Christian era.

Historically, sects are first of all religious groups that are opposed to the dominant thought and who split off from the original Church — a phenomenon common to all examples. Thus, the Essenes represent a Jewish community opposed to the Sadducees and the Pharisees; Christ came from this minority group. Islam, whose esoteric branch is Sufism, gave birth, among others, to the sect of the Hashishins (consumers of hashish, or Assassins), gathered around Hasan ibn Al-Sabbah (1050-1124), "the Old Man of the Mountain." This sect, originating from the

Ismaelians, themselves born from a schism of the Shiites, launched a military and political offensive first against, and then in alliance with, the Knights Templar who were fighting in the Holy Land. They established a veritable empire that ended in the 13th century with the Mongolian invasions but whose imams have succeeded one another up until present times under the name of Agha Khan.[2]

A number of sects have played important political and military roles, without any apparent religious origin. The great Chinese Triad played a considerable role at the time of the Boxer War. Nazism nourished its roots in the Golden Dawn and Vril. The *carbonari* played a powerful role in the advent of the Italian republic.

There has been little study regarding the influence of sects, except to some extent by sociologists who have been quick to define them in contrast to religion and the traditional Churches. According to Wach, any religious body that shows a dynamics of formal protest can move towards becoming a sect.[3]

Studies on Christianity show that sects have multiplied since the Middle Ages, in opposition to the official Church. Sometimes they take the form of spiritual or charismatic movements, or of brotherhoods making vows of poverty (Montanism, Novatianism, the Petrobusians, followers of Vaud, etc.), and play an important political role (Catharism). Sometimes they are organized as true militant movements (Hussites, Joachimites); sects are also found in Protestantism (Mennonites, Anabaptists).

The discovery of the New World helped them to multiply and they prospered in the territory of America (Darbyists, Methodists, Jehovah's Witnesses). Over the course of time, they can acquire the status of a Church, such as the Adventist Church. Others continue to function on a sectarian model, like the Amish. Some give rise to controversy, like the Jehovah's Witnesses and the Mormons, or they fragment into various structures which themselves evolve into sects, like the Davidians. Sometimes they sprout up under new names and combinations to create a new movement.

Catharism is a prime example of this ongoing mutation; it had the status of a Church or sect, but above all has preserved a historical significance. This movement reappears periodically in the form of nostalgic microstructures that combine their rites with those of the templar groups (likewise persecuted), then take on the colorings of orientalism, of Arthurian knighthood, alchemy, esotericism, or tantrism, finally leading to the creation of movements such as the Knights of the Grail, New Cathares or Knights of Montsegur. Another example of the flexibility of the structures is the Black Order of the SS, which fed its Aryan philosophy on themes from the Arthurian legends, developing its rites by copying those of the Thule group, Martinism and Vril.

We have little precise information on the sociological organization of such structures, but one can safely assume that the Thule group contributed to the development of Nazi ideology, even though it was dissolved in 1925. Created by the poet Dietrich Eckart, the Thule group based their ideology on magic and secrecy. This dimension was a part of Nazism. Hitler, Himmler and Hess were deeply immersed in its myths. According to certain authors, Rosenberg and Professor Karl Haushofer (one of the fathers of geopolitics) were ardent organizers of this group. The group's founding myth rises from the existence of Thule, magical center of a lost Scandinavian civilization whose secrets, preserved by a small group of "unknown superiors," are accessible exclusively by initiation to the group. The initiates and the esoteric Nazis believed that between mankind and extraterrestrial beings there were intermediaries who could give the initiates colossal supernatural powers necessary for the fulfillment of their paramount mission, which is to fulfill the spiritual destiny of humanity. However, only those with the gift of being a medium, like Hitler, could serve as a "bridge" between these invisible forces and the common people. And it is the Aryan race, the main branch of humanity, still according to Thule, which is designated to assume destiny over the earth and to govern the advent of future millennia. For this reason, under the aegis of this group, Nazi Germany was to direct the entire world.

According to the same authors, we can link this group with the creation of Ahnenerbe by Sievers and Haushofer. Ahnenerbe, equipped with virtually unlimited funds and under the direct authority of Himmler, was responsible for research in the most various fields, from the so-called medical experiments in the concentration camps to the most absurd search for supposed supernatural phenomena.[4]

While some authors doubt whether Nazi leaders were members of the Thule group, they do acknowledge that the Aryan ideology was built on elements borrowed from groups as diverse as the OTO (Ordo Templi Orientis), Freemasonry, Rosicrucianism and H. P. Blavatsky's theosophy.[5]

Some of the same topics are found in cults today. The New Acropolis has borrowed elitist and Aryanist symbols and ideas; the Aum cult presents similar ideas, from the notion of unknown superiors to the elitist, spellbinding and expansive nature of the group, right up to the prophetic and missionary status of their guru.

Deciphering the affiliation of cults is not always easy; but it makes it possible, when necessary, to predict their behavior. A cult's actions are guided by an oral or written tradition that may be recent or old. Studying these traditions helps in understanding the leader's thought, in anticipating the choices he makes, in penetrating the real meaning of secret rituals that may mimic older ones and, thereby, in preventing criminal conduct.

Consider the sacrifice of members the Solar Temple. Knowledge of their rituals and themes probably would have made it possible to foresee this event as the inevitable result of the requirement of mystical sacrifice, itself an extension of the Templar tradition. Pretending to the heritage of the ancient Templars, the disciples of the Solar Temple see themselves as designated victims, like the Templars who were destroyed by Philip the Fair. This notion of their being potential victims finds its origin in their alleged knowledge of secrets revealed by God and in the expiate nature of their faith.

The past is not of ethnological or historical interest alone, it is also an invaluable means of digging up religious and philosophical roots. The heredity of a cult with an original line of thought often clarifies the choice of terms used in its ideological speech, as well as the dynamics by which it sets itself apart from its doctrinal antecedents.

The only way to elucidate the intentions of "the Messiah of Waco" (Vernon Howell, alias David Koresh) is by studying his "sermons." One finds in their "religious" history the explanation of the pre-cataclysmic and suicidal behavior of the Davidians. The imminent approach of the last judgment, the apocalypse, is one of the characteristics of the Church of the Seventh Day Adventists. This Church split, giving birth to the Davidians under the leadership of the Bulgarian emigrant Victor Houteff, and later to the Waco sect. In addition, the fact that Vernon Howell was called Koresh is significant when it is known that this is an Americanized translation of Cyrus, the Persian king who allowed the captive Jews of Babylon to return to Israel. Thus, Koresh becomes "the king" who will give his disciples, "the chosen people," the power to free themselves from the yoke of American society that is "corrupt and opposed to the true faith." The apocalyptic and millenarian content of the leader's presentations hold within them the idea of a final sacrifice.

The same applies to the Mandarom group, for whom the only rampart against the "lemurs" that are attacking the world is the Cosmo-planetary Messiah, whose biological end is inevitable. Given that this group has no traditional affiliation, and given the divine character of the Lord Mahacharya Shri Hamsananda Saravasti Adinath (real name: Gilbert Bourdin), his death would leave the disciples disabled and without a father figure, and would quite possibly be a signal to his disciples to organize a communal departure for the Aumist paradise.

Sociologists and biblical scholars have proposed several classifications of sects.[6] One of the most traditional is based on the groups' religious origins. This system is not entirely satisfactory because some groups appear to have arisen through spontaneous generation; nonetheless, it is worth mentioning. These researchers have distinguished three main types of sects:

• Sects of Judeo-Christian inspiration, referring to the Bible (Jehovah's Witnesses, Mormons, Christian Science, Universal Church of God)

• Sects of Eastern inspiration, based on various interpretations of Zen Buddhism, Hinduism and Islam. Their practices are centered on the search for mystical ecstasy, organized around the Master, holder of supreme knowledge

• Sects of Gnostic inspiration, which draw their origins from the beliefs and practices of both the East and West. These may blend esotericism, alchemy, astrology and, more recently, extraterrestrial myths, numerology, etc. They do not preach revealed reality, but discovery through study and effort.

Besides religious analyses, it is possible to classify sects by integrating cultural elements of various origins:

– Traditional sects derived from historical Protestantism

– Derivatives of Christianity (Mormons, Jehovah's Witnesses, Family of Love, Plain Truth, Moon)

– Marginal offshoots or parallel churches, presenting themselves as Catholic or Orthodox (Counter-Reformation Catholics, Abbot of Nantes, Cross of Dozule, Revelation of Ares, Community of Frechou)

– Esoteric-occultist movements (Orders of the Temple)

– Prayer and healing groups (IVI)

– Secret and initiatory wisdom (gnoses)

– So-called schools of wisdom (Rosicrucian Brotherhood, Transcendental Meditation, Universal White Fraternity, Holy Grail, Scientology, New Acropolis)

– Groups or practices concerned with occultism (channeling, magic)

– New practices and new messiahs (Golden Lotus, Aum)

– Mental or physical health groups (Iso-Zen, Energo-Chromo-Kinesthesis)

– Ecologists (Ecoovie);

– Neo-paganists (Raeliens, Saint-Erme).

No classification is definitive or satisfactory. Sects and cults are continuously evolving, assimilating outside influences and mixing them with their own. Simultaneously, their chosen themes grow broader or are purified according to the mood of the guru and requirements of growth.

The 20ᵗʰ Century

The sects and cults that are currently thriving appeared after the Second World War; the majority of them correspond to a socio-cultural phenomenon born in the Seventies.

Even though their theses may appear to be anchored to a remote past, their actual mode of operation is the consequence of the questioning of the consumer society; it is the result of a counter-culture of protest that cropped up in the 1960's. This exploded with the *Beat Generation* and fed on end-of-millennium fears, ambient catastrophism and the successive holocausts.

It was in May, 1968, that the framework of a true psychodrama was set, which involved a social and mental shift. Many tried to find a loophole or a therapy in new sects. Some wrongly qualified them as new religious movements.

New Sects

Since ancient times, religion has been proposing Utopia as the alternative to daily problems, whereas politics has been confined to the field of reality. (To be honest, in recent years, Utopia in politics has reappeared, in tandem with the bankruptcy of the great ideologies.) The 1960's and 1970's saw a weakening of "traditional" religious sentiment and the traditional Churches gave ground to the spontaneous communities organized around a guru or an idea that was in fashion.

Sects are located in the fringes of the religious and social architecture. They propose philosophical and religious concepts that cannot be verified from the benchmark of accepted definitions. In place of a plan, they present a systematic criticism of the existing structures. In fact, they create a social diagram built on a psychotic model, developing barricades intended to protect against the intrusion of others, manipulating reality and revising the individual's behavioral and ideological model.

Several sets of themes are distinguished. We need not draw up an exhaustive catalogue but it is important to locate their sources, for these can indicate the development of the follower and clarify his possible pathology.

The traditional Churches are the primary source. In the course of their history, the Churches have given birth to schisms, apostasies and various trends that evolved and blossomed into parallel Churches. Most of the time, these Churches are qualified as sects only because of their minor place compared to the mother Church from which they spring. Occasionally, the paranoiac behavior of a leader of such a Church leads to a cult-like dynamics, but these are individual pathologies. (An example is the Abbot of Nantes.)

The second source is represented by oriental religious movements. In this sphere are found more or less faithful interpretations of the traditional religions such as Hinduism and Islam, but these are colored by their historical avatars (Buddhism, Zen, Universal Bahai Faith, Sufism etc.). The problem arising here is that of the random interpretation of texts and sacred principles, by gurus with a greater or a lesser degree of inspiration.

The third source feeding the river of sectarian movements is that of Gnosticism, Esotericism and Occultism. Religion is based on the revealed truth. On the other hand, the gnostic affirms that individual salvation comes from progressive knowledge of the divine, which is presented by Masters who have received this knowledge through revelation.

The new sects find the engine of their development and success in these global doctrines. Indeed, Gnostic initiation assumes the concept of life-long work and effort, which will bring answers to the questions that trouble the disciples. The Truth will be found only by the zealous. To doubt is synonymous with failure. The solution will be provided only to those who remain in the sect, for there are always new levels to attain before the final enlightenment.

Last, but not the least, are the sects that are born and nurtured from the fertile mind and intellect of the charlatan. In such sects, there is no philosophical or religious alibi. There is only an individual paranoiac mental pathology, which spreads like a contagious disease to the disciples and leads them to collective hysteria, which is consolidated over the passing years (Raeliens or disciples of the Great Cosmo-planetary Messiah of the Golden Lotus.)[7]

The New Age

Today, the esoteric-philosophic-religious field is almost completely occupied by the ideology known as New Age. This movement was born in the United States; its rise has been supported by the decline of the great religious and political systems, due to their inability to respond to millenarian anguishes and to rectify feelings of failure and impotence.

Contained in outline form in the esoteric writings of the beginning of this century,[8] which were built on historical interpretations and the concept of cosmic cycles,[9] "the New Age" corresponds to an astrological vision of planetary development. It is supposed to coincide with "an era which begins when the rising sun, at the vernal equinox, passes from the zodiacal sign of Pisces to that of Aquarius." Slowly and surely, this idea was established in "hip" communities within the United States, then it contaminated the Anglo-Saxon world, Western Europe and, recently, Eastern Europe, which is the new favorite ground of cults since the fall of the Iron Curtain.

The feeling of isolation and dislocation experienced by American youth grew somewhat blurred with the new feeling of being reintegrated with the Great Cosmo-Planetary Whole. The mother planet Gaia[10] was rehabilitated in her role as nurturing mother. This New Age is synonymous with rebirth, where fundamental water acquires a double symbolism: fetal and divine.[11] The New Age, symbolized by the water carrier or its Latin equivalent Aquarius,[12] represents the only chance of salvation from nuclear darkness.[13] It rests on "a new paradigm,"[14] i.e. a different standard, whose components are: "Ecology, soft technologies, holistic science, transpersonal psychology, communal life style, alternative practices, spiritual search."[15] A proliferation of fluid organizations aims to change society radically by proposing alternative solutions in every domain.[16]

Running parallel to this ideology of "returning to the primordial state," tinged with rustic ecology and astrology, there are certain movements that profess more political doctrines or who look toward a global upheaval:

"A prophet has announced the arrival of the Antichrist between 1980 and 1999. . . . Combat is joined between two opposing and complementary forces — the White and Black, the Light and Dark, Christ and Antichrist. . . . Our Mother Earth is in gestation of a new race, the Solar Race. . . . The pains have started, the amniotic waters will break, blood will flow."[17]

These apocalyptic views, more or less publicly proclaimed, are nurtured by an ancient esoteric that is the source of renewed interest in "invisible governments" and paranormal powers supposed to arise "from initiation."[18]

A Fairytale for Adults

Children are fascinated by fairytales. The ogre and the wolf represent the law and the father; the good fairy is a substitute for the mother. However, poisoned needles and magic wands do not fascinate the adult, stripped as they are of their symbolism. Sectarian doctrines are fairytales for adults, where fantasy takes the place of reality, where the dream of power erases social frustration and where divinity is within reach of all by the phenomenon of transcendence.[19] Religion gives super-human power only to the mystics, whereas sects make it gleam in the eyes of the more humble.

An Aberrant Ecological Vision

Environmentalism and ecological activism are outgrowths of the counterculture that appeared after 1968. They represent a naturalist vision that questions all of society. How can we mention ecology, one of the hottest topics at the end of this century, in the same breath as "cult"?

The very word "cult" creates a reflex action of rejection and alienation in a normal listener. Today, everyone says that he or she is an ecologist, without claiming to be a member of a sect. However, these two trends have common points in their operating methods, as well as in their doctrinal basics.

In *The Three Ecologies*,[20] Felix Guattari describes the three stages of ecology: environmentalism, political ecology and moral ecology (or eco-sophistication). The good meaning of ecology has to do with organic and economic constraints, and is separate from the parasitical lucubrations of moral ecology and environmentalism. The last is primarily a limited vision of ecology, resting on the traditional idea that human happiness rests "not in the accumulation of goods, but in the aesthetic joys and the spiritual wealth that is received as a result of a more direct relationship with nature."[21] The danger in this ecology is that the focus on immaterial wealth requires breaking away from the social and economic order. The diffused spirituality preached in this case does not offer a "resolution" to the problem of living on Earth. Excluding Pascal's bet, he who wishes to live fully according to his personal commitment often has to break away from society and move towards the fringe of society, in a microstructure that can become the embryo of a cult if the person leads other individuals to adopt his ideas and choices.

Catastrophism and Millenarianism

There is a disconcerting similarity between apocalyptic predictions (Biblical flood, cataclysms, etc) and the nuclear winter prophesied by ecologists.

In *The Cold and the Dark*,[22] Paul Ehrlich and Carl Sagan are not satisfied with exposing the consequences of thermonuclear chain reactions. They proceed to illustrate their work with graphic color prints that would not be out of step with the religious iconography of last century. They stress the "balls of fire" that will destroy our planet, leaving a vitrified and sterile place recalling Sodom and Gomorra. The irreversible catastrophe and permanent danger illustrated in this report make the reader feel guilty; irresponsibility is transformed into a mortal sin.

This feeling of self-blame is the psychological basis that gives rise to sects. It causes Manicheism, where the sinners are the destroyers of the environment and the believers are the environmentalists. Certain authors have gone so far as to suggest that the ecological upheavals are the expression of the rejections of God and that only by living in Franciscan austerity can we save the planet.[23]

The millenarians believe in a less catastrophic version, but they still expect the worst. They have a vision of history as an eternal series of new cycles.

The doctrine of cycles was very widespread at the beginning of this century, and it continues to pervade the speech of certain sects even now. For example, George Barbarin's spiritual heirs:

> History is like a revolving wheel. The top becomes the bottom and the bottom again becomes the top. In nature, everything happens in circles. The planets turn on their axes, moons turn around planets, the planets and moons as a whole turn around a star, the whole star system turns around a larger system . . . In this way, it takes 26,000 years to complete one period of "nutation" *(sic)* of the earth, or displacement of its axis. Thereafter, the whole process starts again, which is the new period of nutation. Similar laws also govern the life of societies. Each development in society reproduces the principal characteristics of the developments that preceded it. Attentive study of the characteristics of a completed human cycle is sufficient to know the characteristics of the present human cycle and even the characteristics of the future human cycles.[24]

Such doctrines are most interesting when they contain several prophetic elements. Then each group can choose some element from such doctrines to nourish its own imagination. The follower is supposed to discover the great laws of history by re-reading past events. The perfidy of cults is in the choice of the "magic" of the previous cycle that would develop, build and explain the present cycle. Using this magic number, a member of a cult developed for us the following reasoning:

> The One Hundred Years War began in 1337. War is a manifestation of the devil, whose number is 666. Adding them gives 2003; i.e. 1337 + 666 = 2003. Thus, the year 2003 will see the beginning of a new conflict that will last a hundred years. One of the first signs of this future conflict is the opening of the Channel Tunnel between England and France, which is the intrusion of the earth element in the water element, representing the beginning of elemental chaos. . .

Interest in such doctrines is supported by the imminence of catastrophe, which is close to the classical millenarian doctrines.

Back to Nature

Recent history does not end with the Findhorn movement. Certainly, this community in northern Scotland played a fundamental role in awakening the concept of environmentalism and a return to nature. Still, it is hard to deny its cult-like tenor, especially its tendency towards frenzied behavior.[25]

This group cultivates vegetables of unusually large sizes in hostile environments. According to the group's members, they are able to achieve this feat due to the synergy within the group. The social superorganization of the group is supposed to influence cosmic and telluric energies that play a decisive part in the extraordinary growth of tomatoes and lettuce under the blessings of the Devas, or spirits of the plants.[26]

If technology carries within itself the germs of planetary destruction, a return to the natural state may seem to be the most logical solution. Indeed, natural living holds much that is of paramount value. However, excess of everything is rightly said to be bad, and excesses with this ideology can have dramatic consequences as well. This damage was noticed when such groups embrace doctrines that have been rejected by science, such as monovegetalism (the eating of a single vegetable), or "instinctivo-therapy," the eating, raw, only of the food that the person by instinct desires immediately,[27] based on Mosseri's therapies. This concept of eating only one vegetable or only by instinct is unhealthy, and it has placed several followers of Burger in the hospital and their guru in a court of law.

Bucolic Ecology

And rightly, within a few months of each other, two authors have denounced the poetic vision of ecology. Luc Ferry, on the one hand, and Michel Onfray, on the other, spelled out the risks of what the latter calls "bucolic" ecology.

These doctrines hold that "nature gives happiness, truth, pleasure and satisfaction; whereas civilization generates only misfortunes, pain and disease." Technology becomes an evil in itself and it separates the human being from his natural roots. Technology prevents humans from living in harmony with Mother Nature. The bucolic or rustic ecologist develops a phobia with regard to technology and industrialization. The phobia is a typical reaction, born out of the difficulty of confronting a social situation that seems aggressive.

This is not a matter for political or economic theories, but for psychoanalysis. Besides this group's fear of society, respect for the elements appears to be an expression of the desire to be one with Mother Nature. Water, the sea, the ocean; in fact the very blue planet; all possess an inherent mystical and protective power within. This form of environmentalism is a psychological projection. Earth, clothed in her feminine and maternal characteristics, protects her children, showering her bounteous gifts on them. Mankind is a threat, a masculine entity, warlike and destructive. Technology is simply the instrument (phallus) used when man commits a crime against Mother Nature.

Outside the political context, reduced to environmentalism, ecology produces an incomplete and illogical analysis. At this stage, deviant sectarian or cult-based initiatives come into play. The prospect of a planetary catastrophe, if it is described in a charismatic way, can lead to bizarre approaches whether proposed by pre-existing groups with a fixed ideology (a sect) or via tautological rationalizing giving rise to a new ideological approach (a cult).

The absence of a unified global concern for the planet's ecology leads to the cause being taken up by fragmented groups. Certain groups reduce the conversation to one aspect of ecological concern, focusing only on that and cutting themselves off from those who do not share their concern. Gradually, a feeling of persecution may develop among defenders of a single ecological conviction (nuclear power, organic agriculture, saving the dolphin, and so on). Disregard and even scorn for socio-economic realities leads directly to social rejection. Those who do not agree become enemies. The group then closes in upon itself in a retreat tinged with paranoia, and ends up being marginalized.

Social and media pressure are exerted, and lost civilizations become standards for comparison that allow these groups to demonstrate all sorts of ineptitude and uncontrolled behavior.

A sinister caricature of this phenomenon was seen in the coercive cult Ecoovie, which espoused a doctrine that was half way between ecology and worship of the Indian state. The Master or guru of Ecoovie was Pierre Maltese Dorg, alias Piel Petjo Maltest, alias Norman William, and alias Maolin Tiam. The members of this cult followed their guru in a great ecological walk around the earth. These long walks may or may not have achieved something, but certainly they resulted in several followers ending up in the hospital for malnutrition, disease, hallucinations and other general and psychiatric medical disorders. After about fifteen years of these great walks, the remaining followers planted their teepees in Finland, where they led an extremely difficult and almost tramp-like existence. The bulk of the cult seems to have dissolved during the summer of 1994. This kind of pure "hard fundamental ecology" has impressed others too and caused the creation of the Silo sect around its guru, Marius Rodriguez Cobos.

The Silo cult is well known for its petitions intended to save the Amazon rainforest and for taking a strong position in favor of a natural lifestyle removed from any harmful or pollution-generating activity. This personal growth group represents a model of a cult organized around a blind and rigorous environmental doctrine and promoting all-encompassing indoctrination in the name of grand ideals.

Health Hazards

The human body has always been one of the favorite subjects of sects and cults. All religions and mystical discourses contain some aspect devoted to the body and health. *Mens sana in corpore sano*. While this premise is well accepted among today's populace, there is nonetheless a side to the discussion that goes well beyond what is actually healthy. Purification and internal cleansing of the body are presented as essential conditions to attain the divine, to combat the polluted and "unclean" environment.

We have no intention of disparaging holistic concepts of health and warnings against dietary errors from serious practitioners. But how can we ignore the incongruities that crop up among the flourishing new health magazines? Magic is everywhere, in the articles and in the ads praising such and such a diet, contraption, or technique. From air purification through ionization (*sic*) to appliances generating magnetic waves, to "amagnetic" bedsprings, the list goes on to trap suckers. The harm might be negligible if it only touched the gullible person's wallet, but it amounts to a large-scale manipulation founded on a subculture. The paraphernalia gain in credibility as they become fashionable (chromotherapy, gems, crystals, and so on). The product is made to appear magical and fascinating, removing all the consumer's capacity for critical analysis, as he is fascinated by the fact that the desired object is natural, non-polluting, and non-industrial. There is an underlying message on the pseudo-scientific plane that prevents the untutored from distinguishing what is real and what is false.[28]

The siege mentality is the basis for widespread pseudo-solutions to modern health problems — a mentality that is close to fascism. Crisis and danger are always present. Early on, it is recommended to protect oneself against aggressors by developing a strong group. Then the threats from outside the group must be contained, and finally one should destroy the threatening group that is responsible for all the evils.

Corollary to the siege complex is the fascination with superhuman powers. This superman status is achieved through rites of eating, special techniques, clothing, and ways of breathing. It is the worship of man, new and clean.[29] Magic is not far removed from this. The body is regarded as a cosmic entity whose personal "vibrations" are in resonance and harmony with the primordial cosmic vibration. "Pain and disease are signs of conflict, of lack of cosmic harmony. . . . The body is an energy field inside another energy field."[30]

To these dubious meanings suggested by the term "holistic," we can add its Greek etymology (*holos*, wholeness) and a New Age sound (*holy*, sacred). Taken all together, one concludes that health is the expression of the sacred. Following this ideology, the Davidian cult of Waco, under their guru Koresh, predicted that after the final cataclysm a new type of offspring would arrive. They would be free from sins.

Strange Medicine

Drug addicts have been the favorite customers of cults. Some cults have developed dedicated branches in their organizations for the drug addicts. An example is Scientology, which has the Narconon centers that are supposed to contribute to the detoxification of drug addicts, using Scientology techniques of purification.

Other groups seemed, in the beginning, to be doing good work and providing valuable assistance to drug addicts. However, these services were slowly transformed into coercive groups, attracting the attention of the authorities. The French Department of Health and Social Security had to rescind approval for a number of such centers. The Patriarch Association (called Dianova, since 1998), under the direction of Lucien Enjelmajer was even condemned by the Courts for the coercive methods used. Here is an extract of the judgment of the County Court of Toulouse, in May 1992:[31]

> It is obvious that the methods used by the Patriarch Association for the care of their boarders were unusually strong. These methods create an

environment of moral constraint whose real purpose is in fact the conversion of the spirit of the addicts. The methods used in handling the addicts are contrary to the rights of the individual and to the respect for private life.

The ECK, or Energo-Chromo-Kinese, used a panoply of quack medicines. For the ECK, man is merely an antenna that establishes energy current between the telluric cosmos and terrestrial forces. For them, disease is the result of poor energy conductivity or an anomaly that disturbs the energy levels of the individual. The gravest threat from the ECK is that it is usually licensed doctors, dentists, and therapists, graduates of recognized institutions, who practice these treatments.

One may wonder about the validity of this cult's theories when one finds such a dentist tearing out a patient's fillings without anesthesia, under the pretext that lead saps the energy vibrations. The coherent reasoning of such an expert is further doubted when he advises not to install metal prostheses for the same reason. We have treated the former patients of a fellow psychiatrist who is a member of the ECK, and found that in lieu of treatment he had prescribed bottles filled with colored sand to be placed under the patients' pillows. These sand bottles were supposed to give vibrations in harmony with the fundamental vibrations of the patient.

Even though the patients were not cured, one may note a constant running through these practices: they all involve people having high incomes, "the fundamental vibration" of those with low incomes being perhaps to feeble to suit this type of care. We might also note that the ECK has a curious reading of history, whereby the Jewish holocaust appears altogether beneficial, for it must have engendered a powerful release of energy toward the cosmos.

The ECK also sells "nutriments" manufactured in its own laboratories. These are prescribed to the public by kinergists and energeticians, who have been trained at seminars. These nutriments are supposed to increase the individual's energy level. One finds here the traditional theories of the Yin and the Yang, which made a fortune for those peddling Zen macrobiotics and its derivatives.

The ECK apparently has a second, more esoteric tier of operation, similar to the orders of the Templars. They profess a doctrine of energy reincarnation that sparks the interest of patients who may be backsliding.[32] After several months of work at the energy level, the subject may be initiated into the mysteries of light-cosmos-genesis. This ultimate knowledge would enable him to accomplish space voyages to the edge of the galaxy, accompanied by beings of the sixth race.

Periodically, these Utopian medical practices are given publicity by the press when some controversy arises. All of Austria held its breath in August 1995, watching the politico-legal drama of the Pilhar family. The family were members of the Fiat Lux cult, whose female guru, Erika Bertschinger (called Uriella), was a resident of Switzerland. When Helmut Pilhar fled abroad with his daughter Olivia, who was six years old and suffering from a serious renal tumor, the President and the Chancellor of Austria intervened. Uriella had directed the Pilhar family to have the girl treated by a Cologne doctor from the cult, named Dr. Ryke Geerd Hamer. Dr. Hamer had been prohibited from practicing medicine in Germany and Austria, and was even termed a "charlatan" by Dr. Juergessen, the original doctor who had been rendering "conventional" medical treatment to the child. Efforts were made to persuade the father to have his daughter treated only by qualified medical practitioners, and to give up the magical practices promoted by Uriella. The political, legal and human drama caused the matter to become an obsession with the press. The publicity surrounding this case contributed to the reappearance in the general public of myths developed by cults for serious diseases like cancer and AIDS, where prayer and healing groups have always had a strong appeal, in part because of conventional medicine's relative inability[33] to cure certain serious diseases.

In the same vein, the institute of psychoanalytical research led by Maud Pison and surgeon-dentist Galiano — recently condemned by the County Court of Draguignan — developed a theory where religion, radio waves, magnetism, UFO's and cosmo-astrology intermingle. According to Pison (who claims to be a reincarnation of the Virgin Mary) and her associate Galiano, most physical and spiritual problems come from bad influences that reach the individual through the receiving antennas constituted by metal parts in the body, such as lead fillings. A former patient testified to the following effect:

> I went to see Galiano last summer with Anne, my future wife. He affirmed that he was the reincarnation of Jesus Christ. Without eyebrows. Looking at our teeth, he enumerated the persons that Anne and I had been in previous lives. He said that we had been the brother and sister of Jesus and that, under these circumstances, our present marriage would not be possible, as it would be incestuous. My fiancee Anne was terribly shaken by this revelation.
>
> As regards the dentistry itself, as soon as I entered the room, I was settled into the armchair. My teeth were examined and I was informed that it was urgently necessary to remove my fillings as they were causing interference between my astral being and the cosmic being. Without anesthesia, to measure my energy level, the fillings were removed. I screamed in pain, but he carried on. Still, on the way out, I signed a check for 1500 francs. Dr. Galiano also said that to have better communication with the cosmic waves, patients must file their nails with a bur and let their hair grow long.

This is similar to the proclamation made at the seminar of the re-discovered Holy Grail[34] — "Happy are the hairy ones, for they will hear God in stereo."

Extraterrestrials

With so many magazines and groups proclaiming the sightings of UFOs, this phenomenon has become a great attraction for the gullible. One might have thought that, given all the science fiction of the 1950's, the public would be ready to laugh at the earlier idea of life on Mars, or an invasion by Martians. But pseudo-scientists and gurus cash in on a ready market.

The extraterrestrial myth is similar to the myth of the return of the divine, only it is more accessible. To reach the heavens, where Martians, the new gods, reside, Jacob's ladder has given way to space ships. This edifying quotation follows the Scientologist account regarding crossing "the wall of fire":[35]

> The leader of the Galactic Confederation (76 planets around large stars visible from earth), founded some 75 million years ago, solved the problem of overpopulation (about 250 billion inhabitants per planet). He conducted wide scale implants, and mass deportations, including to other planets. He transported the Thetans to the earth and placed hydrogen bombs in the principal volcanoes (Incident 2).
>
> The Thetans of the Pacific region were sent to Hawaii, and those of the Atlantic area were sent to Las Palmas. He was called Xenu and renegades were employed for this task. When the renegades had completed their task, those honest officers who had remained loyal to the people captured him after six years of fighting. He was then placed in an electronic trap located high upon a mountaintop, where he still exists to this day. As for "them," they simply disappeared.
>
> The length and the brutality of this whole episode were such that the confederation was never able to recover, and the location where it took place became a desert.
>
> The implant is designed to "kill" whoever tries to obtain it. However, the technology I put in place makes it possible to solve this problem. I knew that somebody should "make the jump" and, in 1967, I did it. I left there terribly shaken, but alive. I am probably the only person during these 75 million years to have successfully done it. I have all the data now, but you need only those which I deliver to you here.
>
> To approach the implant without preparation and protection leads to death. One must follow the directions to the letter, precisely. A "free approach" will not help you achieve the goal, instead it will destroy your sleep and finally result in your death. Therefore, be extremely careful and follow the leader's instructions precisely as indicated....
>
> Your body is not your own, as the Thetans have entered it and are using it to play out their own drama. You must get rid of these Thetans by traversing Incident 2 first, then Incident 1. The method is long and requires hard work, care, patience and good hearing. You will hear beings. The Thetans believed that they were one. That is the fundamental error! Good luck!"

This myth of the great voyage, known since Antiquity with Jason and Ulysses, has gained momentum in the age of flying saucers. Again, the old symbolic discourse is turned around and offered as pablum to a populace that is low on education and is fascinated by "prophetic" speech.

Lost Civilizations

The myths of lost wisdom and lost civilizations have many common points with extraterrestrial myths. Sometimes they merge. Civilizations that are lost or disappeared are considered to be better, the way people think of those who have died. The present world is regarded as the expression of ignorance and evil, whereas past civilizations, whether real or mythical, are thought to have operated at a higher level scientifically and philosophically.

Certain cults seek to unlock the secrets of the ancient Egyptians, others are interested in the Aztec or Toltecs. Cults rarely base their ideology exclusively on such secrets; usually, these are points that build on or support their main topics and ideologies. That leads to an ideology that may be spicy but is a bit of a stew, as briefly summarized here:

> The Telamones are extraterrestrials in disguise. They supplied the ancient Egyptians with the mathematical secrets that made it possible for them to build the pyramids. These pyramids are in fact esoteric timetables, like Mayan pyramids. By proper understanding of these pyramids, one can read the past, present and future. They are entirely comparable to the great cathedrals, such as Chartres, meticulous study of which makes it possible to posit the arrival of extraterrestrial beings, to discover the secrets of the philosopher's stone, to find the lost treasures of Templars and to achieve eternal youth . . .

Belief in some kind of universal key in the remote past of humanity is part of the lore of all esoteric and initiatory groups. These groups use this vague ancient universal key as "spiritual gymnastics." In full-blown cults, this vague key is developed further, and promoted to the rank of the "revealed truth."

Past Lives and Angels

These two topics sometimes constitute the theoretical corpus of a given group, and sometimes they are used merely to support or illustrate other elements of their ideology.

The theme of past lives is derived from the doctrines of Hinduism and Lamaism, presented by traditional Churches as well as by the most singular doctrines. The old practice of mediums, which was renamed to "channeling," is the preferred instrument. "Channeling" mans that some person becomes the channel, usually the guru, through whom messages from the beyond and from previous lives are passed on to the waiting public. Sometimes, the "channeling" medium is considered to maintain a privileged relation with a spirit or "angel" that provides him the message that is useful for demonstrating its powers. The angel would even go so far as to lift a fog — at least, that is what a certain Marc Schweitzer reported in connection with Maguy Lebrun, the driving force behind one of France's largest healing groups.

> France was drowned in a thick fog. On the road from Bourgoin to Grenoble, the visibility was less than ten meters. Three kilometers from Maguy's place, the fog suddenly split. It was there, under a splendid blue sky without clouds, that I saw from afar the small chapel with no path or way to reach it.

As for the interested party, if she does not maintain that she has the power to change the weather, she does claim to have powers of healing.

> We had in our group a baby girl who was born with an eye problem. The specialists had told her parents that she would be blind. You cannot treat this kind of malady with magnetism. Our guide (the angel) said, "It is too sad. We'll try a spiritual cure." For one month, we awaited the green fire that would prepare us for the intervention. On the appointed day, the mother took her naked baby on her breast and prayed with all her heart during the group's spiritual recitations. A great lethargy fell over her and I could tell that she was participating in some fantastic energy exchange that was necessary for the success of the event — which was stupendous. Today, Cecile is fourteen years old. She wears tinted spectacles to guard against glare, but she follows

a normal schooling and one day I even saw her chasing an ant.

In this trend, we see a resurgence of the kind of themes that fascinated the astronomer Camille Flammarion during the last century and which inspire voodoo groups all over the globe today.

Many such groups promising cures are merely refurbishing for today's tastes the shamanistic practices of earlier times. The guru takes on the status of a saint, that status being associated, in the subconscious mind of the people, with the power to heal. It is similar to the claim that the legitimate King of France had the divine power to cure scrofula. Along the same lines, the guru gains dominance within the group on the basis of his or her extraordinary therapeutic powers.

Witchcraft and Devil Worship

While it is true that this particular source of cult inspiration is minor, observers have noted a recent recrudescence of "black magic." Satanic groups are cropping up everywhere in the United States and Europe. The danger of these groups is that they represent abnormal practices, along the lines of the good old myth of Faust. Taking into account their morbid rituals and their systematic use of prohibited objects, the rift between them and the normal world seems even sharper than is the case with other groups. One of the attractions of these groups is the role playing of satanist characters. It is easy to slip from playing games to practicing magic, which encourages teenagers to test in the real world the effects of the magic ceremonies that they have seen in rituals and which they have tried out in role playing.

Even more worrisome is their practice of sacrifice, whether animal or human. Even if the law prohibits moving on to criminal acts, the dynamic personality and uncontrolled violence of their guru can incite a group to fatal madness. This was the case with Charles Manson, the assassin of Sharon Tate.

A paradox of all these satanic groups lies in the obvious inconsistency of their reference to the darkest age of the medieval Sabbaths.

One of them, in which a patient of ours took part, is called the *Treatise on Demonology,* by a certain Delancre.

> Towards midnight, the ceremony starts, and the Queen of the Witches sits at the feet of the Devil, who has the head of a goat, with horns, hairy body and tail. The fingers of the Devil are like talons of a predatory bird, the feet are webbed like those of a goose. New members are brought before him. They abjure their faith, they kiss his left hand and his shameful parts, and then they kiss the ground beneath his feet. Afterward, potions, powders and ointments are applied to the new members. Sometimes, the wizard makes a horrible mixture, in a pot, of toads, reptiles, the entrails of torture victims, brains of new-born children, bird droppings, gall of goat, eyes of lizard. Then comes obscene dancing, monstrous incestuous couplings, until the cock's crow.

Happily, for now, the group prefers to consume, at the time of its "sorcerers' dinners," a mixture of wine and flour which simulates coagulated blood.

Political Schemes

Cults were probably born with politics. Initiatory rituals have often served as a cover for demanding fidelity or devotion to a cause. In 1861, in an appendix describing the rituals of the coal-producers' Freemasonry (better known as Carbonarism), Ragon, the venerable founder of the workshops of the Three Sinosophes, described the role played by various secret societies that helped awaken the feeling of Italian national unity. He counted ten such secret societies, all interconnected and allying for (or competing for) influence.

Spartacus Weishaupt, the 18th century founder of the Illuminati of Bavaria, gives a historical example of the political projects of cults. His ambition was to create a political elite that would infiltrate Freemasonry and build an instrument of revolution. His enterprise failed, but he had a real influence on the training of certain revolutionaries.

No well-developed sectarian group gets by without political action. Sometimes that is, indeed, the hidden agenda. Today, these platforms are most often tinged with Aryanism, elitism, racism, and even eugenics. Often, they hide behind apparently creditable intentions: to save planet Earth, to end war, to promote equality.

In Japan, the political influence of the Soka Gakkai can be seen through the political party Komeito. It was created after the Second World War as the philosophical branch of a non-orthodox Buddhist movement, called Nichiren Shoshu. Komeito is the third most important political party in Japan, and as part of the governing coalition, it tends to combine with the Renaissance party to make up a core of neo-conservatives. Soka Gakkai, with its ten million members, presently constitutes approximately 10% of the Japanese electorate. It has been accused of holding extreme expansionist and authoritarian views that are far different from the democratic façade portrayed by its political party Komeito. These accusations are good for a rival sect, the Rissho Koseikai, which does not shine as an example of democratic virtues but which also carries considerable political weight, with six and a half million members.

Another example of the collusion of politics and cults is the Unification Church, still called the "Moonies." While it had almost disappeared from the world of European cults, its political subsidiary Causa, created in 1980, took up the cause against Marxism. Admittedly, its speeches in general have become somewhat deflated after the fall of the Soviet Union, but it still finances extreme right wing political parties in Europe. Under the leadership of Moon's right hand, Bo Hi Pak, Causa continues to feed the Manichean dialectics that encourage the fascist right. On one side, we have God and liberalism, on the other, Satan and socialism. This kind of speech still seems to strike a welcoming chord with the antidemocratic right, unless the latter are only seduced by the chance of financing their election campaigns.

Moon's European ambitions have been denounced, but he has increased his influence in Uruguay. In this country, the cult owns the third largest bank, the second most widely circulated national daily newspaper, several radio stations and various agricultural plantations. During this period, the European political scene has been infiltrated by other cults such as New Acropolis, Transcendental Meditation, Silo and other movements. In 1993, Transcendental Meditation entered the campaign for the legislative elections; and also for the European elections. Behind its leader, Benoit Frappe, it gathered thirty thousand voters, with enough contributions to stay afloat for five years, as per the law on financing political parties. A few years earlier, it had proposed to American President Bush a plan of transcendental meditation that would release the American hostages in Lebanon. In 1981, it played up to Philippine dictator Marcos and his wife Imelda, who were described as the father and mother of "the age of illumination" by the sect's guru, Maharishi Mahesh Yogi.

The stakes appear even higher in Mozambique. Completely immersed in the doctrines of Maharishi Mahesh Yogi, President Joachim Chissano appears to have converted to the cult of Transcendental Meditation. After a "study trip" to the Netherlands, the cult's European seat, Chissano signed a contract by which he gave the cult members a concession for 20 million hectares (close to 50 million acres) of arable land for a fifty-year term, without real compensation. In fact, the Finance Minister of Mozambique, Eneas Comiche, has signed a contract allowing TM to exploit an area of waste land in order to create a paradise on earth, and turning over 40% of the profits obtained by such exploitation to the government of Mozambique.[36]

South America also seems to be a promised land for cults. The association "Tradition, Family and Property," a fundamentalist and reactionary catholic sect, is particularly active. Founded by Plinio Correa de Oliveira in 1960, a Brazilian, it is opposed to the Brazilian land reforms and fights against the Marxist and Communists. It wants to restore the monarchy. It played an active role in the anti-militant political repression in Brazil, Argentina and Chile. It also supported apartheid in South Africa. Equipped with considerable financial resources, it has funded well-equipped militias dedicated to combating communism. In France, it is better known by the name of "Cultural Future." It became well known there because of its demonstrations against the film *the Temptation of Christ* by Martin Scorsese and also *Je vous salue Marie* by Jean-

Luc Godard.

In Brazil, it is the Universal Church of the Reign of God (called simply "the Universal" by the Brazilians) that fills stadiums. Its leader is Edir Macedo. It is an offshoot of the Pentecostal Church that succeeded the Assembly of God and the Quadrangular Church. Emerging on the political scene in the 1960's, it controlled President Ernesto Geisel from 1974 to 1979. Presently, it forms the inner circle around Peruvian President Fujimori, as well as the President of Guatemala who converted a few years ago. It has a simple strategy, and that is to control the media, in particular the radio and television. Edir Macedo presently controls 28 radio stations and 850 temples. With its base of one and a half million followers, it has launched an evangelization campaign against animist religions. The campaign is not without some fascist and xenophobic strains in relation to the black population. However, it knows how to weave together perfectly the topics that appeal to its audience — success, wealth and cure by laying on of hands. Its more prosaic intention is to lay its hands on the entire country, and many indictments have been issued. That has not slowed its growth.

The Pentecostal Church and its offshoots like the Universal Church, however, do not appear to be the fruit of good luck nor of Brazil's spiritual quest. In 1984, in a report addressed to the Vatican, the conference of Brazilian Bishops denounced the CIA's hold on the Pentecostal sects and their use for objectives of manipulation and political influence, of which the CIA is so fond.

"I am a man who wishes the truth. In this matter, I obey not the constitution, but the Bible." Thus spoke General President Efrain Rios Montt in March 1982, having just come to power in Guatemala City, following a banal military coup. A follower of the Church of the Verb, a fundamentalist Californian sect, he brought to power with him two other members of the sect, Francisco Bianchi and Alvaro Will. President Montt was to retain power for only seventeen months. Since his departure, various sects have been competing influence in Guatemalan politics. This is particularly fertile ground for sects, with almost 30% of the population belonging to one or another.

Similarly, in the aftermath of the sarin gas attack by the Aum cult in Japan, the international investigation that followed it underscored the close bonds existing between the Russian political powers and the cult. When Vitali Savitsky, the President of the Parliamentary Committee on Religious Organizations in Russia, was asked how the inquest was progressing, he said, in July 1995, "The investigation has been stymied at the highest level of the State. No trial of the Aumists will take place." It is obvious that Moscow did not take pains to clarify the relations between the Aum sect and the services of the State. It seems that Oleg Lobov, Secretary of the Security Council, was among those responsible for the establishment of Aum in Russia. In 1991, he contacted Shoko Asahara for the alleged purpose of collecting funds for the creation of a Russian-Japanese university. During his stay in Russia, Asahara met Ruslan Khasbulatov, at that time President of the Parliament, and also Alexander Rutskoi, Vice-President of Russia.

Today, the faces and the outward appearance of cults is constantly changing — yet one thing remains clear: the will to convert the entire planet, either by free will, through proselytism or, more prosaically, by developing networks of influence based on economics as well as politics.[37]

Money-Making Schemes

The latest transformation in cults, well-suited to the present crisis, is economic performance — a powerful argument for recruitment and one which, furthermore, encourages an abundance of affiliate groups. Scientology, for one, adopted the practice of developing networks in every sector of economic life, without changing its underlying structure. The WISE network (World Institute of Scientology Enterprise) takes care of the cult's marketing. Founded in 1979, it is presented as "a management organization whose aim is to have the administrative technology of Ron Hubbard disseminated on a grand scale and utilized in the business world."

Thus, WISE is overtly the economic branch of the sect. It is manifest in all the hierarchical levels of the sect, and supervises an organization that gives licenses to individuals and associations permitting them to use Hubbard's "prescriptions." Their services include management consulting and the organization of seminars, classes and workshops. The standard written contracts signed between WISE and users of the Hubbard technology calls for payment of royalties that may go up to 16% of the fees received by the members.[38]

Other cults have made a specialty of producing and commercializing various products. Thus, for many years, selling incense has been a significant source of income for the Light of Krishna. Similarly, the Moonies were deeply involved in the sale of ginseng.

Under fire for many years, the EGMP, European Group of Marketing Professionals, was recently dissolved, in France. Created in 1988 by Jean Godzich, this group is accused of raising money by illicit means. The group posed as a champion of individual free enterprise, but was actually a pyramid system that practiced multilevel sales. It was different from traditional sects, where the financial interests usually appear to take a back seat behind the ideology. This one promotes a sales network charged with enriching its members.[39] Although the leaders claim that this is not a sales pyramid (or "snowball,") consumer associations think otherwise. They have revealed practices far removed from commerce. Doug Wead, who was a member EGMP side by side with Godzich and a former adviser of George Bush, is also Pastor of "The First Assembly of God" in Phoenix (Arizona), where Leo Godzich (brother of Jean) officiates. The near-obligatory conversion and baptism in this Church, the "Dream Weekends" during which sermons alternate with public confessions, seem to show more cult-based indoctrination than training in marketing.

At the heart of all these processes is the guru. Whatever may be their doctrines and methods, cults need leaders around whom they can create a structure, and who can serve as guides in their journey towards an illusory ideal. It is the leader who breathes life into the cult and defines its actions.

3.

THE GURU

Imagination, that mistress of error and falsehood, is the dominant part of man, and all the more misleading since it is inconsistent — for it would be an infallible measure of truth, if it were infallibly so for lies. But being more often false, it gives no sign of its quality, and marks with the same character both what is true and what is false.

Pascal.

Manipulation fundamentally depends on fraud. How well it is done depends on the personality and cunning of the guru.

The original term "guru" was derived from a Sanskrit word meaning "worthy." It defines a spiritual Master in the Brahmanic religion. By birth and by essence, this person is above the Kshatriyas (warrior caste) and the Vaishyas (trading caste). The guru is the wise person who teaches and shows the way to divine revelation. In the present context, the term "guru" will be used only in its modern extended meaning, "charismatic leader of a cult," without intending to imply that this charisma is founded on the value or the legitimacy of the affiliation claimed by the individual in question.

The guru is occasionally described as a psychopath whose personality traits include mythomania, impulsiveness, amorality and an imperviousness to others' opinions. We do not completely share this interpretation. Some gurus conform to these nosographic criteria, such as Jim Jones, the guru priest of the Temple of the People in Guyana, L. R. Hubbard, founder of Scientology, and David Berg (alias Moïse David), leading light of the Children of God (Family of Love).[1] Others seem to be simple crooks or individuals "guided" by financial or political interests[2] that leave little room for psychological concerns. One may in any case include among them some who are truly mentally ill, who have succeeded to gain mastery over their followers in spite of their disorders. Or thanks to them.

Jim Jones, through his Temple in Guyana, involved his disciples in a collective suicide, resulting in the death of 914 cult members. L. R. Hubbard was accused by his own family of sadism and sexual conduct typical of real perverts. David Berg was convicted of sadism toward children, and incest with his own.

On the other hand, few psychiatric elements stand out in the profile of Sun Yat Moon, creator of the Moonist cult. It has been well known for several years that the CIA supported him in launching and developing the cult so that it could have a presence in Korea and be used as a bastion against communism by organizing the sale and production of weapons.

In the second group of gurus, the confused nature of their doctrines serves as protection against analysis by society, for the more aberrant their treatises, the less mistrust is directed toward them; they are simply regarded as "mild lunatics" taking advantage of general social misery. A serious look at the discourse of one Claude Vorilhon, alias Raël, leaves little place for mythomania. It is more the conscious construction of a pseudo-bizarre history (contacts with extraterrestrials, trips on flying saucers). His exploitation of the media leaves no doubt — we are not dealing with any psychiatric element here. Studied in terms of its financial implications, the message "transmitted" by the extraterrestrials has very little to do with transcendence or spiritual growth.

Looking back at the last fifty years, we find that there is little in common between masters of thought such as Sri Aurobindo, Lanza del Vasto or Taisen Teshimaru,[3] and other individuals such as Ron Hubbard, Raël or Moïse David. More difficult to pin down are characters like Sri Chimnoy[4] and Maharishi Mahesh Yogi,[5] who profess, sometimes rightly, that they are merely following the traditional path of another divine guru, as a child follows a father. Still, the drift toward culthood is a live possibility — the proliferation of pseudo-gurus issuing from the ashram of

Auroville in India, created by Aurobindo, serves as a reminder of this.

Gurus can be divided into four groups:

• Masters of thought, in the noble sense of the term, which however does not preclude behavioral and ideological oddities;

• Cheats who know how to exploit human credulity to market "products;"

• The mentally ill, especially those suffering from paranoia, hysteria and hallucinations (interpretive mystics and nervous hysterics).

• Lastly, there are some who fall somewhere between the above three categories, who began with a sincere personal vision and slid into a pathological view of reality or who consciously use the awareness thus gained for a lucrative purpose. Michael Ivanov, founder of Universal White Fraternity[6] has been in legal trouble on several occasions for fraud, infractions of the labor laws, and rape; he is a model of this genre as can be seen from this excerpt from his proposition, "What is a Master."[7]

> Different energies and apparatuses are called upon when an ordinary man works and when a Master works. A Master is he who knows how to nourish himself only from the solar source, at the level of this source and not elsewhere.
>
> That means that his is an enlarged consciousness, directed toward the sublime, in order to attract, absorb and accumulate particles and energies coming from very high, which will be used to nourish all the bodies of which he is composed. While the ordinary man, not turning his consciousness or his thought toward noble, honest and outward-directed things, attracts far inferior materials which accumulate in his subconsciousness. Thus he will not be able to nourish all the bodies that make up his being; he lacks the food which the Initiates like to call "celestial" or "ambrosia."

Another extract from the same author shows that the guru's role and status cannot (must not?) be comprehended by the disciples:

> Very few understand that which we wish to say. A Master is one who has applied the four esoteric rules of the manifest world: to know, to

wish, to dare, to keep silent. Knowing how to comprehend the laws of the manifest world, wishing to apply them, daring to do so, in silence, he has realized his evolution in the manifest world. Thus he is at the zenith, like a Sun, and now in turn he can apply his strength to illuminate the consciousness of ordinary man.

A guru must be seen by his followers as participating in a divine energy that places him above his "troops:"

> A Master is a being who has become luminous, warm, inspiring and powerful like the Sun, who is wholly concentrated on the Cosmic Spirit. He knows the ineffable, the unspoken, that which is not manifest; in short, he knows the fundamental principles of Life and the Cosmos. A master is a being who knows the four internal elements and who is obeyed by the four external elements. He is one who can decipher the four languages in which nature is expressed: the seven movements that correspond to the Spirit, the seven colors that correspond to Intelligence, the seven sounds that correspond to the Heart, the seven shapes that correspond to Physics.

The Master is supposed to have completed a path of initiation that confers upon him supreme knowledge.

> A Master has achieved his "second birth," according to traditions of initiation. His philosophy teaches the development of internal forces, so that man is no longer an animal at heart, and so that he undertakes the process of his resurrection: the descent of his spiritual soul. Thus, initiation cuts short the time needed for development.

> The Masters do not develop only their intellect, as men generally do, but rather their intuition which is at the apex of their consciousness, in the causal plane, the Center. By their determination, their life is governed by the law of Providence.

> The Master is one who lives at the mountaintop, on the causal plane (principles). He is above dust (certain thoughts of the intellect, and above fog (certain feelings of the heart). He has reached the higher subjectivity with is true objectivity, the reality of true life.

Having achieved a different ontological status, the guru acts on nature and men:

> The Master has given first place to the Cosmic Spirit, "the Lord," so that everything else will be organized within it. Thus, his future is well-oriented. The Master can become a luminous being to enlighten humanity, a warm-hearted being to comfort humanity, an inspiring being in order to awaken humanity.
>
> The Master knows how to adjust the wavelength of his thoughts in order to set off vibrations in human minds.
>
> The Master, by the means of his spiritual light, knows how to harmonize himself with the Cosmic Spirit.

This harmony is the basis of his knowledge and power. It gives him the authority to assert the law and to claim the role of leader.

> The Master is master of his imagination. He uses it. He is the boss. He knows that that is where the power lies, and he does not plant in his imagination any seeds but the divine, in order to be able to have divine manifestations and divine children. He is a man of synthesis. People do not accept the Truth because they wish for truth to conform to their caprices, to their varying whims. Thus they accumulate things, and cares. Philosophers and artists lead to chaos through analysis.
>
> A Master has only one idea, one Philosophy, the only one, the philosophy of synthesis, which brings everything together and unifies it, connects it, makes life flow. Only he can know the truth, because only simplification allows one to recognize the truth.
>
> Masters think only about fusion with the Cosmic Spirit in order to help others. They are enlightened. Their feelings of abnegation, sacrifice, patience, tolerance, softness, of Love and purity, place them at the apex of this scale of feelings.
>
> But, being of a superior essence, the Master is not always understood, even by his disciples. That is why he is sometimes subjected to unfounded criticisms coming from the ill-informed and ill-intentioned.

But Masters are clairvoyant. They know how to distinguish between people of darkness and people who are enlightened.

They know that in order to make the quality of their emanations more subtle, they must practice vaporization. Vaporization is the transformation of the dense into the subtle; it requires increasing the free surface of the air, raising the temperature, and increasing the internal pressure.

That is why, to verify this law, they work for centuries on their emanations by liberating themselves (more free surface), through thought (air), through spiritual love (warmth), and by increasing the internal pressure (faith). The hearths of initiation that they create prepare the best conditions for all of humanity.

A Master is a repository of Esoteric Science. His morality is the knowledge of the laws of Nature.

The basis of his actions is to harmonize with the Cosmic laws.

His knowledge enables him to manipulate his insides, according to the rhythm of these laws. It does not follow the rhythm conceived by human intellect. That is why people make mistakes and mislead each other through poor judgment and ignorance.

A confused, flattering proposition of generalities.

Truths and Lies

For a guru to be marketable, a past has to be invented for him that is interesting and greater than reality. Russel Miller,[8] a journalist, inquired into the life of Ron Hubbard.[9] In 1993, he published the results of his research:

For more than thirty years, the Church of Scientology has made every effort to promote the image of L. R. Hubbard, its founder, as a bold pioneer and an inspired philosopher, whose early life had prepared him, no more nor less than Jesus Christ, for the mission of universal redeemer (which he proclaimed for himself). The chain of supposed facts that glorify the guru as a superhuman character and savior of humanity can only be concocted with a distinct contempt for the facts. This is the reason why every biography of Hubbard published by the cult is woven out of pure invention, half-truths and grotesque embellishment.[10]

The guru endeavors to make this magnificent history credible and to "sell" it to his disciples, with a degree of success that varies with the strength of their desire to believe, and which does not hold up for long under intense scrutiny. Little by little, even the guru falls into his own trap of lies. Over time, the guru loses sight of what was true and what was invented, and gradually takes on the character that he created, slipping into a state of confusion and madness.

Biography of a Guru

This can be highly significant, when one wishes to assess the authenticity of the teachings lavishly bestowed. There is no discrepancy between the real biography of a true Master of Thought and that which is known to his disciples, or to the general public. Conversely, the fake guru manufactures a legend connected to the history and the roots of the group. The stages of his life are completely re-written. Thus the account of an illusory mystical experience turns out to have been a real episode that was not exactly brilliant. A professional and social failure will be dissimulated behind a panoply of titles and prestigious diplomas — every one of them invented — or a mystical quest around the world may hide a pitiful wandering. Almost invariably, there has been no breakthrough event in the individual's development.

On the other hand, the absence of flamboyant events in the guru's biography is the surest sign that the guru is rendering traditional teachings to his followers. The guru is part of a continuity where his individual personality is not of interest. He is only a link in a chain of thought and a spiritual flow of which he wishes to be the instrument. He is like a telegraph operator who transmits, without corrupting the message that he receives. And while the disappearance of the guru is likely to break the chain of transmission of the message, yet his personality neither truncates nor embellishes the message that he conveys.

From Eccentricity to Strategy

The imaginary biography of a guru conceals considerable information. Fables? Pure invention? Sheer raving lunacy? From these nuances the cult's organizational strategy is derived, its profile — and the choice of methods that may be sued to combat it.

Certain cults rely on a family structure, like the Melchior brothers.[11] Robert, the eldest brother, was a missionary in Bolivia. He lent an aura of moral and religious standing to the Pianto Society, whose aim is to market a rejuvenation product. His joining the society made it possible for them to extend their field of activity by introducing a trade that is more flourishing than the traditional religious symbols and objects. Andre, the junior brother, a chemical engineer, extended his scope to the development of the Pianto elixir that is sold in health food stores; then he went further, making plaster statuary weep and produce miraculous markings (containing phenolphthalein), that were then blessed by the elder brother and sold by the cult. Victor, the third brother, an unskilled laborer, handles all the lower tasks. Roger, the youngest brother, is a doctor of law and a part-time lecturer at the Catholic faculty of Brussels. He is the brain of the cult. He tried his hand at diplomacy before settling down and devoting himself completely to the divine mission of the cult. The combined strength of these brothers contained all the ingredients favorable to delinquency: abuse of public property, fraud, abduction of minors, theft, violence and similar acts — before they were arrested.

Childhood and Adolescence

Often there is a mythical recombining of the birth and childhood of the leader. Certain children are born gurus, others grow into it later in life. Filiation may be biological or spiritual.

The father of Guru Maharaj Ji[12] was the creator of the Mission of the Divine Light. In 1956, he ceded his place to his son, who was only eight and a half years old at the time. Abhay Charan Ji,[13] Master of the Consiousness of Krishna, received "the initiation and transmission of the responsibility for the Consiousness of Krishna" from his spiritual father Sri Srimad Baklisidanta Sarawashi Gowshawari. Other gurus assert their legitimacy by virtue of initiation or cultural relatedness, like Sri Chimnoy through Sri Aurobindo. Similarly Moon,[14] member of the South Korean cult "the Orders of Israel," would take over the messianic role of Kim Mon Pai.

Sometimes, the relationship is limited simply to reference: Michael Ivanov, founder of the FBU, claims to continue the heritage of Peter Dunov and Rudolf Steiner. Others make no claim beyond the banality of their own lives, like George Roux, the Christ of Montfavet.[15]

The Passage to Adulthood

Most often, the Messiah or guru proclaims that he has supernatural powers after he has become an adult.

Ron Hubbard, until the age of 30, was a simple author of science fiction novels, before building the structure that later became Scientology, and from then on displaying an unfailing religious determination. "If you really want to make a million dollars, and not be paid at a rate of 5 cents per line, you should become the founder of a Church," as he stated one day to a group of journalists.

The same conviction seems to have been adopted by Claude Vorilhon (later, Raël),[16] who tried in vain both journalism and singing. In 1973, he met God in the guise of extraterrestrial beings. Yahweh revealed his true origin to him, as follows:

> We selected a woman as we did at the time of Jesus. We took her on board our spaceship and she was inseminated as we had done with the mother of Jesus. We had taken care to have a man meet this woman as well. Your father is also the true father of Jesus. Hence, Jesus is your brother. And the father is standing before you.[17]

However, this account suffers from a basic defect, as it does not offer any bait to tempt the followers. There is no hope for them to attain an achievement comparable to that of the Master.

Religious Training

The religious background is important and it will be discussed below. Iso-Zen and Soka Gakkai[18] draw inspiration from Buddhism; the Light of Krishna, Brahma-Kumari[19] and Bhagwan[20] draw inspiration from Hinduism. Similarly, the evangelical and millenarist cults of David Koresh, Jim Jones and Charles Taze Russel (Jehovah's Witnesses) draw inspiration from Protestantism. The founders of the cult try to give some new interpretation to distinguish themselves from the ancestral religions, but they weave into the jumble of their discourse certain recognizable elements. This process results in a proliferation of religious and philosophical pseudo-syntheses which have more to do with the esoterico-mystico-occult catch-all than with any a true syncretism.

It is like one blur over another. A lack of cultural knowledge makes it difficult to verify the affiliations that are claimed, because they relate to domains that are themselves not well understood, with mythical figures, sometimes real but generally long since dead, ancient, forgotten and a blur. Thus there is little chance of seeing a guru repudiated by his pupil. Little by little, the story is built up, and the guru will gradually acquire the aura of wisdom and holiness, which will be his path to promotion.

In *The Hell of Cults,* François Cornuault describes the environment in which Michaël Ivanov (FBU) revolved:

> In 1938, the most enlightened esoteric spirits of the time, Leadbeater (founder of the Theosophy Society), Rudolf Steiner (founder of Anthroposophy), and several other famous visionaries testified in his favor. They recognized Michael as the one "who was expected," the holy Archangel Michael in person. In no time, FBU became the most well-known cult in Paris. Everyone followed the Master like a new Christ and sought his legendary radiance. It was whispered that he was the "19th Grand Master of the World" or "the Alchemist of Aquarius."

Jean-Paul Appel, founder of Iso-Zen,[21] was so impressed that he ascribed to himself a divine filiation. The work written to glorify him writes:

> The copulation of the congenital parents of his physical body was accomplished with the immersion of the energies that control the favorable chromosomal conjunctions.
>
> He knew the early childhood of the exceptionally gifted, programmed as he was by the cosmic powers. The programmed vehicle would be stabilized on Earth 3 and would enjoy an accelerated development.
>
> When the child was twelve years of age, he received his first direct contact with the cosmic powers. This contact was in the form of a radiation coming from the sky and crossing the brain. This contact would not show its effect for six years, as the cosmic powers say — Investiture Successful. Flash forward six years into the future — Earth 3 time.
>
> Between the two dates, this cosmically programmed being would be initiated by a spiritual master, up until the age of eighteen, where he arrives in an intensely mystical state.

It is difficult to contradict the author of such gibberish. We will see more of this clever use of language and words by cults to avoid any dispute. Every follower finds his own meaning to the words and sentences used. The argument put forth to support this clever oratory is that it is not really a language at all, but is really a symbolic speech.

Cultural Level and Diplomas

It is impossible to authenticate the value of the diplomas held by gurus. Some are real, some are completely fake. Whether they are false or genuine, these diplomas do provide invaluable indications of the graduate's concerns. Ron Hubbard's alleged qualification in nuclear science is a kind of precursor to the therapeutic pseudo-indications later recommended by the Church of Scientology.

After several successful journeys around the world, on returning back to United States in 1929, Ron Hubbard again took up his school education. He took courses at the private college of Swawly in Manasses, Virginia, then graduated from Woodward, the boys' school in Washington. He was registered at the George Washington University. His father and destiny directed him toward the study of mathematics and engineering. This knowledge of engineering and mathematics was to be of particular use to him in later life. This knowledge later enabled him to conduct research on the mysteries of life and the spiritual potential of man according to scientific methods. He posited that the world of subatomic particles could provide indices of the thought process. He was enrolled in one of the first courses in nuclear physics taught in the United States.[22]

The followers of the cult, without batting an eyelid, credit Hubbard with the discovery of quarks(!). However, that view does not appear to be unanimous. Professor Galle, of the laboratory of biophysics of Inserm, studied the method of "purification" given by Ron Hubbard in his public documents of Scientology. He concluded flat out that "it is nothing but an amalgam of quotations from fantastical articles. It combines fatuous propositions and disconcerting 'scientific' justification."[23]

This opinion seems to be shared by Doctor Nenot of the Commission of Atomic Energy,[24] whom we questioned about this same protocol:

> Ron Hubbard's text does not seem to be a scientific document so much as a collection of strange jargon. It appears that the author has not fully assimilated the basics of physiology or physiopathology. In the field of radiopathology, he misses the general sense of this science and his remarks lack any medical value.

In order to assert supernatural powers, the guru must appear to be more advanced in all fields, including the most prosaic. Thus he readily claims to have fictitious diplomas, generally in fields that fascinate him but of which he understands not an iota. The topics and areas of interest are selected according to the fashion of the day, but they generally have to do with "waves." Many gurus allege competence in nuclear science, electronics, and electromagnetism. These disciplines are all sufficiently complex and evolutionary to be beyond the understanding of common followers, and lend themselves to theories of para-scientific extrapolation.

Another favored field is parallel medicines. Here, the guru has triple benefits. First, these fields allow for the most absurd speculations; second, establishments exist that manufacture doctorates "honoris causa" for the most outlandish reasons. Finally, disciples are fascinated by the underlying myth of eternal life, promised by the healing techniques offered by the guru.

Gurus are very keen on diplomas. Take Mr. Moon: "After primary education in his native village and secondary education in Seoul, he went to Japan to study for a diploma in electrical engineering at Waseda University. He could not obtain the diploma and he changed his line of study." Young Kwan Pak, the author of *A Critiques of Cults*, a work published in Korea, has affirmed that the Unification Church embellished the story — as proof, "the Japanese newspaper *Manichi*, could not find the name of Mr. Moon in the list of former students of the university..."

With or without the diploma, the young Moon returned to Korea and worked as an electrician in the construction industry. This early cohabitation with ions and electrons would leave traces in the Moonist doctrines. The Unification Church is constantly making references to positive and negative concepts to explain the universe — a reference which must owe as much to electric theory as to the Chinese heritage of the yin and yang. Similarly, without any biblical or theological education, the plant biologist turns himself into the pastor of a charismatic Christian community in Pyongyang, capital of North Korea, under communist rule. Thereafter, he claims the title "Reverend." Under his aegis there are long prayers, much singing and hand clapping, speaking of strange languages, laying on of hands for healing purposes, celestial revelations, and communication with the world of spirits.

Medical History

It is edifying to analyze the medical past of gurus. A number of them have extensive experience in the medical world. Not as experts, but as patients, during periods of confinement for psychiatric reasons.[25]

At the request of the Austrian government, a psychoanalytical analysis was undertaken on the writings of Otto Muhl, founder of the cult AAO[26] (Organization of Actional Analysis), known in France by the name of the Kommune. The conclusions are beyond dispute:[27]

> The author was a problem child, so much so that he tried to strike his father with a chair. The horrors of war during his childhood had obviously traumatized him and left its impact on him.

> This man was prey to a very marked inferiority complex. At the same time, he was a paranoiac and a pervert. He speaks of the wrong and the injury done to him by his parents, his education and the low middle class upbringing. His actions show that his whole being has revolted against society.

In 1968, Otto Muhl introduced himself as an "anarchist" painter. He displayed himself nude, oozing lemonade, in the Austrian literary clubs, from which he was banned immediately.[28]

The Disguised Truth

This taste for disguising the truth, for embellishing it, or even for transfiguring it altogether, is no game but a vital necessity. Only the real and recognized value of the individual can make people forget the condemnable or petty elements of his life. However, the guru is only a poor individual, and setting out his true past in clear daylight would immediately throw discredit upon the person and his ideas. Thus there is a vital obligation to observe absolute secrecy on the elements of reality likely to tarnish his image. This has been explained in complete clarity by Livraga, guru of the New Acropolis,[29] in a small handbook strictly reserved for the most trusted followers:

> Secrecy, the central commander's principle of propaganda and maintenance of law and order, is necessary for harmonious development of the New Acropolis.

> The exaggerated virtues ascribed to the teachers and leaders of the cult

allow the students to divinize them, and to ascribe to them further virtues, powers and achievements imagined simply by extension of smaller truths.

The New Acropolis member who does not have sufficient seniority or access to the sources of information or to the supreme leadership cannot have a very clear idea of the why's and how's.

Spiritual, mental and even physical contact with the top leadership, in fact with the guru, can only be significant for the disciples of long standing, who are closer to the solitary summit. At the base, a healthy psychological coolness must prevail, for friendship is a heady wine for the young, and it separates them from the whole of the cult, making them lose the unity that is the fundamental axiom of the pyramidal system.

The pyramidal structure must be established everywhere in the cult. It will be veiled, as we shield the eyes of the newborn baby from strong light.

A man is better able to lead when he is little known.

The chief of information may be well known to all, but his activities and his contacts must remain hidden both inside and outside of the cult.[30]

The concept of secrecy applies to the guru's biography as well as the working procedure of the cult. This is why J. A. Livraga devoted whole chapters of his leadership handbook to the strategy that should be implemented in the event of internal or external crises. In both cases, the follower should remain unaware of the reality of the facts. Secrets, denials, even lies conspire to maintain the survival of the myth.

Things must be kept as quiet as possible. Use propaganda and the Intelligence Service to give out a version of the story that will minimize the effect of any adverse event, which could even be denied altogether, if necessary.

Along with this strategy, the courses and services must be maintained, giving the impression that nothing is amiss. . .

Guru-Speak

If a guru were content to construct the theories of his hysterical ravings for his own benefit, he would be nothing more than a kook. However, to exist as a guru, he has to convince his close relations and then increase his following through sparkling and attractive remarks. His speeches have to be a subtle balance of dubious reasoning (that may elicit hysterical laughter or a perplexed frown) and a proof, of supposedly irrefutable cogency, of his theories. The speech is built on paralogical reasoning that starts from a clear and concrete proposal, is then built up little by little, subtly distorted, and finally reaches an aberrant conclusion that would ordinarily be rejected.

To illustrate the principle of paralogical distortion, we will repeat an environmentalist joke that has become a classic: "Nature is threatened, because the trees are dying. The trees must be saved. However, the beavers cut down trees to make their dams. Thus, to save nature, the beavers have to be killed. All among you who love nature must follow me in the campaign to kill the beaver..." The proposition is precise, and so are its consequences, except for just one — "The beavers have to be killed," since beavers are also part of the natural balance. And the logic of the entire discourse falls apart.

Most gurus use these paralogical distortions, which go together with paranoia and megalomania. In every case, the most elementary Manicheism is at work — the guru puts all lies and evil on one side, and himself and his trusted partners, mirrors of truth and light, on the other. It is this dynamics of exclusion of the other, the outside, that gives the cult its aggressive and proselytizing dynamism. The biography of the guru has only one goal, to glorify his person as a figure of truth and justice in a fight against malefic powers.

The contemporary palm-reader and seer, Hanussen, combines all the ingredients of occultism. He is allegedly the illegitimate son of an astrologer of the same name, well-known under the Third Reich. He derives the paranormal powers, of which he is so proud, from the history of his father. This new Messiah opposes the harmful forces of the black occultism of Nazism. His role is to save the righteous from suffering and to inform humanity of its errors. The illegitimate birth of the guru is doubly interesting. On the one hand, it precludes any serious investigation into the alleged relationship; in addition it confers an "unusual status" that is the mark of an occult transmission of the powers claimed. As if throwing opprobrium on Hitler was enough to be seen as a supreme enemy of Evil, the guru establishes his character by playing on the unanimous revulsion caused by Nazism and the Jewish holocaust — with the side-effect of providing an attractive setting for those who feel they are persecuted.[31] Here the version of the facts given by his followers:

> Hitler was born in the same year and in the same country as Herman Steinschneider. The latter was at the peak of his glory when Hitler reopened the Reichstag.... Hitler's entourage took dim view of the greatest prophet of the era captivating the public with his clairvoyant gifts. He was a danger to the regime. Hanussen was assassinated sometime in the night of 24th/25th March, 1933.... Hanussen died, but his memory and spirit survived for decades in the hearts of his followers, until his last prediction came to pass, which was — "In less than 30 years, the world will listen to a new Hanussen, my only heir, my direct successor." The first Hanussen had the courage and strength to hide, until his last breath, the fact that he had an illegitimate son. That was the only way of protecting the child from threats to his life because of his Jewish origins. It had saved the young Hanussen's life, but his childhood was particularly difficult, painful, solitary and often dramatic because of this withholding of identity. His mother informed him of his paternity only on her deathbed. The new Hanussen owes to this ensemble of circumstances, both mysterious and logical, the development of a personality that extends and exceeds that of his father.[32]

Paralogical Reasoning

Paralogical reasoning is the mainstay of gurus' discourses, and are counted on to convince the followers. Annick Lasalmonie, in her thesis, has provided examples in her analysis of the Moonies' talk:[33] "Sexual sin is the most serious sin of all, since it is the original sin, Lucifer having seduced Eve." The first paralogical conclusion: "All marriages since creation are the result of Satan's evil." The second: "If Jesus had married, he would have been able to correct this situation." Remember the Moonie postulate: "Moon is the new Messiah." Conclusion: in March 1960, he marries an eighteen-year-old girl, Man Malega. This marriage places Moon in the same position as the first Adam marrying Eve, who was immature at the time of her union.

For all these reasons, one can become member of the Moonist Church only by being a son or daughter of Moon through membership in a mortal life where only marriages between "a son" of Moon and one of his "daughters" is tolerated, and that only after a period of probation:

> And so, each of you will have a period of seven years during which you will be linked to the father. You will thus return to the position of seed in the perfect body of Adam still unwed. We can see that the seed comes from the father of the man who is not fallen. The seed is conceived, it must begin in the body of Adam. Only I have achieved this role to date.

Moon is thus presented not only as a father, he is also the symbolic husband:

> We can be dissolved in the marrow of the bones of the Messiah and we can become a seed of the Messiah. Then this pure seed will be sown in the uterus of the woman who is without sin. By entering the marrow of the bones of the Messiah, a woman can become a seed of the Messiah, without sin. If the two parents are without sin, their daughter will be without sin: that is the change of a lineage.[34]

The paralogical reasoning of the guru makes it possible to legitimate any attitude; his speech betrays his major desires. This para-logic underlies many cult themes. Here again, it is difficult to differentiate between pathology and simulation, since this reasoning allows for so much fakery.

Paraphrenic Elements

Psychiatry describes "paraphrenia" as a mental illness that completely cuts off the individual from reality. He is projected into a fictitious universe that is built around the most absurd interpretations, the haziest theories and the most elaborate hallucinations.

Many theories developed by cults are derived from fantastic elements borrowed from myths. They reflect the megalomania of the guru and his skill at marrying the imaginary to the most varied sources. He tends especially to restore magical thought, while borrowing from esotericism and sorcery. In this catalogue of the strange and the occult, one meets the Masters of the world and their forbidden cities (Agartha, Atlantis, Tibet and so on), extraterrestrials and their messages (UFOs, drawings of the Andes cordillera, megaliths and so on), lost words and secrets (pharoahs, Templars, alchemists and so on), communion with the beyond (Belzebub, Saint Michael). It is true that these themes are also found in a number of initiatory societies that are not coercive in the least, and whose organizers are generally healthy of mind. In such cases, they are used only as supports to development and for the maturation of an initiatory "search." They are read for their symbolic value, and not taken literally.

Levitation was recommended as a way to reduce criminality, by Maharishi, in his address to his followers in Transcendental Meditation:

> Maharishi spoke with the first Purvsha in Boppard. He proposed that in order to increase coherence, they should coordinate the moment of levitation, so that the maximum possible number of the five thousand German sidhas should practice their flight simultaneously.

As for Raël, after being received with great pomp by the little green men, he returned to Earth with this message:

> We are very pessimistic. Your earth is condemned. It is going to destroy itself and nobody will be able to help, nor to prevent its suicide. Unless Raël discovers the solution, which he is not far from doing, because he alone has the capacity to read and interpret the sacred texts....
>
> By order of Yahweh, a man of God went from Judah to Bethel. He said, "Here the altar will split,... thanks to a disintegrator." One of the creators destroyed the altar and burnt the hand of one of the men who did not obey the creators. The creators cannot eat in the open air be-

cause of their space suits. They can extract the essence from various offerings when necessary by using flexible tubing.[35]

The Scientologists use this sort of doctrine, mixing all sorts of wild imaginings to make up the "historical account" of their cult. Similar cosmic gestures are found in the speeches of Harry Palmer, a dissident from Scientology, who teaches similar oddities in his "Magicians' courses in metamorphosis":[36]

25,000 years ago,... the beings of the Galactic Confederation were able to concentrate their thought with a high degree of accuracy without effort..... In the Confederation, wisdom was measured by the number of beliefs one held. Each generation of the Confederation increased the mass of knowledge. Over a period of time, this mass of learning became so extensive that no member of the Confederation could live long enough to learn all of it. At this point in time, the Confederation adopted the technique known as indoctrination by stimulus. This process was like a trip to the movies, but in place of popcorn a hyper-sensitizing drug was given and the room was filled with a plasma of synthetic mental energy at a high level of vibration. The images scrolled by on the screen at a rate several hundred times the normal. The data were thus loaded into the mind of the viewer.

Later, the Confederation started to experience disturbances. The films became instruction manuals for military and political indoctrination....

The galaxy was expanding and new forms of gravitational pull began to upset the stability of the collective consciousness of the central worlds. An error of judgment led to the contraction of the Confederation of the central worlds. It was like the snake in the Garden of Eden. The snake represents the innermost beliefs that act like a stimulus coiled in the spirit and ready to strike. The Garden of Eden is the collective consciousness of the central world before the disturbances....

The external edge of the Milky Way slowed down, which caused violent gravitational disturbances and events.

Many civilizations died and fell into oblivion...

Nevertheless, Karsak of Triton inherited the science and culture of the Confederation and was the agent of scientific and technical knowledge. A civilization appeared, only one, where the collective consciousness was released from the chains of fixed beliefs, in an enlightened age. Its name was Companion of Estro.

Karsak of Triton became a large gray rock. The majority of the population was dying of hunger. A glimmer of hope survived, that was the Companion of Estro.

A growing circle of Companion test pilots accepted the responsibility that destiny had entrusted to them. They swore to bring wisdom to the middle worlds.... They explored time from the beginning to the end.... Here is their mission — to help every civilization that has attained technical maturity to pass without hindrance into a state of enlightenment, so that they will not destroy themselves.

I remind to you that the Earth is a seedbed of life, that its process of photosynthesis is always intact. Welcome to the course for magicians!

In many of these speeches science fiction stories coexist with identifiable cultural elements (the loss of Eden, the apocalypse, science without conscience and so on). They can be reproduced *ad infinitum* and indicate the extreme fertility of the gurus' visions and, especially, their capacity to respond to the desires of their "subjects."

4.

HOW CULTS ARE ORGANIZED

Every clear idea that we form decreases our slavery and increases our freedom.

Alain

Become that which you are. Do what only you can do.

Nietzsche

The cult develops around the guru. The aspiring followers enlarge its ranks like a snowball. However, not all the followers have the same status — far from it. They do not maintain the same relationship with the guru, nor do they derive the same benefit from their membership. There are two groups of individuals — those who are unconscious and manipulated, and those who are conscious manipulators.

The unconscious manipulated ones function like a flock, which can be described as spherical. Whatever the status of the individual, his place is identical to the others', except for "the leader" who plays the part of the intermediary between the base and the summit. The person who is in charge can be further developed or may be replaced, according to his competence. He is interchangeable and serves as the leadership's "telephone" and the "fuse and circuit breaker." Actually, there is no hierarchy among the handled unconscious ones; the individuality that would otherwise make them behave autonomously is suppressed.

The conscious manipulators are distributed like a pyramid. The higher one rises, the fewer the members are, and the more demanding and reliable they are. The further up one goes, the more the moral sense decreases.

The Pyramid

The pyramid structure is fundamental for the CC. Guarantor of secrecy, it is also the indispensable condition of coercion, for it supposes a hierarchization of knowledge, power and benefit. Between the bottom and the top, the recruited and the guru, one observes:
- the higher one goes, the more the benefits increase;
- the lower one is, the more coercion he faces.

Generally, the individual will know only as much as he is told. He has less information than his immediate superior. Progression from one stage to the next is slow. Accession to a higher stage is a sign of fast promotion; the contrary also exists — downgrading and sanction.

Such a system aims to keep the individual under constraint. On the one hand, he finds it impossible to get out of a model of which he knows only the direct demonstration and, on the other hand, the impossibility of attaining the higher levels directly. The way up is the follower's only means of access to the guru, who benefits from isolation because that protects him from unfavorable assessments that might emanate from the bottom of the pyramid.

The guru controls the flow of information from top to bottom. He also has means of gathering and controlling information from the bottom up.

When a follower rises in the structure, it should be noted that the rewards for merit generally include certificates and status, but it also happens that material advantage may be added in a way that can be taken away again if the disciple falls out of favor. It remains essential that the chosen members be dependent. And this can only be so if the psychic dependence is accompanied by a real financial dependence on the part of the follower so that it becomes impossible to leave.

The system is analogous to that used by networks of drug addicts. A drug addict is like a cult member. He has to provide service, unless he pays for the drug. In the cult, work is the payment. Purchasing drugs or services implies selling or proselytism; the sale brings benefits which are used for personal consumption, and the cult's knowledge prevents any treason because the follower is himself a link in the chain of the network — going down, as a user (or member), and going up, as a dealer (or proselytizer). Just as few drug addicts escape becoming dealers, in the same way the manipulators of one level become the ones who are handled at a higher level. This structure of interdependence leads to the total loss of the participants' individual ethics as one rises in the hierarchy. The cult organization is in this sense an organization which can be interpreted only in the light of a criminological vision.

The pyramid structure is of double interest for the cult member. It gives him a feeling of pride when he climbs up the hierarchy. It also strengthens the feeling of membership and dependence. Further, it "also allows the mystification of the secret to be maintained over a long time, by allowing only gradual contact with the initiates."[1]

Consequently, the manipulators, who are themselves handled by others, do not feel any scruples when their turn comes to exploit the lower level of followers.

> In the New Acropolis, the pyramidal structure must be established everywhere. Any exaggerated unity of two or three comrades separates them from the ensemble, making them lose the fundamental Union, principal axiom of the pyramid.[2]

Thus at every level of the system, from the supreme chief to the simple executant, nobody feels the least guilt. Each executant knows he has no personal responsibility. He can perform any act without feeling the least regret. This was the position of the accused Nazis during the Nuremberg trials, who answered: "Those were the orders, the indisputable and anonymous orders which it was inconceivable to not execute."[3]

The Web

Certain cults function in a structure that is like cobweb. Several pyramids are combined, each having separate functions. The web structure also has rigidity. A member may progress in one pyramid and stagnate in another; he is always dependent on the hierarchy, whatever his level. Only a small minority, the elite, escapes this circuit by becoming part of the guru's inner circle. Scientology provides a model of this type, with interlocking flowcharts of pseudo-religion, of auditing, of purification, and of the group's secret service operatives as well as for every other subsidiary.

An attack on the cult is therefore likely to fail, because the target individual, even if he seems essential to one pyramid, is only readily disposable in another. He will be sacrificed at the least sign of danger. The structure that was destroyed will then immediately be repaired from a parallel structure that is, in a way, its shadow.

The Star

This model is like a bicycle wheel, with the guru as the center and all the followers as the rim. Messages go from the center to the periphery and vice-versa. This structure is often seen in the initial stages of development of a cult, or in small sects like channeling, prayer or healing groups. Everyone has direct contact with the medium or the guru, who dispenses energy to each member. Sometimes, this structure develops at a given stage within a pyramid; there may be a few separate functional wheels around specific individuals.

The sects that develop on a large scale are usually not satisfied with this star structure, which does not allow for absolute control of power and on the contrary exposes the guru to the followers' judgment by creating opportunities for communication.

The Sphere

This structure is usually found in cathartic groups, rather than in true coercive sects. Indeed, the emotional and relational exchanges are such that each participant plays a similar part without hierarchy nor real directivism. This type of structure does not allow for effective control of the group. Although it can be integrated into a more traditional sectarian organization, it entails a risk of instability and removes any possibility of control.

When this spherical structure exists in a coercive cult, the structure is used provisionally or for some specific simple organization within the more complex pyramidal organization.

Group Dynamics

Whatever the structure of the cult, it observes three principles of group behavior:[4]

• Lack of differentiation of the individual and the group. The follower loses any autonomy of existence and thought. There is no possibility of individual thought, even though the follower's thought may have been identical to that of the cult in the first place. The follower functions and thinks within the group apparatus. He has no say in the life or development of the group; he is a non-autonomous part of this life and this thought. He is a member of the body illustrated by La Fontaine in his fable *Les Membres et l'Estomac*. Any hint of individualization can be dealt with only through exclusion — such a follower is a danger to the cult;

• Self-sufficiency of the group. This is what develops the psychotic dynamic of the cult. It leads to the progressive and complete isolationism characteristic of the cult. It creates barriers with the outside world which, seen first of all as being nonessential, is gradually perceived as dangerous, then aggressive. This self-sufficiency prohibits the contribution of constructive criticism or any questioning of the sectarian logic;

• Delimitation of the external and the internal. All facts, thoughts and actions come to be qualified on this basis. Everything that is a part of the cult ideology or inside the cult is positive, constructive and dynamic. All that is external to the cult is negative, destructive and lethal. The group assumes, in the place of the participant's own ego, the transactions of analysis of external reality and compromise between that and the sectarian plan (internal reality).

All positive feelings tend to strengthen the illusion of group unity. All the negative feelings are projected onto some individual, who is gradually isolated from the group and made a scapegoat. Little by little, through this illusionary phenomenon, the group ego replaces the individual ego of the follower. At the same time, the paternal image of the guru becomes the ideal of the follower.

Didier Anzieu[5] stressed the similarity between group behavior and dreams. This similarity is even more pronounced in sectarian groups. The individuals expect the group to fulfill their hidden desires, first of all in the imagination (doctrines) and then in reality (society). This explains the frequency of the allegorical topics found in cults (discovery of lost paradises or eldorados, reconquest of a holy place, embarkation for extraterrestrial Cythera, construction of a utopian city, forgotten treasures, lost words, the Holy Grail, rebirth of the chosen people or a tribe of essentially divine people).

The danger of the cult is that it proposes to make this dream a reality, which it presents as accessible by denying confrontation with reality, which it represents as the expression of evil:

> You are the most powerful movement on the surface of the earth today.... Scientologists are the most intelligent people in the world. A civilization without insanity, criminals or war, in which able beings can thrive and decent people see their rights respected, and where Man is free to reach high goals — this is the aim of Scientology.[6]

The Rule of Comparison

One of the obstacles that the cult confronts in its endeavor to persuade followers is the need to cross the barrier of "the rule of comparison." This rule, in simple words, holds that the future cult member has to compare his past beliefs with the beliefs of the cult and has to assess whether or not they match up. From this analysis, three different results can emerge:

• If there is total dissonance between the individual's beliefs and the CC's propositions, the latter is immediately rejected;

• If there is agreement, then the individual is a likely recruit and only some effort at reinforcement is needed;

• Lastly, the most common situation is that the cult's propositions cause introspection, and the cult has to set up more complex procedures of conditioning. The follower must be exposed to new ideas at a pace that takes account of his ability to assimilate them and to confront them with his old convictions.

> Even if what I say is a lie, you can lose nothing by following this way of life. Suppose that I created a whole new theory to unify the world, a theory God never thought of; then God would come down and bargain with me to buy it.[7]

This matching up exercise provides an apparent ability for resistance on the part of the follower vis-a-vis cult recruitment, which has been noted by some authors. In this respect, some believe that religious belief — in a recognized Church — helps resist cult recruitment. Still, the former religion would have to be one that the subject does not criticize or reject; the proposed cult product does not harmonize with the old beliefs.

We must also consider that religious belief is, on the contrary, an element that supports joining a cult whose overt goals are in line with the subject's beliefs. For example, a transition may be made from a fraternal Christianity to the pseudo-Christianity of the Children of God, or a gnostic search may lead to Scientology. This deviance is notable in prayer groups, where the charismatic alibi often poorly hides the cult-like character of the group and the paranoia of the leaders.

The sectarian group's autocratic methods lead to several types of negative behavior in the followers. When the individuality, thoughts and personal actions of the follower are negated, members of a CC are subjected to permanent mental pressure that can lead to reactions counter to the desired outcome:

• the follower takes refuge in passive obedience, by adopting a behavior close to disinterest and apathy;

• or the contrary — tired of being confronted by the group or its intermediary, the guru, the follower allows his aggression to filter out, which leads to immediate repression if it is identified in time;

• or the aggression may be suppressed until it explodes, breaking out within the group in fits of collective rage that may lead as far as murder or suicide.

Cult Speech

The word "cult" conjures up images of enlightened turban-wearers with shaven heads, dressed outlandish garb, of which the followers of Mandarom are only the most recently televised images. Even though such model may exist, it is a more perverse and discrete model that succeeds better at recruitment.

Any practice, even the nuttiest, can be rationalized. Any behavioral aberration can be justified in philosophical, pseudo-scientific or pseudo-medical terms. This leads to the flourishing of doctrines pertaining to food, medicine etc., around which gather certain followers — such as the FBU, which worships the sun:

> The sun consists of small intelligent particles that enter man's brain
> and help him to understand the secrets of creation and creatures on
> earth.

All the CC's practice *scotomization*, that is, they focus all concentration on one or two main ideas; this cuts the followers off from the general public, due to the discipline required, and clouds their thinking.
Certain sects develop theories of purification in this way:

> All our ills are the result of our own technological choices. These
> choices are made unconsciously by those who have not had the revelation and are, in fact, sinners. [Ecoovie].

Other sects even suggest that the evil in the planet is already too advanced, and that it is necessary to create a completely new world (or sections of it) to allow survival or transition to a world that is hypothetically better:

> Christianity is for snobs who like English tweed, French films and American whisky. The conditions of life are difficult today and our contemporaries are very disturbed. It is, thus, the ideal time for encouraging Buddhism, which offers radical solutions to these pressing problems. [Soka Gakkai]

Reducing Cognitive Dissonance

The ability to reduce cognitive dissonance, to use American sociologist Festinger's term, is one of the essential characteristics of cults.

Festinger suggests that sectarian groups have the capacity to "recalibrate" their objectives or their thought when a confrontation with reality shows the thought to be false. When there is "dissonance" between the thought and reality, the group tends to reduce the discordance by experimentally revising its thoughts and analyzing the results.

Cults have an stunning capacity to reduce dissonance. Traversing their recent history, one notes that the followers are not terribly shaken by the non-realization of their frequent prophecies. The failure of the world to come to an end, as frequently predicted by the Jehovah's Witnesses, does not seem to slow down their enthusiasm to convert others.

Festinger infiltered and closely studied the millenarian cult in the suburbs of Salt Lake City led by Marian Keech. Festinger noted the group's astonishing capacity to reduce this cognitive dissonance. Keech had announced that the end of the world would occur on December 21st, 1954. The group, reduced by then to some twenty-five followers, had been convinced that a flying saucer would rescue them from the final flood. This conviction was based on the many messages that Marian Keech is supposed to have received from extraterrestrial beings in visions and even in written form.

The followers waited for the flying saucer for several days, and performed multiple rituals that were intended to facilitate their departure. The followers were then surprised to be given the happy tidings, through Keech as usual, that a divine update had been received. The great faith of the cult had saved them from enormous suffering and the final cataclysm had been postponed to a later date, whose exact time would be communicated to the followers later through the usual channels.

While ordinary logic would suppose that the group would be much shaken in its conviction, on the contrary, Keech's followers were able to recruit more than two hundred new followers within a few days of this incident. The apparent failure of the cult had been changed to advantage by reducing the dissonance by amending their message. Notice of an impending apocalypse was converted to a message of love from God and a warning for the future. The failed experiment was interpreted as a pledge of faith of the followers and a proof of the effectiveness of their prayers, since they had caused the postponement of the fatal date.

If a given activity fails and it causes the death of a follower, it is because the rest of the group had insufficient faith or that it was done too late. Should the extraterrestrial beings not descend at the appointed time, then it may also be explained as due to their being frightened by the non-believers. Thus all plots and prophecies become possible — the capacity to reduce cognitive dissonance is the cement of the cult when it confronts reality, and this is why the layman is helpless before the nonsense that is spread by these speeches.

Magical Thought

The pre-eminence of magical thought is the decisive element that differentiates a cult from a "normal" coercive group. The Western populace has a growing feeling of diffused anguish caused by several contemporary crises (unemployment, social exclusion, social conflicts, wars, nuclear threat, etc.); this reinforces the primitive need to seek refuge in the irrational. Accepted religions and ideologies have not properly addressed this contemporary feeling of anguish. Thus, the anguished individual tends to be drawn unconsciously towards magic. It allows the confusions in his mind to be explained in the contemporary context and popular culture. The boundary between his delusions and "magic" is thin, which makes it possible for the cult to exploit the individual by crossing the line.

In 1975, while working as hospital psychiatrist in a French province well-known for its lingering belief in sorcery, I came across one such evolution. A forty-year-old woman had barricaded herself inside her home and the worried police called us in to help. The woman lived in a small farm located in the center of a clearing, close to a spring (strong symbols of magic). The farm was the subject of litigation between the owners and a neighbor known for his ability to remove spells. Upon my arrival with my team, we were surprised to find present not only all the inhabitants of the village, but especially the priest, accompanied by a children's choir. The "exalted one" attacked everything that moved, shouting incomprehensible comments, mixing mischief, spells, deviltry and references to the Malignant One with topics borrowed from sorcery. Any discussion appearing to be impossible, the police had to intervene.

After a few days, the woman calmed down enough to explain to us that she was the victim of bad fate and that the Malignant One material- ized every night on the roof of her home. I tried to convince the woman of the inconsistencies in her story, but without success. I took my team back to the spot to see if we could discover some explanation. An exami- nation of the house and the surrounding environment having failed to re- veal anything out of the ordinary, we decided to camp overnight to see if we could hear the phantom. The house was secluded and some distance from the village, and this was in misty November — all factors that made the situation eerie. The more so as, on the first evening, we did hear something on the roof. At end of three nights of meticulous inspection, we had arrived at an opinion — "perhaps there was something." We would need the services of a mason to take apart the floor of the attic to understand the enigma. It was ultimately found that stealthy rodents had collected sweet chestnuts that rolled between the beams and simulated "the steps of the Malignant One."

Convinced of the origin of the noises, our patient was quickly re- stored. She realized that she had been the victim of an anguished state of mind that started from a misinterpretation of natural facts. However, her wisdom did not extend to the neighbors. Considered "haunted," the house was exorcized, and is now the property of the local sorcerer.

This is the type of confusion that cults exploit to the hilt. They are able to identify easily influenced people and to rationalize their fears in order to integrate them into absurd speeches that form the cult's basis of thought.

What has disappeared, or is beginning to disappear, are the gothic accoutrements like cauldrons, love potions and death's heads. All that has gone to join the old moons, fairies, bogeys and charming princes. However, magical powers, magic energy and faith in magic remain everywhere, and stronger than ever. The life of this magical illusion is everlasting, for it is closely connected with the life of man, the rate and rhythm of his being, with the weave of his handiwork.[8]

In *Totem and Taboo*, Freud showed that magic corresponds to a primal psychic mode of operation, founded on contiguity, like dreams.[9] The process by which an individual takes part in magic is identical to the obsessed individual who thinks he can affect the external world and transform it simply through his thoughts and rituals.

The process of magic is organized around the concept of absolute power conferred on the individual by virtue of his narcissistic libido invested in his ego. Magic gives the individual a new identity that takes him away from his past, that was seen as unsatisfactory, and gives him a new character that is free from the obstacles and frustrations that plagued him since childhood.

Interpretation of magic, which gives a pseudo-logical interpretation to facts that cause anxiety and distress, relieves the doubts of an individual who has generally failed to cope with existential questions. Society is seen as threatening and oppressive, because of the logical and rational character of the answers that it proposes. This fear and anxiety are fought by the new reality and solutions offered by magic.

How Cults Grow

Cults grow and develop according to the following stages, which are usually concomitant:

• the development of a counter-culture that is in opposition to the usual accepted social models; this proceeds from a need to feel oneself a part of society — but opposed to it;

• talk for the purpose of recruitment or for expressing commitment are based on arguments that are pseudo-logical, pseudo-scientific, or even more of concern, because they preclude rational criticism, arguments that truly are scientific;

• in addition to such discourses, misguided philosophic-politico-metaphysical conclusions are elaborated that then combine to form a doctrine;

• the doctrines lead to the formation of a totalitarian "ideology" as well as establishing a way of life that becomes compulsory and serves as the primary system of constraint with regard to the follower;

• the theorization and the withdrawal from the outside world requires the development and use of a neo-language and a meta-language by the cult;

• the refinement of the doctrines goes hand in hand with a more elaborate theorization, and the imperatives of recruitment require intervention in associative, political, or philosophical areas, depending on the initial theme;

• Lastly, the development of a dynamics that makes the unconvinced or the deviants feel guilty, accompanied by a victimizing perception for the "misunderstood" followers, which generates a paranoia and progressive turning inward of the group on itself.

Cult Psycho-Dynamics

The cult functions as a maternal entity. The cult is the mother, the guru is its father, and the follower becomes the child of this couple that is substituted for the natural parents. The whole is governed by its own laws which are those of the father.[10]

All the techniques of conditioning used by the cult have the aim of erasing the follower's original speech, and to substitute for it the new language of the cult. Alienation from society will be fulfilled when this substitution is entirely accomplished, and the imagination "provided" by the cult begin to fill the gaps in the follower's "personal" imagination. These gradually build up to make his original imagination "unrealistic." The follower's dependence on the cult becomes total when this phenomenon merges with his personality, and he loses all critical capacity.

For this reason, new cults are more powerful for they know how to use the dynamics of group restraint (which was done by empirical methods in the past). Their themes support the introduction of maternal symbolism and suggest merging with an "ocean" of life, which ties in with "a mother-like fusionary model," referring to an all-encompassing whole.[11]

The cohesion of the cult is ensured by the unity of the speech, which represents a new symbolic law, voluntarily followed or unanimously imposed. Membership in the cult is accompanied by the symbolic, ritual and imaginary building of a new family for the disciple, where he nestles with his brothers and sisters in the love of the mother, under the law of the father.

> Following Yvonne, 250 IVI walking in Christ's footsteps, behind those of Yvonne, our mother. A being of light, with golden hair, all dressed in white, an admirable figure robed in light, beautiful leader with flowing hair: the gentle and fair Yvonne.[12]

The Guru-Father

Only the laws of the father (the guru) really constitute the doctrines of the cult, but as in a family structure, the laws are sometimes shared. The mother (the cult) assimilates the initiatory speech and creates a second symbolic law that is less powerful, but that governs the operation of the organization.

To become a disciple is thus like returning to childhood and accepting the introjection of prohibitions imposed by the parents, particularly the father. This acceptance of the introjection supports the identification of the follower in the cult structure, without which there would be no hope of attaining the parental deification. The disciplehood represents the adolescence of the disciple, who, if the cult is to function, will never be an independent, complete adult as long as the father-guru lives.

The speech of the mother-cult and the law of the father-guru must correspond in order to support group cohesiveness. Any lack of coordination between the two puts a question mark on the authority of the cult and the followers begin to criticize the system and escape from it. A follower's questioning the cult's presentations is equivalent to patricide, which cannot be ventured without breaking the relation with the mother as well. To criticize is to risk being separated from the family. This situation is not a pleasant one for the follower, as all the sectarian logic aims to make him cut himself from outside society and leave him with nowhere to go. In these circumstances, to leave the cult is like death to the follower. Thus, at an early stage, the follower gives up the prospect of leaving the cult.

The cult operates in a field where there is confrontation between several contrary tendencies. The follower is torn by conflicting loyalties. He may wish fully to adhere to the cult, and at the same time to maintain his normal interaction with the outside world. However, the cult requires him to abandon all those elements that bind him to his past, especially his natural family. The family and past constitutes the hierarchy of the individual, which is potentially in conflict with the substituted new family of the cult. In addition, the cult functions in a closed environment, where all personal interactions are carried out under the control and constraints imposed by the guru. Moreover, these constraints are exerted by the guru on the cult as a whole that in turn generates its own dynamics.

The collective representation of the cult is like that of the "Bund," i. e., the group organized around the chief in German sociological terminology. The cult acts like a primitive tribe, having a system to protect the restricted group that it represents. It acts and thinks with a warlike vision. It identifies itself with an assembly of savage warriors (*Bund*) that are collected around an omnipotent chief who is the holder of the tribe's values (*Fuhrer*), who is the only one who knows the direction of the action undertaken and monopolizes in fact a historical legitimacy. The similarity between the *Bund* and certain aspects of secret societies was stressed by Anzieu, who noted that the discipline is very strict in the latter; the traitor, the weak follower who reveals the fundamental secrets, beliefs and secrets to the outside world, will find himself dead. The *Bund* makes its members into heroes, martyrs, and raises their stature to that of expiatory victims.

This warlike bent to their personality, alternating with a feeling of being victimized is obvious in the strategies observed during any legal action carried out against cults.

The follower is subjected to a variety of complex influences that can be summarized as follows:

- double bonds, internal and external
- filial ties with the natural family
- "filial" ties with the guru-father, a paternal-like relation
- "filial" ties with the cult-mother, a maternal bond
- submission to the hierarchy of the cult
- conflicts with fellow disciples over the achievement of the objectives of the cult and winning the love of the guru-father
- fraternal "implications" with fellow disciples, contrary to or in conformity with the wishes of the cult-mother and guru-father.

The Cult-Mother

The whole of these relations becomes still more complicated by the fact that the cult itself is in the process of identifying with the guru-father, and that the responsibilities and the identifying images is never entirely fixed.

The individual members are fused into a common whole, so that the life of the group becomes the life of each one, and the goal of each member merges with the goal of all. This merger results in the prohibition of any individual act that would be prejudicial to the life of the group. Indeed, the member has his own body, but he participates in life as part of the whole, which becomes for him a kind of higher body. Any wound inflicted on this higher body is like wound inflicted on his personal body. The complexity of these relations of the member to the group is fed by the ambiguity of the status of the co-adepts, so that the member cannot solve his relationship with his co-members in a simple way himself. The group is viewed with ambivalence by the disciple, which recalls Melanie Klein's concept of the Good and the Bad Mother.

The group is a good mother when it is the sought-after surrogate mother. However, it is also a bad mother when the group opposes the privileged relationship with its leader. The group becomes an obstacle to the realization of Oedipal desires. It will be at the origin of all the disorders related to the primitive Oedipal anguish, a persecution complex. One suffers distress at being persecuted, losing control of the body, depressive syndromes, and anxiety in the face of the risk of symbiotic fusion within the group and the annihilation of the individual personality.[13]

Classifying Cults

Cults fall into two main types according to their social dynamics — the father substitute and surrogate mother.

Groups Representing the Father Substitute

In this type of group, the guru is fully invested with paternal powers, and the follower is like the child of this father. All actions and speeches of the guru would aim to reinforce and strengthen this identification by alternating between sanction and gratification. The follower is like a good or a bad son, according to his merits. These groups block the follower's autonomous ego, and especially his individual impulses. They constantly reinforce feelings of guilt.

The guru is viewed as the holder of the law, and more — he has the authority to punish the bad son or bad daughter who has the audacity to violate the holy regulations that come out of the mouth of the guru. This symbolic projection of the guru makes it possible for the follower to cross the major taboo of our society, that of incest.

The prestige of the disciple is enhanced by any possible sexual relations with the guru. Thus, the transgression of the taboo is accompanied not by a guilt feeling or of sin but, on the contrary, to the acquisition of a privileged status. The guru has moreover a dimension of knowledge which is conferred upon him by the transposition of his personal myths into the mythology of the group. All the fantasies and delusions thus become testimonies of his knowledge. To the extent that he identifies with the guru, the follower has the illusion of participating in the fullness of the knowledge and power of the guru. He becomes as passionate as the guru when he fills himself with these filial feelings.

> In a family, the world revolves around the father because he is the head of the family. There is dislocation and disorder when any member of the family is not related or pays heed to the head of the family. The family starts to go downhill. Similarly, if the head of a country disappears, disorder ensues. Even bandits and animals feel the need for a head to give direction. So then why intelligent people have failed to understand this simple truth that in spiritual life, too, a leader is indispensable?[14]

The follower's truth is gradually reduced to that of the father-guru. This identification is made possible by gradually fulfilling, at least in part, the follower's fantasies initially, through the guru but, gradually, if he is worthy, through the follower as well. Progressively, antiquated illusions begin to intrude in the life of the follower.

The guru can exist only through his mass of followers who, like son-slaves, shower him with enthusiastic praise, transforming him from an imaginary identity into a real identity. In return, the follower benefits from his association with the guru and manages to live out some of his major fantasies. However, "direct" contact with the guru can never be enjoyed completely for the identifying transfer of the follower requires the reconstitution of a new interdiction which can be summarized by Nietzsche's aphorism, "The Truth kills." To know the guru is to embrace the truth. However, this knowledge destroys the pact between the guru and the follower.

To safeguard this bond, the guru stays behind a mask of rituals and prohibitions, which are for the follower like new veils of Isis that disguise the truth, but which also protects the truth from being fully discovered. Thus, the sexual intercourse that could bring them together is "re-interpreted" in the context of the new law enacted by the guru. The sexual relation is explained differently by different sects and it becomes sensual initiation (Rael), tantric transmutation (Iso-Zen), revelation of the Great Father (Children of God) and an act of conversion (Three-Sacred-Hearts). The act thus loses its sexual connotation to become an act of truth and knowledge. Sex finally takes on a mystical nuptial dimension that exploits the divine character of the guru and the exaltation that derives from the sexual act.

The transfer in identification from the follower to the guru takes on a number of related meanings. One is the father-child relation, which links the master with the follower, implies that he should lead the follower to initiation and knowledge. Another meaning is that the guru can appear to the follower as someone possessing miraculous healing powers that the practice of magic confers. This power is founded on a precept of total obedience, which does not authorize any transgression or criticism.

> I will push you into the irrational. There is no other way, you must be pushed into the irrational; and in that way, everything can be done effortlessly. The readier you are, the more I will place in you things which will seem insane to the eyes of others. At this time, I see that you are ready to be insane, that you are no longer frightened of others' regard and their opinion, that you no longer fear even your own reason. [Bhagwan[15]]

Groups Representing the Surrogate Mother

Every cult serves as a maternal substitution, to one extent of another. The cult is the mystical wife of the guru, and is the family rebuilt around him. Moreover, certain sects are organized around a female guru, who doubly plays the role of substitute mother.

The cult may only adopt the role of a substitute for the family, or share it with the guru who plays the role of the father. The maternal group is ambivalent; it is at the same time the good and the bad mother. It represents a place for protection and regression. Certain sects particularly develop this maternal aspect in regard to the follower. These groups are usually small groups that support the direct transfer between the follower and a female guru.

> The most complete incarnation of Adi Shakti now lives on Earth to begin the golden age. This incarnation is named Shri Mataji Nirmala Devi, or simply "Mataji." [She is the sacred mother].[16]

Many healing groups function on this model, which increases the phenomenon of regression by placing the follower in the position of expecting physical care, which encourages ties of infantile dependence. Cult dynamics are dominated by the phenomena of infantile regression and fusion in the maternal bosom of the cult.

In contrast to groups of paternal substitution, in the surrogate mother groups the follower is not inclined to identify with the guru. The followers maintain an infantile state of dependence that prohibits the possibility of their identification with the guru, which would, in fact, represent a risk of unauthorized autonomy. The cult-mother, all-powerful and nurturing, exerts a psychotic mothering role over the follower, stifling and seemingly overprotective, denying any possibility of self-development. The follower loses his separate personality, especially as the cult prefers group regression over rational analysis.

The inability to be identified within the group is accompanied indeed by a serious phenomenon of depersonalization. Little by little, the follower loses sight of the boundaries of his being. He finds himself at the stage of the unweaned infant who is unable to perceive the boundary between himself and the other. His individual psyche becomes diluted in the psychic apparatus of the group, which is likened to the primary education of the family psychic apparatus. He participates in an undifferentiated entity, composed of the fusion of individual psyches regressing within the cult's maternal psyche.

The loss of the boundary between oneself and the other is initially accompanied by the pleasure born of the buoyant feeling of fusion with a sea of others through the dissolution of the ego. With time, this feeling gives way to anguish at the dilution and loss of identity, leading to a desire to escape. At this stage, the techniques of conditioning will intervene to remove any illusion of independence.

5.

RECRUITMENT

Poor lamb, you were thoroughly seduced. Wolves abound, who lure the flocks from the Path of Righteousness and turn them toward evil ways.
Clement Marot.

There are three phases in the recruitment of a new member, reeling him in gradually, creating a certain intellectual and emotional dependence. Step by step, the new member will be attracted, persuaded, and finally fascinated.

Seduction

The seduction phase is the prelude to the process of indoctrination. No recruitment can take place until the subject's attention is caught by the ideas or illusory spectacles suggested to attract him. Just as "you can't catch flies with vinegar," it is unlikely that a future cult member would be attracted by a recruiter with the cantankerous attitude of a drill sergeant. To seduce is, above all, to be pleasing, but also means distorting the truth. All the work of the cults aims at proposing a brilliant Utopia instead of the drabness of daily existence. The recruiter-seducer sets the scene for the cult illusion; he serves as a conjurer to attract potential followers; he offers simple answers to complex questions; he charms the interlocutor, creating the illusion of an emotional exchange; he constantly exploits the register of emotions, omitting any reference to logic;

he opposes the morbidity of reality with the prospect of an idyllic love, that which reigns within his community. A former Moonist calls this phase of seduction "setting the hook":

> I met some nice people on the street, I filled out a questionnaire, I saw a poster for a seminar. . . .They listened to me. They think like me. They seem to have interesting things to say. I have their address so I can meet them again.

Generally, the cults take the initiative in creating the first contact with a target. It is an active selling process: they go after the prey. Usually, it is done one-on-one, even if — and this is increasingly common — the ground was prepared by an earlier bit of advertising: a brochure, a meeting, a mass mailing, etc. However, to sell a product, you have to establish contact with the potential buyer. This contact must start the process of identification between recruiter and recruited, in order to cause the latter to start comparing his life with the recruiter's. Thus, during door-to-door sales, the Jehovah's Witnesses present themselves as a "family" (whereas they may have no real family ties). Conversely, the Scientologists' image as "dynamic young activists" is more suited to canvassing in university cities, gyms and popular hangouts. Another cult will hold conferences in a university city, adopting "the student look" and choosing its topics according to the material taught: existential angst for people in the arts, "how to increase your dynamic potential" for economics students, "Egyptian civilization" for fledgling historians, etc..

In the exhaustive instructions CC give their recruiters, a very particular emphasis is laid on choosing the place of recruitment. Places where there is a lot of foot traffic are preferred: shopping streets, large public squares, campuses, theater exits. These places should be close to the CC's headquarters or meeting place, so that the subject is not turned off by the distance.

The targets of choice, beyond those in the immediate vicinity (family and friends) are people who give the impression of having time on their hands, and few relationships. It is hard to pay attention to a solicitor if you are waiting to meet somebody or you are in a hurry to get home or to get to the office.

Recruitment techniques depend on the postulate of "the potential for identification." "What is good for me is good for you. If I can do it, you can do it." It is a question of finding between the two interlocutors a possible footbridge that makes it possible to direct the speech towards the concept of common history. Once the link is established, the recruiter will try to develop an emotional empathy.

Scientology has established an actual chart of the attitudes to assume, through what it calls "the scale of tones." For example, for a sad-looking potential recruit, it is good to display a sympathetic face. In the Association of Unification[1] recruiters' handbook, one may read the following advice:

> You have to be a psychologist, know how to read a face. You must impress people with our calm, our safety, our concentration. To move others, we must be moved ourselves. We must believe absolutely in what we say. We must speak with strong feelings. Give your face, particularly your eyes, your mouth, an expression that makes an impression. We know that we are superior to other people, but we must keep a humble attitude. Nobody should think they are losing something. You must give people the impression that they will gain something by listening to us. You must leave them satisfied and wanting to come to see us. . . .

Moïse David, founder of the Children of God, recommends *flirty fishing.* He lavishes advice that borders on the comical, when it does not suggest an unambiguous attitude of sexual aggression.

> Even if they are married, girls must go out dressed in see-through clothing. Bras are prohibited. In the discotheques, they must dance to arouse men. . . . If somebody refuses to buy, offer him the letter for free and he is likely to make an even larger gift. . . .Don't dress in jeans, but wear clean "middle-class" clothes, that impresses people. The look is very important; look at somebody with love and you will see the immediate effect. . . . Pay attention to your breath. . . . Clean your teeth regularly and suck mints, bad breath can discourage many

contributors.[2]

In a series of letters going back to April 1974, Moïse David spells out for his disciples the technique of "missionary soliciting," comparing the woman to bait that the future member will swallow. Sex is the hook which will catch the prey. Note that the word *teaser* is used in fishing as well as in marketing.

> Every time you go into a hotel late in the evening with a man, he should give a good tip to the receptionist when you go in. That usually discourages the receptionist from insisting on checking your identity. Making love includes sleeping with them, sucking them, cuddling them, fondling them, jerking them off and kissing. Please, be very precise in your reports. Say exactly what you did, how and how much. Include any odd behavior, any unusual position or abnormal perversion... to warn the next girl. . . . Always take petroleum jelly, tissues and if possible talcum powder and a bottle of strong wine, whisky or sherry. Bathe him before sucking, or insist that he does it. When you make love, it is good to have a little eau de cologne or toilet water close to the bed so that you can wash your hands without having to get up and go into the bathroom to do it, in case that wouldn't be practical.[3]

Each CC has its "market," and the products correspond quite precisely to the demand. Without emphasizing the caricatural character of the disciples of Krishna, it has been observed that members of a given cult tend to look the same and to dress in similar ways. It is not a matter of chance. This is both a sign of recognition and membership, and a walking advertisement for the cult. Who does not recognize the young Mormon evangelists, with their close-cropped hair, their eternal navy blue blazers and their discrete club ties? Who could miss the conservative, outdated style of the Jehovah's Witnesses? All this is done deliberately. And needless to say, the best places for soliciting are the cities, where the population concentration is higher:

> Go to the cities where most of the people are, and let them (the Catholics) evangelize the villages, the jungle and the hamlets. It is not writ-

ten in the New Testament that we must return to the depths of the jun-
gle to unearth some little savages in order to inherit the earth gradually. . . .The Church's plan was to send missionaries to the principal
population centers, the regional centers where they could reach the
masses as well as the majority of people.[4]

Seduction is intended to expand the cult through its representatives.
They will be all the more attractive if society is painted as an aggressive
milieu, indifferent to the most intimate concerns of the potential recruit.
This internal-external opposition crops up at every stage in cult conditioning.

Persuasion

Persuasion requires two actors: the transmitter and the receiver.
They established a specific relationship that is defined by the message.
The transmitter or convinced cult member is the persuader; the receiver
is the target, the potential member; and the message is embedded in the
cult speech presented by the transmitter.

For the persuasion to be effective, these three elements must meet
specific conditions. The goal of persuasion is for the transmitter to get
the receiver to agree to a specific proposition summarized in the message.
It is a multi-stage process: attention, comprehension, ability to reformu-
late the message, integration of the message, acceptance of the message,
change of thought or attitude.

The whole process is called the ELM (Elaboration Likelihood
Model). The ELM starts with the message transmitted. However, this
message is never simple; it takes direct and indirect routes. Directly, a
specific theme and its implications are presented in cognitive terms. Indirectly, the central message cannot be separated from a general context,
and what it means depends on the listener's desires and the speaker's objectives. The message conveyed by the central route can be read directly,
it is accessible to rationality; the indirect message is a swirl of irrational
and emotional impressions and deceptions on the part of the transmitter.

If it looks like it will be easy to get the receiver to accept the message, the transmitter will use the direct approach of the ELM; or, if he has strong defenses and seems hard to convince, the manipulation will be done indirectly. The transmitter must be credible and must inspire confidence. He feigns sympathy in order to create empathy, using the ELM's indirect approach.

The transmitted message meets complementary conditions. To use the central approach, the transmitter must be rational, capable of producing arguments that stands up to analysis, while causing emotional reactions in order to free up the field of promises, setting aside intellectual concerns.

The listener is the most variable element in the ELM. The success or failure of the venture depends mainly on him, and he is the one, especially, who determines how the message will be presented and which persuasive techniques can be used. The greater his analytical ability, the more the message must be conveyed indirectly and the central channel must be avoided; conversely, the more credulous the receiver, the more likely the central channel can be used.

The transmitter may be more than one individual: it can be a group, even the cult itself in its totality. But in every case, the two-fold requirement of credibility and attraction leads cults to use figureheads who are constantly spreading the word. This is the basis of Scientology's "celebrity centers." In the absence of such symbols, the recruiter will have to acquire credibility, so his image is important. The first impression he gives should be of seriousness, poise, success. The transmitter's credibility is due to his apparent worth as well as his interaction with the receiver. Competence arises from the persuader's position relative to his target, and this hierarchy will succeed or fail in producing the desired result.

Since, obviously, the real goals of a cult are contrary to the message conveyed, the transmitter shows nothing of his real objectives; he limits his actions to the expression of sympathy and to pseudo-transparency to avoid revealing his real plan. Only one thing matters: to attract and beguile, to the greatest possible extent, by exploiting the processes of identification and similarity.

The Persuader's Game

The persuader has a double status. He is the speaker-sophist who convinces through equivocal and ambiguous speech rather than through answers and evidence. He also builds myths, using dreams and Utopia as costumes and scenery in the theatre of collective illusion.

He founds his art not on reason and logic but on affect and feelings. He does not prove: he provokes; he does not give answers: he upsets. He constantly violates the social and tacit pact of true communication: an assumption of sincerity and truth. His entire discourse is intended to mask his intention to indoctrinate. He has to present lies and deceptions as reality. He puts on a continuous show, a fable that drives out reality, gradually invading the space of communication. The goal is to get others to go along. This is the first real stage of handling. At the earliest stages, the persuader overcomes the momentary reserves of his interlocutor without breaking the established relation and, if necessary, will back off, in order to try again later.

One of subtleties of the maneuver consists in pretending that joining the group is up to the interested party and depends on his free will. It is this perverse claim that causes difficulty for close relatives and therapists when they try to talk with an individual who was "involved" in a cult. This alleged personal freedom inhibits efforts at "dis-indoctrination."

The techniques of persuasive communication have been written extensively, mostly with the intention of helping advertising, marketing and publicity specialists. Here some of the "tricks" described in these works,[5] used by cult recruiters:

- Force sympathy
- Hide your moods and ignore of those of the others
- Give the other person the impression that you are interested in him
- Look people in the eye
- Talk with your mouth, i.e. externalize your speech and don't stay lock up in yourself
- Get people on your side by talking about the subjects that interest

them, and especially about themselves

• Give the illusion of sincerity by having your speech coincide as often as possible with that of your interlocutor

• Always carry out the ball, but know when to break off if you encounter too strong a resistance

• Never defend, always attack, never doubt

• Keep catching the person's attention with new tricks

• Always suggest two possibilities, in order to get agreement on at least one

• Always be attractive; dominate without showing it.

The result of these precepts is what an ex-follower of Moon calls "surrounding:"

> You enter a universe where everything is controlled, the room itself, the group that surrounds you, the information that is given to you. You are the most important person in the world. You are so happy to be finally recognized for what you are. The group is very devoted and you wouldn't think of doing anything against it.

During this period, little by little, one replaces the recruit's identity with the cult's thought. Analyzing the techniques of occultist Stanislas de Guaïta, another occultist, Matgioi, wrote in 1909:

> To suggest is to give birth, in the brain of a subject, by one means or another, to a thought of foreign origin, whether a likely thought or not, either of an action or of a series of actions to be performed. To replace a subject is to expropriate his organism from the triple perspective of his will, his intelligence and his emotions, and to install one's own will, one's own thought, one's own feelings.[6]

Fascination

Fascination is the driving force in enrollment, fascination is what tips the scales. After a phase of doubt, the candidate is definitively convinced he has made the right choice when he is faced with the masterpiece of cult dynamics. Confrontation with the guru (or his deputies) breaks down his last reserves.

Then a new stage begins in the process of indoctrination. It introduces a magical character into the relationship between the future follower and the cult group. The relationship is detached little by little from reality and becomes established more in the symbolic universe of the sacred and the divine. This fascination will remove any possible inclination to withdraw from the influence of the cult and its members. It is accompanied by a request for complete commitment:

> You have discovered a group that wants to build a better world, purer and more beautiful. You know that the group has a fantastic leader who enables you to foresee the future of humanity. You learn that the group and the leader need you to fulfill their mission. You decide to commit yourself, to give your life for such a beautiful cause.

The follower's fascination is founded on a symbolic projection onto the guru, who is invested with a supernatural power that approaches the divine. At this stage, the recruit's free will starts to deteriorate in face of the doctrinal pressure. His final conversion will depend on the balance between the coercive power exerted by the cult and the strength of the recruit's earlier bonds with society.

The process of fascination is comparable, to some degree, to that of hypnosis. When fascination takes hold, it is a sign that the empathic relationship has taken precedence over rational analysis. Fascination indicates that the disciple has become dependent.

Who Are the Victims?

Recruiting and indoctrination techniques are effective only on subjects with receptive personalities. Cult-based pathology may have affected populations the world over, but few systematic analyses have been conducted. Indeed, the psychological examination of a universe of subjects presupposes their acceptance of the study exerted on him — which is far from being the case for the CCs, which screen and cull the information they provide, to ensure that the only items that get through are those that are compatible with the image they want to disseminate.

The rare studies on the psychological profiles of cult members[7] have covered only a universe of marginal subjects. It is impossible to conduct a comprehensive study since most potential subjects refuse to cooperate. Existing studies relate to individuals turned up by the medical or legal system in conjunction with criminal investigations, former cult members who have "repented," volunteers "offered" by a cult,[8] or subjects under-going psychiatric treatment who are, therefore, marginal. Only a long-running practice covering followers of a variety of cults and having un-dergone different courses of experience would allow to us to identify spe-cific factors of psychological predisposition.

The Profile of Likely Recruits

Still, we have observed some general trends in the course of our therapy practice, medical-legal consulting, and advisory sessions with parents.

Cult members are generally recruited between the ages of eighteen and twenty-five. Older followers usually belonged to a cult earlier in life as well. At the young end of the scale are students finishing their secon-dary education or beginning their higher education. Full disciplehood usually means curtailing formal studies, and the true cultural and educa-tion level of the members is slightly lower than it appears to be. The dis-crepancy between the biographical cultural level and the real cultural level is an indicator of socio-cultural maladjustment.

Family or social conflicts often contribute to a person's decision to join a cult. The group is a shelter from the aggression that has been felt and it provides a model of conflict resolution that intellectually satisfies the follower. He refuses any self-analysis and transfers all responsibility onto the external world, and more particularly onto the social or family unit. Entry into a cult is often a way of responding to the social pressures to establish one's autonomy from the family, especially during adoles-cence. Sometimes this move is taken in response to crisis situations —

divorce, job loss, mourning — or to a disturbance of what used to be "normal," either personally, or within the family. Going into a cult, in such cases, serves a pseudo-therapeutic function. This element of "asking for help" makes CCs take a strong aggressive stance with regard to recognized psychiatrists and psychotherapists, who are the only ones likely to bring the subject to a real analysis of his actions and his responsibility in family and social conflicts.

Factors that increase one's psychological predisposition to join a cult include schizoid characteristics, but more often traces of the so-called "Kretschmer" syndromes such as hyperactivity and hyper-sensitiveness, at levels that are not actually pathological. Moreover, likely victims often exhibit broken or strained social bonds and difficulty with socio-cultural integration. There is a general lack of interpersonal relations, and emotional exchanges are minimal.

The cult's ideal target population is young people who are depressive or who have broken off from their family and society, who feel they cannot handle day-to-day life and who are searching for substitute solutions.

Certain phases are more favorable to cult contamination: on the one hand, periods of conflict, failure at school, university or work, divorce or personal or parental separation; on the other, all the elements that test the family and social structure by straining emotional ties or by creating a total or partial sense of alienation: the death of a loved one, serious illness, financial difficulties, unemployment, etc.

Of course, there are also plenty of cult members who show no sign of these characteristics. The latter will be held up as public examples by the cult, which uses them as cover.

Overview of the Victims

Cult pathology has long been known and has been considered in general studies since Freud and Jung, but little "field work" has been done. Our approach to the study of cult victims is based on the examination of actual victims, using a universe of some 300 cases including simple participants, people who have attended courses, thoroughly convinced converts, people who have left a cult, and those who are currently in therapy.

The overall dynamics that links a CC and its practitioners can be understood only if we look at the average profile of the members. The recruiting and indoctrinating techniques only work on a given segment of the population; they have no effect on most people. These practices strike a chord with individuals having a specific psychological structure. Depending on how convinced, and how subservient they are, these subjects will become proselytes of the cult and their personalities will be changed, first in terms of social expression, then in their more intimate aspects.

Only certain individuals are "cult material." An exhaustive study by Galanter defines their profile, mostly confirming our observations. We could not, alas, conduct true statistical studies. Indeed, it is not always possible to collect complete biographical and psychological data for a subject. The major interest of the data that we collected is to obtain a transverse structure (the whole cult at one specific time) and longitudinal (the cult in its evolution over about a ten-year period). A summary of these data may be useful:

• The followers come from the middle well-to-do classes of society, very rarely from the modest classes;

• Their level of schooling is generally primary or secondary. These social segments are also more likely to belong to a religion, as other studies have shown in a more general context.[9] The distribution of cultural levels within the cults is similar to that seen in the population at large;

• Joining a cult is a response to social or family conflicts. The cult group becomes a shelter from aggression and a way of responding to the social pressure to become autonomous that starts with adolescence. The follower passes from the family protective structure, which disaggregates through conflicts or appears unsuited, to a cult structure which offers a refuge during a certain lapse of time and gives him the feeling to reappear in a new community;

• The cult member has trouble achieving the social status of an adult; disciplehood represents an easier-to-attain substitute;

• Hyperactivity and hyper-sensitiveness are clearly supporting factors;

• Depressive young people experiencing a feeling of inadequacy, even of revolt, are frequently targeted prey. They feel lonely, rejected and sad.

According to Galanter,[10] about 60% of cult members are "depressive."

Entry into the cult has a double resonance: individual and family. Before joining the cult, the potential recruit is in a weak and unstable position within an apparently stable family structure. Joining the cult reverses the relationship: the follower gets relative stability within the cult, while by contrast the family structure is shaken and partially disorganized. The social bonds that pre-dated entering the cult are considered to be generally bad or incomplete by the interested parties themselves. In spite of an apparent stability, the family ties are often weak: couples breaking up, divorced, separated; rebellious children; widowers or widows. Even in the absence of conflict, the family structures are often strained by disease, unemployment, financial or professional problems. The follower, and often those close to him, have a feeling of personal or family failure.

Generally, between the ages of 25-35 years, there is a profound sense of loneliness. An older age bracket, also distinguished by the feeling of loneliness (50-60 years)[11] forms the preferred target for prayer and healing groups. Lastly, the antecedents of addiction, drug use or alcoholism often return. Actually, for recruits, the cult constitutes a stable system. It offers a new point of reference compared to an environment that is little by little falling apart.

However, one does come across completely atypical followers: Scientology, one of the most virulent and the most tightly structured CCs in the current "market," termed "evil, dangerous and corrupt" by the United States Supreme Court, regularly publishes the list of its members, amongst whom one finds a well-known lyric singer, a famous actor, a jazz musician, a race car champion and a tennis champion. It would be stupid to believe that these followers enjoy the same status as the *vulgum pecus*. Some are completely isolated from cult reality and are convinced of the good faith of their "Masters." Others relate a personal history that defies genuine analysis because of their prior experiences (heavy addiction, for example). Still others are part of the group of manipulators that make a profit from the system and see the cult as just a lucrative scheme.

In every case, nevertheless, the cult will try to strengthen the ties in order to make sure the new follower has no possibility of turning back. For this purpose, the cult will call upon a whole battery of techniques of persuasion.

6.

COERCIVE PERSUASION

At the same time that a man, by the very development of his powers, is led to discover greater and loftier goals to strive for, he tends to become dominated by the object of his conquests, and he ends by adoring the very object that he was fighting.

Pierre Teilhard de Chardin

Strategies of Persuasion

Persuasion is founded on the persuader's ability to seize the opportunity to move someone. Usually, it corresponds to the latter's frame of mind, as he tends to be the kind of person who is easily influenced. However, in the case of cults, persuasion is coercive. The person is deprived of any free will, he gives in to an imposed decision.

Persuasion known as "normal" assumes the exercise of free will on the part of the person being persuaded. Four criteria apply: the credibility of the message, its consistency, its coherence and finally its congruence.[1] The message must be credible and coherent: it must be shown to be based on proof, logic, demonstration. The persuader must be consistent, i.e. his remarks should not vary from one moment to another. Lastly, "the product" proposed must adapt to the potential customer and correspond to his needs at the moment when it is proposed. Selling a space heater in the Sahara Desert or refrigerators at the North Pole would not be congruent.

The first three criteria do not apply to coercive persuasion. The

product proposed may be utopian, the demonstration aberrant, the remarks changeable: only congruence must be respected. The opportun-
ism of the persuader leads him to adapt his words to his audience and the
situation, without any preoccupation with the truth. It is congruence that
confers unity on the persuader and makes him "the right man for the job."

The cult offers "a product" supposed to meet a need given (the deficiencies of the recruited person) at a given moment (that of recruitment).
The "sales" pitch can include any subterfuge, any lies, any illusions. This
is a resolute step away from the free play of democratic free choice, and
even has undertones of a totalitarian process of imposed pseudo-choice.

The speech of coercive persuasion rests on a fundamental given:
mystification. The speech is a made-up discourse whose goal is not communication, but in fact the conversion of the listener. The strategy of
mystification consists in moving gradually from reality to illusion, without triggering rejection.

The mystifying discourse is based on several elements:

- Fabulation: the persuasive speech must disguise reality, make it a
myth. Fabulation proceeds from the white lie. The speaker is not satisfied to disguise the truth, he invents a fable intended to attract the interlocutor, to allure him and to start him down a false path;

- Simulation: the speaker acts, he creates a tempting character. He
replaces doubt and analysis with certainty and conviction. He invents
facts to support the transmitted fable;

- Dissimulation: the speaker masks his own questions, he hides his
doubts. He changes and adulterates reality. He becomes the fable that he
tells. He materializes his illusions and denies his concerns;

- Seduction: the speaker cannot tell his tale if the listener is not willing to hear him through to the end. The speaker must thus support his
speech on both cunning and on courtesy, "the most acceptable form of
hypocrisy" according to Ambrose Bierce. "Courtesy is artifice in service
of persuasion, for it is the agent that produces approval at a good price.
Polite words and gestures of courtesy achieve an emotional capture and
they seal a consensus of feelings."[2]

- Contempt: any true communication postulates a natural identity between the interlocutors. The persuader not only disguises reality through his speech, he also fakes the relation. Asserting a similarity between himself and his listener, on the contrary he places the latter in a hierarchical relation where he exerts the power of manipulation. The ultimate goal is not to establish a relationship, but indeed to exert power over the listener.

One of the driving forces of coercive persuasion is the speaker's faculty to make people accept irrational concepts. Whereas reality caused the anguish and the feeling of incompleteness that led the follower to the cult, the irrational concepts that are proposed to him are reassuring, because they offer shrink-wrapped solutions to everything.

The Influence of Beliefs

Persuasion is addressed more to belief than to reason. To believe is to give one's approval to a proposal that one takes to be true, either in a mediate way, after reflection,[3] or in an immediate and unreasoned way.

Belief is opposed to reflection and analysis; the process of indoctrination cannot be based on logic. Any hesitation, any reasoned examination of his situation by the follower can only lead him to question the system into which he has been "recruited." Consequently, joining a CC means implicit acceptance, without reservation, of a myth or a founding fable of the group thought. The future follower will be expected to believe in the history that is told to him and to consent to any actions that derive there from. Questioning just one such action is synonymous with treason. Conversion means absolute subservience.

Identification and Imitation

To belong to the group, the follower must model his behavior on that of the others. This imitation erases his individuality. By replacing indecision, born of the free will, by automatic conduct learned by example, imitation wears away the feeling of uncertainty and replaces it with

113

the sense of urgency around a mission to fulfill. This is a true psychological make-over, typical of the behaviorist techniques, that gradually creates a new personality better adapted to cult dynamics.

Imitation fuels a competition between the followers, who must reach their goal as quickly and as perfectly as possible. Once he has become a model disciple, the subject is ready for the total identification with the guru, the climax of belief and the ultimate goal of coercive persuasion.

Self-Persuasion and the Reduction of Dissonance

Every individual has a natural tendency to maintain his internal equilibrium and to reject external elements likely to threaten the unity of his being. Either one rejects these elements, or on the contrary one tries to assimilate them by attempting a slight modification of his equilibrium. When a follower shows unexpected resistance, set off by too great a discordance between his former state and the future state suggested by the cult, he has to be convinced that the proposed product makes sense and he must be allowed to reestablish his equilibrium, before a new, more powerful attack can be carried out. This new offensive will take advantage of the relaxation of the defenses that were stimulated by the earlier attack. The subject is convinced that his opinions are respected, while the new tack is only a strategic prelude to a new offensive.

Propaganda Tools

In 1985, a multi-disciplinary scientific congress held in Wisconsin on "cults and coercive groups" proposed the following definition:

> A coercive cult is a totalitarian movement displaying itself in the form of an association, of a religious, cultural or different group which requires total devotion of its members, and devotion to the group more than to any other person. This movement employs techniques of manipulation, persuasion and control intended to fulfill the objectives of the group's leader and which cause among followers a total dependence on the group, to the detriment of the family and social entourage.

Note that the central point of this definition is the totalitarian character of coercive cults. Carl Friedrich, a scholar on totalitarianism, distinguished its constituent components. Similar traits are found in the operation of coercive cults.

The essential functions of coercive cults negate any individual benefit from the structure and repress any deviance. Thus, they affirm their totalitarian character.

Cults use the traditional tools of propaganda:[4]

- use of stereotypes that exploit people's tendency to generalize and to project themselves into an imaginary group;

- distortion of language and use of specific words intended to mask the truth or to create a stronger impact;

- control of information and selection of facts and the ideas, choosing only those that are favorable to the defended ideology;

- systematic lies and falsification of the truth;

- endless repetition of invented information to obtain assent or to change ideas;

- constant reaffirmation of the totalitarian thought as the only true one, and rejection of divergent thoughts;

- designation of a standard enemy or scapegoat presented for the group's opprobrium;

- total subservience to the authority and constant reference to him as the source of truth.

The Process of Assimilation

"Integration" is the preferred term, and indeed we favor it both in the sense of "assimilation," and in the biological sense of "phagocytosis" [*Editor's note:* in which leukocytes attack and ingest other cells]. Indeed, to integrate somebody is to regard him as a full member of a group, while preserving his identifying marks. Integration into a cult, however, is accompanied by the loss of these elements of identity.

Assimilation in the physical sense means using the elements of the

TOTALITARIANISM ACCORDING TO FRIEDRICH	COERCIVE CULTS
All-encompassing ideology	All-encompassing ideology
Led by a single dictator	Led by a single guru
One party conveys the ideology	The cult conveys the ideology
Monopoly of communication	Suppression of external information
Monopoly of weapons	Monopoly of strategies
Official monopoly of the economic	Collecting of individual work for the
Repression in the event of diver-	Repression in the event of opposi-
Fight against other ideologies	Vilification of outsiders

assimilated organism for the good of the assimilating organism; it is in the sense that we compare it to phagocytosis, in other words to the capacity of a simple organism, like a bacterium, to simply assimilate another organism by contact and by destroying its borders. Phagocytosis once achieved, the organism rejects waste at the end of the digestive process. In the same way, the CC will reject useless human "waste" after passage through the destructive system.

Which individual, collective and spacio-temporal factors influence assimilation by a coercive cult? The speed of assimilation is a function of the techniques applied, of their force of application and of the subject's resistance. All these factors hinder any resistance by the external milieu and, above all, by the subject's social and family environment. In this sense assimilation, the process of acquisition of the individual by the cult, is the result of the application of the techniques of coercive persuasion.

For J. G. Clark and M. D. Langone, there are three successive degrees in the process of coercive persuasion: persuasion, conversion and indoctrination.[5] Rodriguez Carballeira[6] proposes a different sequence, making it possible to establish a parallel between McGuire's analysis on persuasion and his own work on coercive persuasion. McGuire describes five stages in the process of persuasion: caution; comprehension; acceptance; retention; action. Carballeira holds with the following five stages: seduction; inveiglement; conversion; indoctrination; action. The stages are not rigorously distinct in chronology. On the contrary, they are overlapping phenomena. They mix, fade and reappear, recombining progressively throughout the process of assimilation according to the resistance exhibited by the subject.

The CC can hold back during one phase and emphasize another, sometimes even starting the process over again with an earlier stage that was not fully completed.

The essential difference between traditional persuasion and coercive persuasion is the cult's need to annihilate the individual quickly, by crushing any inclination toward criticism and analysis.

Seduction

This phase is only an extension of the seduction that took place during recruitment. The future cult member's aspirations, suggested to him earlier, are made to seem more attainable and real. The recruiters must lend further support to the suggestions made when they first latched onto the potential recruit, and expound on the cult's themes without revealing its principle ideology. The CC will present the future member with the tantalizing possibility of increasing his wisdom, his power and his wealth. It goes on to persuade him that the structure being proposed is reserved for the elites, who are devoted to noble tasks.

> Scientology works with the individual and allows him to improve himself, by developing his consciousness and his aptitude to solve life's problems. It differs from other religious philosophies in that it provides the means of developing his aptitudes, and to resolve the difficulties and the situations that confront the individual and the people around him. Because you are a spiritual being, completely distinct from your mind or your body, Scientology will help you to control and manage your mind, in the same way that it will help you intelligently to exert your power of control over the various aspects of your life.[7]

The seduction is based on two complementary emotional processes. On the one hand, a positive emotional phenomenon is activated by the sympathy generated by the transmitter — a preferred means for encouraging the processes of identification. In addition, negative emotional phenomena reinforce any conflicts that set the potential recruit against his normal environment. The transmitter's *love-bombing* on the receiver is accompanied by "hate-bombing" by the transmitter-receiver pair, with regard to third parties, society, family, etc.

This Manichean approach to the potential recruit's relations with, on one side, society which is shown as evil and, on the other, the cult which is shown as the only alternative, obliges him to make a choice. The demand of total and final dedication is certainly not formulated at this moment, but passing the "essential test" is suggested with such a force that it leaves little place to the recruit's free will. In place of a distressing future, a dehumanized world, an indifferent society, the CC proposes a congenial organization and a fraternal structure.

The second stage of the assimilation will set the potential recruit's intention by addressing all the arguments he might use to challenge the illusory character of the suggested solution.

Captivation

This is the stage where the famous "love bombing," cited by every author and recommended by cults, begins in earnest. Once the prey is caught, the next step is to engage him in the sphere of the group to begin the process of conversion. The captivation phase exclusively consists in drowning the subject with reassuring emotional ties that give him a feeling of belonging. The recruit must be convinced that, from now on, he can count on the support of people who claim to feel sympathy for him. The cult is presented as a cocoon, as a substitute family that is more accessible and understanding than the natural family.

At this stage, the process of assimilation is based not on rationality but on emotional dynamics. The feeling of belonging to the group is transmitted by ceremonies in the course of which the new recruit is welcomed and flattered in front of everyone. He has the illusion that everyone is looking forward to meet him. The ritual of initiation, where a climate of mutual support prevails, corresponds to this strategy. The newcomer must get the feeling that he is participating in a collective energy. Then he will be more disposed to start a intellectual search in order to give more solid bases to his new identity.

This phase is fundamental in the process of assimilation. At the same time that a feeling of belonging is being created, a slight frustration is triggered as well: the initiate should start to feel that he has not yet reached the degree of friendship displayed by the others. This emotional lack reinforces the feeling of missing something on the intellectual plane. There is, at this stage, an inability to grasp all the mysteries of the system and a dissatisfaction with not having all the elements that enable the older members to demonstrate their calm and flourishing lives. Consequently, the ground is prepared: the CC will start the emotional and intellectual handling that should lead to full conversion.

> Scientologists are persuaded that exchange is a necessary principle. If somebody only receives and never gives, he will not be happy and will lose any personal dignity. This is why all the charitable plans sponsored by Scientology also encourage those who benefit from its charity to contribute in one way or another, for example by helping their peers, so that they can retain their dignity.[8]

Conversion

Conversion is the apex of assimilation into the cult. By now, the future convert has exhausted his defenses to reduce the dissonance between the standards of his former life and the new one proposed to him. His conversion implies that he has made a compromise between his past and his future. Still, he must prove his unerring devotion. The surest way is by becoming a recruiter himself.

Conversion is basically a bet on the part of the follower. He is exchanging a painful past for a brilliant future that is accompanied by heart-

and-soul dependence on the structure. Accepting this bet signals the pact of final commitment, "without criticism," towards the guru. Proselytizing by the disciple will be not only the proof of his conviction, but a means of reinforcing the bond and an element of coercion.

> Scientologists strive to make technology more widely available because they want others to benefit from the gifts that they have known. The Church wants more people to know and apply work of Ron Hubbard.[9]

Every cults uses recruitment statistics as evidence of their members' fidelity and devotion.

> Things that are regarded as offences include:
> - omissions leading to a loss of reputation or a financial loss;
> - insufficient or declining activity or income in a section, a unit, a department, an organization, a sector or a division;
> - supporting such insufficiency or decline.[10]

Conversion confers a new identity upon the follower. The new identity is affirmed in front of the group, in baptismal ceremonies, the granting of diplomas, or the transmission of powers by the master or a senior-ranking member. It is accompanied by a reaffirmation of the cult's rules, through recitation of oaths, commitments or contracts. Sometimes it is based on "evidence" given by the new member (hallucinations or delusions that take on the character of supernatural demonstrations). The cult will interpret any psychotic experience as a sign of the follower's advancement along "the path of truth."

Indoctrination

Indoctrination consolidates the conversion. It aims to eliminate any remaining critical thinking that might still be lurking in the subject. Indoctrination integrates the individual more and more thoroughly into the cult's network of relationships. The new member is drowned in a multitude of obligations that abolish his personal space. From a recruit, the follower becomes a recruiter, from a subordinate he becomes a leader.

However, the real status is only vaguely related to the apparent status. The more one's responsibility seems to grow within the cult, the stronger grow the bonds of dependence. The dependence becomes multidirectional: not only does the follower depend hierarchically on his superiors, but he depends morally on his inferiors and, economically and socially, on the structure.

Action

From this point forward, the follower will be making his new membership clear to the outside world. He is completely implicated in the cult's social network and takes part in the CC's actions. Through action, he participates in the extension of the group at the same time that he continues to lose his own autonomy and to substitute the cult's rules for his own earlier morals.

Coercive Techniques of Persuasion

Coercive persuasion attacks the individual from four sides, using behavioral, emotional, and cognitive techniques, and at its most effective culminates in techniques for inducing dissociative states.

Behavioral techniques modify the individual's relations with his surroundings and aim at controlling the follower's interactions with the former relational system. They limit the information coming from society, the family or the pre-cult socio-professional environment. All the individual's vital statistics are rearranged and every field of his life is governed by new rules of food, sleep, sexuality, work, leisure, etc. The clearest break with the past is the geographical: the follower must exchange his residence for a monastery, an ashram or another place specified by the cult, either in the country of origin or abroad.

Emotional techniques establish an empathy between the individual and the cult by creating a continually emotional climate that tends to remove all the emotional ties and all the emotions linked to the past. The follower is progressively absorbed within an organization with high emotional dynamics, reinforcing his identification with the guru.

This feeling of fusion is the basis of the group dynamics, and more precisely of the dynamics of restricted groups where the cult-society relationship is painted in black and white, in terms of conflict. The fight against a supposed aggressor accentuates the group membership and accelerates fusion inside the new social body. Doubts a follower might express would be seen as signs of collaboration with the enemy, which would engender a powerful feeling of guilt.

Cognitive techniques: The intellect represents the only barricade to the cult's ideology. As it is difficult to annihilate an individual's intellectual abilities, the cult's strategy consists in saturating the information channels with false data. At the same time, the cult will endeavor to disparage any critical attitude.

The use of lies and deception tends to recreate an unreliable intellectual space that is made up of arbitrary rules and distorted reference systems. Judgment gradually loses its objectivity and takes on the cult's subjective perspective. The control of attention and of language, the manipulation of symbols, the recombining of values are the instruments by which the cult member's internal make-up will be redesigned.

Techniques for inducing dissociative states: These techniques are intended to destroy an individual's intellectual and emotional equilibrium in order to lead him into delirious or hallucinatory psychiatric experiences; we will consider them at greater length, below. These psychotic or pre-psychotic experiences are represented as states that should be sought by the follower, for they are synonymous with spiritual growth.

The Symbolic Triad of Coercive Persuasion

Coercive persuasion is built on three symbolic elements that encourage the follower to believe without criticizing. In *The Brothers Karama-*

zov, Dostoyevsky writes, "There are three forces, and only three, that can conquer and subject for ever the spirit of these rebels... They are miracles, mystery and authority."

The mysterious nature of the cult and the guru attracts the new follower; he is fascinated by the out-of-the-ordinary world represented by the new practices of the group. The plan for acquiring knowledge or specific powers creates the illusion of an existential search. The guru's authority enhances the relation at the same time, by offering an role model as an ideal. In combination, they prohibit any initiative of criticism or deviance. The miracle — or rather the created illusion — is a bait for the follower. It testifies to the power of the cult, removes any dispute, reinforces the guru's authority and stresses his mysterious essence. The authority conferred on the guru enables him to work miracles and create mysteries at will; and the mystery that surrounds him masks his inadequacies.

The cult environment, magical thought and the application of well-tailored techniques are the elements of the conditioning that will turn a recruit into a whole-hearted follower.

7.

CONDITIONING

*If the code of rewards and punishments is clearly written and
expeditiously implemented, it serves as a handle by which
you can use the multitudes of men.*
                                            Sun Tzu

Education by Brainwashing

In clinical psychology, conditioning covers "all the associative operations by which one can cause a man to have a new behavior."[1]

> Conditioning is a technique of training by association. It is the basis of
> military training, and of any education aiming to substitute disciplined
> automatic behavior for the imagination and spontaneity of the individual. Propaganda that intends to shift opinions and behaviors in a given
> direction also takes its inspiration here.[2]

The objective is to change an individual's behavior and lead him
toward attitudes that have been defined by other people. Conditioning
may be mild or coercive. Education is a model of mild conditioning, at
least in our Western democracies. Coercive methods are called brainwashing, mind control, mental handling, coercive persuasion, indoctrination, thought reform, forced conversion, re-planning of the thinking process[3] and so on.

While the techniques of conditioning are well known, fortunately
their effectiveness leaves much to be desired. Research on conditioning

125

more or less began in the United States, starting in the 1940's, following the public interest created by the confessions made by the defendants during the purge trials in the USSR. These trials were launched in the USSR after the great purge of 1936. From Kamenev to Zinoviev, stalwart militants reversed themselves and admitted to being traitors to the Party and the Fatherland — self-criticism that was so surprising that it cast doubt on their sincerity. Similarly, in 1949, the trial in Hungary against Cardinal Mindszenty was surprising, given the prelate's character. It was several years before the "penitents" revealed the torture that had been inflicted to extract such confessions.

During the Korean War, from 1950 to 1953, nearly seven thousand Americans were taken as prisoners of war. Shown on TV, the faces of these wounded men moved the public and put a bee in the bonnet of the military authorities who began studying "brainwashing" and "mind control." Under the control of the CIA, Cornell University researchers tackled a program named M-K ULTRA[4]. The aim was to establish the reality of this mental handling, and to develop "offensive and defensive information techniques." This program would include 185 researchers, divided among 80 institutions, mainly from the well-known Mac Gill University in Montreal.

Doctor Cameron, head of the psychiatric care unit of Allen Memorial Institute, conducted his first experiments on conditioning and reconditioning at Mac Gill University. These experiments lasted from 1953 to 1963, but ended with an acknowledgement of failure. Rightly denounced by human rights organizations, especially Amnesty International, these tests were carried out on Korean prisoners of war and mental patients. The experiments failed to prove that brainwashing could be accomplished, even though the most sophisticated techniques were used, with the greatest contempt for the human person.

The procedures were systematically divided into two stages. The first phase consisted of "washing" the brain of its existing information through a series of repeated electric shocks, several hundred times in a few weeks. The second phase consisted of filling the mind with new information that is repeated ad infinitum by recorded sound tracks. Other methods consisted of administering drugs that were intended to block sensory perceptions and to inhibit brain activity. One of these drugs, PCP or monohydrochloride of piperidin, was used by drug-addicts during the 1970s to get high. This method might be supplemented by electric shocks, or by insulin or amphetamine shocks. These methods and experiments would cause amnesic disorders, space-time disorientation and then a loss of identity. After the subject was deprogrammed or "washed," he was ready for reconditioning (psychic driving). During the reconditioning, new information would be repeated incessantly, allowing it to become implanted by means of theory of the "dynamic implant." For sixteen hours a day, twenty to thirty days in a row, the human guinea pig had to listen to recorded messages. The dynamic implant was carried out in two phases:

• the so-called auto-psychic phase, during which the subject listened to his own taped voice repeating in a loop;

• the so-called hetero-psychic phase, during which the external message was repeated by the "re-educators."

However, neither "dynamic implantation," "psychic driving," nor "reconditioning" ever managed to fill the mental vacuum created by deprogramming, and dozens of prisoners died after the sessions of electric shocks. This did not prevent Doctor Cameron from theorizing as follows:

> By repeating a message one can predetermine, in broad outline, a persistent tendency to act in a given way. In other words, repetition of the message infallibly causes the patient to fixate on the message. Other components of this bundle of tendencies go as far as the subject's conscious level. Dynamic implantation, especially if reinforced by repeated sessions, tends to activate more and more aspects of this bundle of tendencies that are linked together. These elements reach the patient's consciousness and facilitate the process of reorganization.[5]

While the persistence of the message "established" during conditioning could not be carried out, certain principles of mental handling were defined:

The qualities of the dynamic implant [the new way of thought and behavior wished by the experimenters] are a function of the quantity and the repetition of the manipulation, of the intensity of the reaction, defenses, and tolerance for stress, particularly with regard to sensory deprivation.[6]

Needless to say, these techniques were condemned wholesale by the medical profession. The paradox today is that the CC, which themselves use coercive techniques, use this black page in the history of medicine to feed their campaigns against psychiatry.[7]

If one carefully studies Cameron's experiments, several conclusions stand out:

• Mental conditioning cannot be achieved through one preset, identical technique for everyone;

• Each individual has a distinct personality, a random factor which throws off even the most sophisticated model of conditioning;

• Even the most brutal and most inhuman technique has its limits, and it can cause the death of the subject;

• Whatever the success of conditioning, it is not permanent, and once the coercion is ended it is followed by progressive and spontaneous deconditioning;

• This natural "deconditioning" is accomplished fairly quickly and the psychiatric after-effects will vary in severity, depending on the prior state of the subject.

Alienation

The first symptom of alienation is the individual's loss of his own speech, which "is fed by a reservoir whose substratum is human anguish and which forms the main part of the process of personal development, or that of the narcissistic function of individual."[8] Alienation is seen as "the product of a rupture of one's communication with oneself, a rupture by which speech can no longer feed at the unconscious level."[9]

In cults, conditioning invades every field of the activity. It is used in three complementary ways:

- Cultural conditioning: it replaces the subject's usual system of references with a new matrix of behaviors that, at the same time, satisfies the group imperative, and that makes him lose his former identity;

- Emotional conditioning: the cult cuts off the subject from his past and makes him subservient to the guru;

- Physical conditioning, with a view to remodeling the personality.

The conditioning techniques used by a CC lead to an alienation of the individual and a loss of individuality in favor of a more or less complete dissolution into the CC's group structure. The progressive breaking away from his past leads the subject to breaking away from himself. Alienation is accompanied by the subject's loss of all his usual systems of reference. They are replaced by the cult's fantasies, an extension of the guru's personal fantasies.

The purpose of mental conditioning is to alienate the follower in the sense defined by Hegel. For him, as for Marx, alienation is the state of the individual who ceases to belong to himself, who is treated as a thing or as an animal, and who becomes the slave of the external conditions which are imposed upon him. This state results in the loss of the basic individual rights and, above all, the right of free expression, a reflection of his own will.

Dependence on Authority

The follower's subservience to the cult, or more precisely to the guru through the instrument that the cult represents, has been made startlingly clear by Stanley Milgram's experiments on obedience to authority. In 1974, Milgram, a professor at Yale University, put an ad in the paper to recruit students eager to earn some money, and he asked them to take part in a series of experiments.[10] Then begins an audacious stratagem described thus by its author:

> Two people come into a psychology laboratory that is conducting research on memory and training. One of them will be the "monitor,"

the other the "pupil." The experimenter explains to them that he is studying the effects of punishment on the process of training. He leads the pupil into a room, installs him on a chair with straps that hold his arms to the chair and prevent any movement, and fixes an electrode to his wrist. The experimenter then tells the pupil that he is to learn a list of word pairs; every mistake will be sanctioned by electric shocks of increasing intensity. The true subject of the study is the "monitor." After watching how the pupil is set up, he is taken into the main room of the laboratory, where he takes a seat in front of impressive shock generator. The equipment holds a horizontal row of thirty levers ranging from 15 to 450 volts, increasing by 15-volt increments, with labels ranging from "Mild Shock" to "Warning, Dangerous Shock."

The official purpose of the experiment is to test the learning ability of the "pupil," who must read and memorize pairs of words. Any failure is punished by an electric shock of increasing intensity. These shocks are administered by the "monitor," who selects words from the list. The experiment is conducted under the supervision of Milgram, who embodies the scientific and moral authority and the referent. In the course of the experiment, the errors add up and the monitor is confronted with a choice: to stop the experiment or to continue it by increasing the intensity of the current and running an increasingly risk to his partner.

Of course, the victim was an actor simulating the pain and the electronic "torture" instrumentation was not real. This ruse was not known to the students, and the results are worrying: according to the results of the experiment, 47.5% to 65% of them delivered shocks up to 450 volts — i. e. fatal shocks. Under certain conditions, many individuals apparently can transgress prohibitions and commit severe, even criminal, acts. This passive obedience is explained by the symbolic power granted to the supervisor of the experiment. The student acquires a power over the alleged victim, through the implicit authorization to act that he receives from the supervisor. This is a translation of the "scientific authority" held by Milgram, who refutes any argument the student might raise. Ethical questions are overpowered by the process, and the fact of making a decision implicitly devolves to the scientific authority that supervises the experiment and "pardons" the "criminal."

> Our subjects are completely carried away by the details of the experimental method. They read the pairs of words by articulating them as well as they possibly can and they actuate the levers with the greatest care. The desire to show themselves up to the task is accompanied by a considerable reduction in their concern for ethics. They give up to the experimenter, whom they are assisting, all concern for directing the action and guaranteeing its morality.... The obedient subject does not see himself as a human actor fully accountable for his actions, but as an instrument at the hands of an external authority.[11]

Milgram thus highlighted a phenomenon that he called "anti-anthropomorphism," in other words, "the propensity to confer an impersonal quality on forces that are originated and perpetuated by humans. For some, the systems set up by society seem to have their own existence whose sphere of activity is located beyond and above human contingencies." In fact, he shows that, sometimes, the boundaries of man's free will can be eroded in favor of a passive obedience to ideas or symbolic representations. This ideic illusion manifests in reality and takes the form of individuals, situations or structures that are used as supports and ties to this supramoïc dynamics. Milgram also highlights the fact that the performance of acts that are considered condemnable by common ethics is accompanied by a preliminary devaluation of the victim. Wasn't the genocide against the Jews preceded by a systematic campaign against the Jews?

In the same way, when cults engage in illegal acts, they start with a program of systematically condemning the noncult milieu.

The Mental Shift: From Being Free to Being Controlled

Integration into the cult's organizational pyramid and subservience to a hierarchical system require a change of state on the part of the subject.

If, in a given group, each individual functions autonomously, the group will have to obey rules of operation that are enacted via compromise; the result will be the establishment of a system that supports individuality as much as possible, to the detriment of group unity. The group will then function on the lowest denominator common to the individuals. However, cults cannot survive under such conditions, where individuality is allowed to be expressed. The coercive system thus aims to reduce any inclination toward independence. This "unification" of the group will be carried out only through a change of state of the individuals, which Milgram calls "agentic change."

Integration into the hierarchy can be achieved only through an internal change on the part of each individuality. Individualized control of action, a reflection of autonomy, must be abandoned gradually in favor of the hierarchical directives issued by the coordinating agent. The progressive structuring of the coercive group must include a remodeling of the domains of autonomy and dependence. The subject functions on two models simultaneously: an autonomous and independent model where he is only motivated by the sole aim of satisfying his own desires, and a systemic mode that integrates him into a structure where his action must ensure the longevity of the community.

The increase in the coercive character is accompanied by a progressive change of the individual, who passes from the state of total autonomy to a state that is wholly agentic, or controlled. Resistance to conditioning and to integration into a coercive system is born from the confrontation of these two domains of action. Gradually, the subject loses his free will and his freedom of action in favor of dependence on a system; he no longer sees himself as an organizing agent responsible for his actions.

According to Milgram, "An individual is in an agentic state when he accepts total control by a person holding a higher status. In this case, he no longer considers himself responsible for his actions. He sees himself as a simple instrument carrying out the wills of others."[12]

The same author also hypothesizes that the passage from the autonomous state to the agentic state is accompanied by a biological change at the level of the neurotransmitters and cerebral mediators. In addition, a natural or artificial change (through psychotrophics or drugs) of these mediators would reduce resistance to aggression, and more generally to stress. The variability of resistance to conditioning and to indoctrination probably depends on the rate of concentration of these neurotransmitters. This explains why Soviet psychiatrists turned to psychotrophics: they counted on haloperidol, and more generally on nerve sedatives, to bring *refuzniks* back into line.

Transposed into the cult milieu, Milgram's experiments show how well the guru can control the followers. Invested with a superhuman knowledge and power by the cult, he generates, by his very presence, by his writings or his word, a powerful presumption in favor of the correctness of the action undertaken — which opens the door to every transgression.

Milgram adds that agentic states are limited in the field of application even in the case of venerated authority. An agentic individual will recognize the authority of his superior only in proportion to the competence he ascribes to the latter. For example, a soldier's agentic state involves his total acceptance of military orders but it does not extend to the field of private life — at least, in theory.

In the cult, the agentic state applies to every field, and the legitimacy which the follower confers to the hierarchy applies to every sector of his existence, without limitation.

Consequences of the Agentic State

The agentic state gives rise to a syntonic phenomenon which impels the individual to accept without reservation everything that comes from the authority, while external elements are minimized or denied. Milgram also attests to the existence of a potential ideological form that he calls the "definition of situation."

The agentic subject is "regulated" in a pre-defined situation whose significance is determined by his relationship with the authority and by the elements of interpretation and of judgment resulting from it. Every action takes on its own meaning, coming directly from the setting in which they are carried out, this setting being itself defined implicitly by the standards resulting from agreeing to participate in a hierarchical system. For a cult member, no act can be interpreted until it is integrated in the dogma and ethics, which devolve from accepting the guru's authority and the cult's power. An act that would be condemned by the general public can be interpreted in the cult environment as a demonstration of faith or as zeal in the fight against external evils.

Ethical and ideological abdication are the cognitive basis of obedience. If the world is as the supreme authority defines it, actions take on a different significance and any plans that support respect for the authority become legitimate. In the agentic state one loses the sense of responsibility. The subject no longer sees himself as responsible for his actions, because he is bound and dependent on the leader. Ethics and critical thinking do not disappear, but they change upon contact with the new systems of reference. On the other hand, the concept of responsibility does, indeed, disappear, to be replaced by the pride derived from fulfilling one's duty.

The replacement of the former ego ideal by the cult ideal is a sign of the controlled state. There is a fading of inhibitions related to the culture that was followed prior to entry into the cult. The agentic state thus allows the hierarchy to demand acts of obedience from the subject. However, in order for there to be obedience, there must still be adequate correspondence between the order given and the "level" of the agentic state that pertains. The stronger the agentic state, the further the limits of moral transgression may be pushed. The power of coercive cults consists in pushing this limit to the extreme.

Maintaining the Agentic State

Once the controlled state is established, the coercive structure will endeavor to keep the subject there. However, confrontation between personal ethics and the constraints of obedience will create permanent conflict in him, when the taboos transgressed grow in number and degree.

His critical faculties would quickly lead him to refuse too reprehensible a plan — if allegiance were not a permanent practice.

The essential point, here, is that no personal decision is requested of the follower. The repeated constraint against making one's own decisions is, in itself, a destabilizing element of the agentic state: it is essential that obedience be continual. Moreover, within the cult, questioning obedience is penalized by the loss of the acquired status. The agentic state is thus further reinforced by the former privileges and by fear of punishment. This is what is known as the carrot and the stick. To refuse obedience is to refuse to identify with the guru, to break the potential emotional tie between the guru and the follower:

> First of all, we must release ourselves from our own personality, culti-
> vate permanent values and our capacity to assume risks and responsi-
> bilities. A healthy spirit of adventure is essential. Cowards will be
> never free. Without obedience, freedom is useless, since the wisest of
> freedoms is that of choosing our form of obedience to the Universal
> Law, represented by our instructor or master, to insert ourselves into
> the harmony that gives birth to the Just, the Good and the Beautiful....
> A stone at the beginning of the path says, "I belong, I obey." Anyone
> who does not follow this thousand-year-old prescription can only be a
> bystander, curious about the philosophical subjects.... He will con-
> tinue to be a clown, a man dressed in clothing that always will be too
> large for him.... So freedom and obedience are harmonized in disci-
> pline. The discipline is to accept oneself as one is, while trying to
> improve, by eliminating any fantasy that, with time, exhausts the
> heart. We all are necessary, but in our natural place. That is freedom,
> that is obedience, that is discipline, that is the path.[13]

Refusal to obey and deviance sometimes lead the cult leadership to claim that the follower is mad. This is a practice well-known to all dictatorships.

> If there is any doubt concerning the mental health of a baptized person
> who has committed an action for which he can be excluded, a legal
> committee must examine the facts. Evaluate the evidence and the ex-
> tent of his mental deficiency, then decide whether or not it is neces-

sary to make a communication or if, in fact, he should be excluded. Although there may be reasons to show consideration and patience beyond the ordinary, the elders must nevertheless protect the purity and spiritual health of the congregation (*I Thessalonians*)[14]

Imitation

Imitation is a factor of social training. In normal "society," the phenomenon is limited by the multiplicity of choices and models suggested. In the CC, choice no longer exists and only one model is offered. Imitation of the other, or of the guru, takes on a character of ineluctability that blends into the process of indoctrination.

Bandura[15] described two phases in the process of imitation: a phase of observation and a phase of performance. Jointly, four sub-processes come into play during imitation. Attention, or sensory recording of the behaviors to be acquired; retention, which results in a mnemonic representation of the elements to be reproduced; physical replication, which has to do with repeating and integrating the behaviors to be acquired; and finally motivation, which influences the three preceding sub-processes.

One can easily see that all the sub-processes are reinforced in the cult. The process of attention is covered by the selection or absence of information. The intensity of cult life is like "being hit over the head," saturating the follower's perceptive and sensory system. The processes of retention and motor replication are constantly stimulated by rituals — repeating "holy" words, memorizing texts, reciting prayers — which lead to automatic behavior and thought. Motivation is supported and strengthened by the obligation to produce results.

Bandura also stresses the decisive importance of symbols in the process of training. If one takes road signs as an example, the symbol carries information which determines a behavior, the latter being the result of training which concerns intellect (learning the code) and imitation (learning the behavior). Cults are the perfect breeding ground for this type of symbol. Symbols trigger behaviors that pre-exist analysis and that destroy it. The sessions of prostration in front of a "holy" picture are revealing in this respect: repetition takes away the meaning of the image and, at the same time, of the gesture.

The phenomenon of imitation is always facilitated by the feeling that links the follower to the copied milieu, and mainly to the guru. Conditioning is especially effective since the imitation is voluntary and tends to establish a close similarity between the subject-follower and his model-guru.

The process of imitation culminates in the phenomenon of contagion. According to Wheeler,[16] there are three types of obstacles to this phenomenon (an example of which, within the cult, is the collective trance):

- those coming from the membership;
- those from a repressive authority;
- those born from the individual's super-ego.

When it puts group dynamics before individual initiative, the cult abolishes the first two types of limiting factors and sanctions those which emanate from the individual.

Conformity

The follower's behavior depends on his acceptance or rejection of the standards established by the group. Entry into a cult is accompanied by a change of the rules associated with the world in which the follower usually circulated. These rules must be re-established, becoming more rigid and constraining since respecting them is a condition of survival of the cult minority vis-à-vis in the social majority. In society, people influence each other mutually to work toward the construction of an overall accepted normative system, but in the cult, the standard emanates exclusively from the guru and does not brook any modification. Here, the normative dependence is especially powerful since it is accompanied by complete dependence as regards information. The refitting of the standard presupposes the subject's capacity of choice. To have a choice, there must be judgment over various and sometimes contradictory data. The monolithic and exclusive character of cult information prohibits enlightened choice and reinforces the imposed standard. Disobedience to the standard implies a penalty for the subject.

The rigor of the cult standard tends to create a behavioral and psychological uniformity that goes hand in hand with the suppression of the usual social comparisons. This is why the general problems of conditioning rest on the rule of conformity, which is imposed on all the cult members. Whereas society tolerates (to some extent, depending to the degree of democratic expression) minorities' expressions, the cult cannot accept in its midst the sprouting of any individualistic ideology or feeling. Indeed, while defining itself in terms of counter-culture, it cannot allow the development of thoughts different from those of the guru, since such thoughts would be likely to sunder its unity.

An individual is traditionally subject to two types of dependence: on the one hand, an informational dependence that leads him to seek information from the outside, to develop his capacities of judgment, to establish a synthesis and to draw conclusions; in addition, a normative dependence that encourages him to accept the group's rule without wondering about its validity, since it is an obligatory condition of joining the group.

How well an individual fits into a group depends on the balance that is established between these two forms of dependence. In the case of the cult, the desire for outside information is voluntarily suspended, since that is a critical factor for the coherence of the group. By contrast, the normative dependence is pushed to the extreme and prohibits any mental or practical initiative. The cult group "exerts a pressure toward uniformity," in the words of Festinger.[17]

Stages of Conditioning

Indoctrination is incremental, according to the following stages:
• Belief in a simplistic and acceptable philosophy;

• Rationalization through pseudo-scientific explanations or pseudo-histories;

• Integration of the cult's own "absurd" ideas into the core curriculum;

• Use of unusual (and, therefore, beyond criticism) physical or psychic techniques;

• Use of a vocabulary that has been distorted from the common meanings, and the creation of a neolanguage;

• Emotional isolation, loss of all sense of reality and scotomization of the subject (evidence that the new ways are not reality-based is met with denial), leading to isolation caused by the aberrant beliefs;

• Training in rituals that defy commonsense and that are of dubious moral and legal standing, thereby inherently prohibiting the subject from sharing his doubts with other people;

• Loss of identity by fusing with the cult and identifying with the guru or with the ideal of the cult.

Each one of these methods must be studied as a specific instrument using a technique that is part of the general plan of destabilization of an individual and reconditioning according to new standards.

Ideology, the Basis of Conditioning

The sole purpose of conditioning is to remove prior reference systems and to put in their place a new matrix of values and an ideology set forth by the guru.

A study of the texts of Shri Mataji,[18] conducted by the parents of English followers of Sahaja Yoga, clearly shows how the gurus create, either consciously or by trial and error, a system of conditioning behaviors. Without systematically resorting to brutal techniques, the cult sets up a continuous flow of false information that all aims toward one goal: to persuade the follower that, in following the example of the guru's conduct, he is freely determining his own actions.

The parents of Sahaja yogists, analyzing Mataji's remarks, noted the dialectical elements of conditioning. By extrapolation, they then used the same methodology to identify how cult groups talk.[19]

1. The leader of the group asserts his divine character and ascribes to himself superhuman powers, or at least a specific mission entrusted by God.

> I am Christ, sitting in front of you. I am the Holy Spirit, I am Adi Shakti, I am the first who came to Earth in this form to achieve my mission here.

2. The group shows warmth and friendliness in order to recruit. The information given to a newcomer does not enable him to form a real opinion about the group and the risks incurred:

> You must first of all present them with a pleasing and gentle image. Do not frighten them. Show them only the pleasant aspects. At the beginning, they are apprehensive, they are nervous, they are too ego-centric. Be nice with them. Attract them gradually. If you have seen how I lead my Gurudom, do the same.

3. The new followers are promised various specific advantages, especially security.

> Kundalini is a sleeping energy. Sahaja Yoga is the only School that can awaken Kundalini, without pain and struggle, allowing you to attain the state of being within a short time, which would take several years for the traditional Schools that practice austerity and purification.

4. Members are kept in a permanent state of suggestibility through various forms of deprivation: loss of intimacy, sleep deprivation, diets, etc.

> You must practice meditation every day from 4 to 6 o'clock in the morning, this is vital. Most important is group meditation.... You should not eat too much. You should eat enough only from time to time. You should not have memories of food. You should not remember when nor how you slept.

5. Followers are made vulnerable to authority through suggestion, in ways that recall the techniques of dissociation (states of trance, meditation, repetitive songs, breathing methods and visualization). These techniques are intended to create blind devotion to the leader and to the group, and can induce euphoria or pleasant feelings, thus forging true dependence.

> I entered a different dimension, the room had changed although it remained the same one. A great silence came over me. The noises of my mind were quieted. Everything was very real, very intense.... After several months of critical observation, I concluded that I had mastered Kundalini.[20]

6. The leader is skillful enough to produce altered states of conscience during which it is possible to take advantage of the subject's suggestibility.

> As soon as he touched me, I felt vibrations that radiated from his body and filled me with a feeling of peace and happiness.[21]

7. The leader demands total devotion to his person; he predicts trouble for those who question or who would disobey.

> You must give yourself entirely to me, not to Sahaja Yoga, but to me. Sahaja Yoga is only one of my aspects. You must give in entirely, without question and without hesitation. The total Gift must be made in meditation. It is not for your good, but you must do it. ... Those who are not useful will be rejected gradually. They will be rejected so far that they will never be able to return. They will have several chances, several opportunities, but in the end, if they are without interest, they will be rejected completely, definitively.

8. The group becomes the follower's new family. He is exhorted to break any contact with his family and his friends.

> Among the many obstacles are your family, your relations, all the ridiculous distractions that you do not need. They are stones in your way. Go forward, no matter what you have to do, do it, but have nothing to do with them. In your voyage, you have neither loved ones, nor brothers, nor friends, you are absolutely alone. Drop your old life, it

represents darkness, and darkness is hell, this darkness can be terrible, it is danger.

9. The group and the leader put barriers between the follower and his spouse, his children, his home.

> There are all these people who believe that this is my wife, this is my fiance, this is that, or any kind of nonsense. Why are you here, for what reason?[... If you cannot rise above that, then I cannot help you.... At first, everyone says, my wife is like this, my wife is like that, my brother is like this, my children are like that.... That is OK in the beginning, but when you grow, you must give up all of that.

10. Certain groups organize unions between their members, through specific rituals, and these ceremonies become the only thing that is valid in the eyes of the group.

> We now have a great plan for marriages. You should not organize your own union, that is dangerous. The marriages which we organize are more harmonious than those which you organize yourselves.

11. Children are often regarded as belonging to the group and not to their parents. The leader can begin his teaching from the earliest youth.

> Anyone can make a child. Even a dog can produce a little one. There is nothing great in that. Your only duty is the duty that you have with regard to all the children of Sahaja Yoga, and not exclusively to your own. You must give up your family first of all, give your child, give everything, until the end.... Our relationships and our identities must be abandoned completely.... Now there are children who have been born. But because their fathers and mothers are overactive, they develop a new disease, the over-activeness of the child. Then these children must be removed immediately from their parents, mainly from their mother so that they are not subject to her influence. They must be sent to other ashrams to develop harmoniously outside their parents' influence. Thus the child will develop on his own account, not on account of us.

12. Women play a subordinate role.

If you are a man, and you are a dominating man, then everything is fine. But if you are a woman and you want to dominate, then Sahaja Yoga will have difficulty in curing you, because you have lost your womanly quality. If you are not even a woman, then what do you want us to do with this third kind of people who are neither men, nor women? Women should be more docile, domestic.

13. Reason, objectivity, individualism are forbidden and are replaced by the intuitive feeling of the group. The end justifies the means:

Stop rationalizing, stop arguing, stop looking for reasons. Analysis is one of the diseases of the West. Because of science, your mind is always confused. Especially in the West, people have developed their brain too much. As long as you want to be a unique individual, you cannot be good Sahaja yogist. Stop being individuals. If they [the followers of Sahaja Yoga] kill somebody, it is Dharma, nothing is not evil, they are absolutely pure... If they hurt some people, in the absolute it is perfect... To achieve the ultimate goal, they must carry out humbler tasks.

14. Followers are expected to provide financial support for the activities of the guru and the cult.

The size of your bank account is meaningless. Your wealth is represented by the presence of Shri Mataji on this earth. But there are international programs that must be financed by the families: Sahaja Yoga programs, Shri Mataji's travel, ceremonies, gifts. Use your money solely for the glory of God and the development of Sahaja Yoga.

15. The group does not tolerate and does not respect the great religions. Their forms of worship are violently condemned:

The Jews asked that Christ be crucified. You know the state these people are in today. Mister Pope is that guy with the thing on his head, some kind of hat, a dunce's cap with diamonds around it, like a pop-star.

16. The group must offer a good image to the public. It must be

shown as a new religion, a charity organization, a School of Thought that you can attend for free.

> It is completely false to make believe that young people are encour-
> aged not to see their families. There is no recruitment in Sahaja Yoga,
> no hypnosis. Sahaja Yoga is not a cult. A private Sahaja Yoga clinic
> is opening soon in England. Since 1970, we have systematically de-
> nounced phoney gurus, false religions and fundamentalism while not
> hesitating to call a spade a spade.

One such conditioning speech is not, however, enough to seduce people. It becomes the backdrop for the physical and psychological techniques, of which it is both one of the elements and the ultimate goal.

8.

PSYCHIC CONDITIONING

Techniques for Conditioning Individuals

While it's true that some cults resort to the severe methods of totalitarian regimes to subjugate and reindoctrinate rebellious members (sleep deprivation, starvation, constant exposure to light, compulsory labor and reading, daily public confessions, etc.), while they may sometimes use tricks (sexual entrapment, drugs), most cults in Europe use more subtle techniques. Only the protestors or rebels already within the cult undergo harsh treatment.

> The society wishing to control the greatest number of people offers religion in place of the mind. Now we know more about psychiatry than psychiatrists themselves. We can brainwash a subject more quickly than the Russians (in 20 seconds, we offer total amnesia, compared to three years just to make someone a little shaky in his loyalties).[1]

The Dynamic Approach to Conditioning

One can imagine the personality as a sphere whose core is the most secret part of an individual, over which he exerts some level of control at every moment, and which makes the person inaccessible to

145

others. This is impregnable center is sacred, and it external forces tap into it, the subject recoils and collapses inward. (In schizophrenics, this field is insulated with barriers that prevent external information from coming across.) Around this core extends a permeable area that outside information and other people can broach. There, some intrusions are allowed, such as social interchange and the concessions resulting from a desire to be in harmony with others. From these compromises and concessions comes an increase in the area of sharing.

The more introverted is an individual, the more the field of exchange is reduced and the more the core or personal self extends. Conversely, an extravert narrows the size of the core while extending that of the external sphere. In the specific case of dependent followers, the core expands, submerging the negotiable field. Criticism of the cult's syncretism leads to rejection and collapse inward to this sacred core. The phenomenon of conditioning and cult dependence is proceeded by the conquest of this core, the original personality, which tends to merge with the ideology of the cult. The cult gradually alienates the subject until the transferable relational field is gone. The cult field then merges with the personal field of the follower, whom it annexes completely and isolates from the outside world by rules and doctrines.

This process of indoctrination works in three ways: it attacks the subjects ego, the subject's convictions, and the subject's environment. The new personality created by the cult imagination becomes untouchable, too busy to pay attention to anything not related to the cult, and indestructible, designed to follow a model of interdependence built around services, convictions and scenarios. With the core of the personality entirely occupied by the cult's convictions, the subject in unequipped to deal with his or her situation logically.

Isolation Inside the Cult

The development of aberrant doctrines within a CC (for example, a thetan's claiming to be able to go through walls, labor contracts extending billions of years, relinquishing all life prior to joining the cult, communicating with extraterrestrials, the combat against the lemurs, etc.)

which cause laughter when exposed to the public, only come up at a more advanced point in the path of the "initiate."

Since the doctrines usually generate disbelief, the disciple of an CC avoids exposing them in public. This leads to an increasingly marked departure from reality and feelings of persecution that accentuates the paranoia and mistrust of the fold towards the outside world. The followers believe themselves to be members of a Church persecuted by nonbelievers.

"Scotomization"

Outside of ophthalmologic language (scotome = a blind spot), the concept of scotomization refers to the mental process that makes an individual who is confronted with an obvious contradiction between spoken words and actions to scotomize (not see) this difference. This process of denial works to avoid conflict with the entourage, or to avoid a waste of energy in repeated or tentative explanations of conviction. Emotional insulation and isolation from family and friends go hand in hand with confirming this theory. If we take, for example, the Church of Scientology, one can see that most of Dianetics put the bulk of responsibility for a thetan's failures in life on his or her parents. Thus Ron Hubbard makes parents the true criminals[3] by making them the only people responsible for their child's dissatisfaction with his or her life. The theory of the thetan actually reduces parents to being merely the instruments that produced the thetan. They are usually, however, seen as parasites, since they cut the "ideal person" from his or her true potential by "socializing" him. The majority of painful experiences in a Scientologist's life are blamed on his or her parents, particularly the mother: stress is placed on any abnormal behavior of the mother before the child's birth, this conduct supposedly being the origin of the subject's failures in life.

The parents' influence is therefore suppressed (and is considered an obstacle to the CC's success in initiation) and eventually eliminated. Any opposition from them is considered the same as persecuting the Church. The emotional vacuum that results from this sends the subject to seek relations only within the Church of Scientology, thus allowing the creation of a substitute pseudo-family.

However, the subject can progress if he manages to attract the members of his family into the Church: this is the theory of dissemination and planetary evangelization.

Distorting Words and Language

The dialectical technique used by the cults is founded on the widespread use of nonsense, both in doctrine (its architecture and symbolism) and in words themselves. The cults employ an esoteric language whose purpose is to warp the meaning of words into nonsense and to strengthen the closed character of the cult by making the language accessible only to it members. This new language protects the cult from revealing its doctrine and secrets to outsiders and is used as sign of recognition between followers.

Learning New Words

Under the cover of giving words their precise significance, the CC manufacture neologisms or give ordinary words new meanings. For the Scientologist, "to handle" means "to manipulate," but it can refer to either an individual or to reality. It is usually used is when discussing how an individual is "handling" old and new "truths"; a "button" is a distressing word or expression that works like a push-button that rings a loud, surprising bell.

The use of a vocabulary understood only by initiates causes the subject to gradually adhere to a different way of thinking. Language is the support of a culture, and a standard definition of words and phrases is necessary to a comprehensive exchange within a group. The progressive amendment to words' definitions allows a cultural rebuilding to take place. This amendment to the common direction is supplemented by the creation of words like "Dianetics." Other vocables are modified by breaking them down and discussing their origins, and are gradually replaced.

For the Scientologist, comprehension comes from Affinity, Reality, and Communication (ARC), which leads to the concept of the destruction of ARC-a fall in mental energy or in Tone ARM. What ordinarily represents a difficulty of comprehension becomes, for Hubbard, a fall of Tone ARM visible on the electrometer; thus, any problem of comprehension can justify an auditing process using the electrometer...QED. In the same spirit, "reality" means: a) what is real and solid; b) the degree of agreement between two people. A thing is not real because an individual thinks it is. A thing is real because two people agree that it is, and that the majority agrees it is real as well. Thus, the thetan, the ARC, and the doctrine become reality because the majority believes it to be real.

The creation of vocabulary is often accompanied by symbols that further complicate things, and render the language inaccessible to anyone but the initiates. These symbols can be interpreted in various manners according to the level of advancement in the CC; for example, the first raëlien symbol is made up of a star of David interwoven with a swastika and is interpreted as an expression of a religious syncretism that poorly masks an underlying Aryanism.

Affirming Obedience

At any stage of advance within a CC, rising within the ranks always requires a series of sworn oaths and written commitments. Their absence in a subject's file prohibits ascension or even establishment within the hierarchy. Among Scientologists, a letter of success is delivered to the cult hierarchy in which a follower reaffirms his conviction and confidence in the organization; these can remove any previous criticisms noted in the initiate's file.

The repetitive oath of honesty is used to various degrees in all types of groups, from sports teams (slogans, songs) to bystanders (oath of entreated) on seeing pictures of terrorist groups or crack corpses. But in a cult, that which does not adhere to the ritual is suitable for exclusion. Its oath is solemn:

I promise to accept and to assume my station as well as the responsibilities that are entrusted to me, regardless of their nature, and regardless of where they will lead me in the achievement of my mission.[4]

Rules of Hygiene

Rules of hygiene represent a diverted form of intrusion of the
body. Possession is established by progressive prohibition on managing
one's own body and personal appearance. Some cults make it criminal
to disobey stated rules of hygiene (prohibition of condoms and blood
transfusions), while other CC intervene in choices of food, medicine,
and disease prevention. Disease is often regarded as the expression of
bad acts or bad thoughts, i.e. harmful to the CC. The patient has to
amend himself in a public confession. To call a doctor is thus a condemnable gesture and viewed as an attempt to deny fault and escape
penitence. The greater the illness and the weaker the individual, the
more subservient the initiate becomes.

The questions of hygiene and health are thus solved in Zen
macrobiotics:

Ten days are enough to look after the disease, whatever it is. Diseases
are conveyed by blood. They run in our veins. But each day we eliminate a tenth from our blood. In ten days, with an adapted diet, all
blood is changed and all disease has left. Babies can fast several days
without becoming ill; they lose weight and regain it at once. Mumps,
scarlet fever, pneumonia, diphtheria, and small pox disappear in a few
days if one does not give in to hunger. According to Jehovah's Witnesses, "blood should not be infused (as in transfusions) to reconsti-
tute the vital forces of the body, not by human creature or a domestic
or different animal placed under the authority of a Christian."

Lastly, families are offered this advice when dealing with a sick
loved one. "If a child is harboring a disease, separate it from the others
and ask for his cure in prayer according to the word of God." These rec-
ommendations give an important level of control to an individual under

the guise of offering medical assistance, where ancillary medical techniques are the specific domain of the guru.

Sexuality

The CC frequently enact sexual codes of conduct. They range from abstinence to unrestrained copulation, to prostitution designed to control the choice of partners.

The Family of Love, ex-Children of God, recommends free sexuality at even the most tender age of childhood, independent of possible family bonds. All practices are recommended, including incest. Moïse David, the founder, claimed the right of cuissage (taking virginity) on his followers (even children) and recommended spiritual growth through prostitution.

The second dynamics of Scientology, or 2D, was, in essence, the discovery of sexuality in all its forms:

> One could say that there are eight impulses in life which we call "dynamic." The first is the survival instinct. The second is the impulse to procreate. The third is the survival of the group. The fourth is humanity. The fifth is as a living organism. The sixth is as part of the physical universe. The seventh is in the spiritual universe. The eighth is through a supreme being.[5]

Under the pretext of controlling the libido and following the second dynamic impulse, multi-partner sexuality breaks the last protective barrages of the body's integrity. Refusing to be in a relationship becomes "poor control of 2D. Refusing to participate in a degrading or perverse scenario can be punished if it falls within the scope of implementing 2D."[6] Even though the rules of a number of cults claim officially that they practice monogamy, this is contradicted by many reports from ex-followers.

The Moonists declare themselves to be in favor of marriage, but under specific conditions and according to the goodwill of Sun Myung Moon. They organize ceremonies where several thousand followers are married under the blessing of the Master.

Whereas ceremonial orgies are a fact of life of a number of cults, right of cuissage is generally the privilege of the guru. Raël sings the virtues of sensual initiation. The cosmo-planetary Messiah chooses its elected. Moïse David sleeps with his grand-daughter. Ron Hubbard was devoted to perverse practices. In all the cases, sexuality seems a means of subservience after having been a considerable tool for recruitment.

In an interview published in *Marie-Claire* in 1981, Marie-Blanche Arnaud, ex-follower of AAO (Analytical Action and Organization) — a cult based on the principles laid down by Wilhelm Reich that are halfway between the search for the proletarian Community ideal and the attainment of a state of Nietzchean superman by achieving the ideal orgasm — thus described the daily life in the group:

> One hundred-fifty people implement the principles of Reich, i.e. more family, more couples, more personal life. The children are shared. There is no owned property. Everyone lives in autarchy... heads are shaved under the pretext of saving shampoo, everyone wears overalls. Possessions are prohibited, there is no privacy. The doors on even the toilets are removed, everything has to be done in the open. There is "the mat," *Selbstdarstellung*, the display of oneself.... You get up, you take off your overalls. If you don't, you are helped, either with music, or with words. It is always necessary to go farther, with cries, vomiting, gestures, dance, in the final analysis to lose oneself. When you are lost, cheerful music is played to revive you, and you are applauded.... sex is the compensation. The first two principles are that if you do not kiss three or four people per day and if you do not do it on the mat every evening, you are regarded as an individualist. If you do not do it, they make you feel severely guilty or they reject you completely. You are congratulated when you have a completely infantile sexuality, that you practice anywhere, with no matter with whom or how. Couples are separated. If you want to see the man you were with the day before, you are told it's not allowed. This is love without predilection, sex for sex, as animalic and as much as possible. Homosexuality is a very serious disease, homosexuals there want to be cured.... The men suffer more than women: a woman can make love several times in the course of the day, but for a man, it is more difficult to hold the course. The man who can perform well has power, but

humiliation if he does not succeed.

Deprivation of Identity

Cults often coerce their followers into giving up their birth-names. Names are the sign of membership in a family and/or a social group. The first name conveys the fantasies and the wishes of the parents or the family; it represents an additional identifier that functions, by analogy, either on the meaning of the first name (Desiree, for example), or by the signified bond with a relative, a godfather, a friend, or a role model chosen by the father and mother. Names also serve to assert the parental origin: for example, Ben means "son of." Group membership is reaffirmed by baptism, which is a public confirmation of membership. Baptism generally does not abolish former affiliation: it creates additional affiliation.

Certain cults preach the abandonment of the patronym and the adoption of a ritual name. This also serves to "erase the trail," in case the follower's close relations try to seek him or her out. The Children of God constantly change names and borrow new ones from the Bible. They often bear several names at the same time, so that when they change locations they can reuse old names to help them to find their fellow travelers. Legal identification is made all the more difficult.

A second major function of name-changing is to break the symbolic bond with the initiate's family. Symbolically, the person the initiate was prior to joining the cult is "dead," and is reborn within the cult — the new family. In *Totem and taboo*, Freud noted: "One of oddest, but also of the most instructive habits of taboo referring to primitive mourning practices, consists in prohibiting members of the group from pronouncing the name of the dead." [7]

Reprehensible Rituals

The practice of making reprehensible acts done by individuals a shared responsibility of cult members strengthens the dynamics of protection within the cult against the outside world, making all members accessory to the acts of the individual. The practice of public confession and keeping files containing evidence of crimes effectively turns individuals into slaves of the unit. Any escape would involve the disclosure of such files.

For example, let us cite the actions of the Scientology called "Black Propaganda." Black Propaganda aims to defame opponents of the Church by using all social avenues possible to harm the declared enemy. If an enemy is liable to be a long-term threat, a Black Propaganda campaign is instantly organized in order to destroy the reputation of the responsible person and to discredit him or her in such manner that they are effectively banished from society.[8]

> Such a person is considered Fair Game, and any other Scientologist can confiscate his or her belongings or harm the person without being liable to any disciplinary measure by the Church. You can mislead a Fair Game person, prosecute him in court, lie to him, or destroy him.[9]

In system Minute Man, a messenger conveying coded information from the OT Committee (Committee of Operative Thetans to the followers, allowing the formation of spontaneous demonstrations or the passage of information not detectable by the legal channels:

> If you are attacked, arrange it so that the attack is publicized. Give the impression to the public, to the government, that they have stumbled into a hail of bullets, an electronic bombardment, and that if they continue in this vein they will cause their own disintegration....Convince them that Scientology is the only game where everyone wins. There is no harm to putting things in good order.[10]

Psychiatrists, especially, are choice targets for Scientologists; they represent a constant threat to cults, for they recognize when a patient has been brainwashed and are able to oppose them through diagnosis and therapy. As this passage included in a number of Scientologist publications explains:

Some people are oppressors. Often they are able to rise to stations of responsibility, and then everything goes to pieces. They are primarily psychopaths. People such as Genghis Khan, Hitler, psychiatrists, and criminal psychopaths want only the power to destroy. They are there, as a monument to the cowards and reasonable people who did not stop them while they were still small and vulnerable.

Gradually, certain rituals are introduced, then little by little integrated into daily behavior. They acquire a different significance. That is how "hello" becomes "sieg heil."

The international meeting of the Acropolitans in Buenos Aires in 1975 made saluting a requirement, recommending holding the arm out at a 45 degree angle from the body.

The historical "explanation" for this was given:

Since the foundation of the movement, it has generally been practiced, and it is considered that the gesture had historical connections with the Roman empire. The word *ave* ("sacred" in Latin) which accompanies the physical salute strengthened the idea...

Matched with the new esoteric "explanation":

When you raise the right arm where you can't see it, with a sacred intention, a positive accumulation of energy occurs that enables you to give physical dignity to your body, while making it a receiver and transmitter of the life force fundamental for the birth of the new man: the Acropolitan.

However, the true explanation lies embedded in the intricacy of the text, although it may be difficult to prove "officially." However, the elitist and Aryanist doctrines of the cult leave little doubt about the claimed historical tradition.

Throughout history, societies have used a variety of physical gestures in salutation, and most are variations of the right arm held out. Its current antithesis is to greet with the left fist, in the manner of the Marxists who thus reflect the selfishness of the closed hand and the continual threat of their fists, a gesture that defies Heaven and denies God.

Any society that believes in God and in the ideals of a world where the spirit prevails is always more advanced than any that denies these principles. Believing in God and the soul is what separates Man from primates.

Emulation

The followers of a CC are in a permanent competition with the outside world. Racing towards the ultimate truth, they seek to progress without being outdistanced by their peers. This race's objective, however, has the hidden objective of circulating Scientology's philosophy through conversion of outsiders.

Monthly or quarterly CC recruitment statistics are given special attention, insofar as they reflect the internal dynamism of the community. The same applies to management reports, where the attribution of notes, points, ranks and titles is carefully noted.

Imitation

The guru, or the supreme initiate, or "the enlightened one," rules the group from the top of a pyramidal system. This system works on three principles:

- culpabilization of those who are at the bottom of the pyramid, far from the Master and the truth and therefore impure;
- the promise of obtaining powers or absolute knowledge by the observance of the rules;
- elitism and isolation from the external world: the truth belongs to the elite, and is reserved for beings able to devote themselves to the steeping themselves in the truth.

Many gurus assert themselves to be reincarnates of religious figures: Christ for George Roux and Galiano, the Virgin Mary for Yvonne Trubert and Maud Pison, the Son of God for Raël, Buddha for Bhagwan. By claiming to be reincarnated, a guru adopts certain traits for his or her followers, such as that of the prophet or an ancient sovereign. A rebellious subject will be described as bad reincarnation of an inquisitor or a criminal. There the doctrines of karma, former lives and channeling find acceptance that is limited only by the follower's level of credulity.

Identifying with the Master and Shared Essence

To identify with the Master is to progress toward the truth: at initiation, the disciple joins the Master and becomes in turn the supreme Truth, an expression of the primordial force. Before arriving at this stage, disciples are supposed to take part in the same parapsychological force, the same energy or the same supra-human essence. The doctrines create a "blood tie" between the followers, making them members of the same "energy family" after being given the title of "brothers in thought."

Analysis

Either passed along orally or written down in ritual or technical books, the CC conversion methods mix several classic techniques, minus their therapeutic function.

Analysis, first of all, it is a true distortion of a didactic and therapeutic technique. In the CC, the usual technique is summarized in an initiatory connotation: "You have to kill the old man, to find the new man." The exercise does not aim to identify the sources of conflict or deficiency to eliminate them, but to recover information by the means of confessions made to the guru in private or in public. The material collected makes it possible to better understand and control the subject, and also to effectively blackmail rebellious subjects.

Another function of the pseudo-analysis is to support the transfer of the follower's loyalties either to the guru, the cult, or the co-adepts. The transfer to the guru proceeds with the creation of a paternal substitute. The guru-father is invested with an omniscience, an omnipotence, even of an omnipresence which give him right of life and death over the follower. The cult represents a surrogate mother to the initiate: there are phenomena of regression and recomposition, starting from the new birth represented by entering the cult. Lastly, the positive transfer on the more advanced "followers" is accompanied by a negative transfer on the outside world.

As compared to the therapeutic analysis, which endeavors to control the transfer of affections to keep a relational balance between the psychoanalyst and his patient with a counter-transference, the cult heightens the perverse effects of the transfer and pushes the identifications into caricature, manipulating the subject's dependence and his fears of breaking away.

In the analyst-analyzed relationship, this transfer of affections as interpreted and diagnosed is viewed as reality in cults. The guru is not only a father substitute: he *becomes* the father, and all group dynamics support this development. The guru and the cult's speech make no effort to demystify this analysis by separating reality from the imaginary but, on the contrary, tries to integrate them into the cult illusion.

Hypnosis, Sophrology and Hypnopedia

These classic techniques are ordinarily used to make use of and to awaken the subject's reasoning powers. Hypnosis can be interpreted as another way to help a patient amend previous impressions of a situation. Hypnotized subjects do not perceive real information, but information transformed by the hypnotic process. On November, 1992, CNRS [the French National Center for Scientific Research] met at Salpêtrière Hospital in Paris to discuss the heart of the problem: the existence of a subject's "multiple personalities." Sometimes, one individual has several personalities encased within in each other, like nested dolls. To use Isabelle Stengers's expression, it is as if the hypnotist had the power to "zap" from one personality to another to reveal hidden or unknown elements of the subject. According to Martin Decorates, one of the fathers of experimental hypnosis, hypnosis does not only "zap" from one personality to another, it builds "a truth," the combined fruit of the desires of the therapist and his patient. You can see how dangerous this technique can be in the hands of the cult manipulators. The latter may suggest to a hypnotized subject a history based only slightly on truth, which will become essential to him at the expense of reality.

Hypnosis is allowed today, after much dispute due to the mysterious aura surrounding it and which gave it popular success (with Mesmer's theories of animal magnetism, from which it was derived). In spite of the new favor it enjoys, no real study has made it possible to specify the fields appropriate to its implementations. Studies carried out in Europe as well as the United States came to only one conclusion: some people can be hypnotized while others cannot. In addition, it is known today that being hypnotizable has nothing to do with pathology nor mental balance: hypnosis only reveals more or less hidden characteristics of a subject that have nothing "magical" or supernatural about them, and which correspond to the conscious or unconscious desires of the hypnotized person. These revelations can be just as easily acquired in a traditional study of the personality.

The recent techniques of cerebral investigation, which call upon quantified electro-encephalography, using positron or photon tomography (SPECT), as well as measuring the blood flow in the brain, seem to highlight a change in cerebral activity during the process of hypnotic induction and during the hypnotic state. They suggest hyperactivity of the left hemisphere during hypnotic induction. This hyperactivity leaves the left hemisphere and moves to the right during the actual state of hypnosis.[11] For Brenman and Gill, hypnosis can be compared to a regressive process started by a reduction of ideational and sensory-motor activity or by the creation of a relationship (of dependence) with the hypnotist.[12] Freud believed that hypnotic sleep was equivalent to a numbing of the consciousness, a paralysis of the will.

Hypnosis used for other than therapeutic reasons is a major interest to "magicians," inside or outside of cults. It is likely to start by accessing buried subjects surprisingly recoverable by the hypnotist.[13] It causes in particular catalepsy (if you change the body position of the hypnotized subject, he preserves the new position in this state); age regression (used by cults in their "esoteric" processing); an impression of time distortion (one minute seems to last several hours or several months, creating the illusion of astral projection); the "reflex" of automatic writing, i.e. carried out without the subject being aware of what he writes; sensory distortion (sensations of cold or heat, finding pleasure in eating soap); positive and negative hallucinations depending on the suggestibility of the patient; changes to memory; and finally, post-hypnotic behaviors, which are not excluded from the realm of hypnotic power.

Thus the world of cults discovered an ideal instrument in hypnosis. Used by the esoteric-mystic, this method becomes extremely useful in breaking down the mental conditioners that might keep a subject from being successfully converted.

Sophrology is a specific form of hypnosis created in 1961 by Doctor Caycedo, who connects it, by the etymology of the word, to a state of consciousness described by Plato. Caycedo claims to have borrowed from Buddhism, yoga and phenomenology to create certain techniques of sophrology. Leon Chertok sees it as nothing but a version of hypnosis with no specific characteristic but its name.[14]

Hypnocatharsis is a method that encourages reviving suppressed conflicts and age regression. Its effectiveness depends on a mixture of a cognitive process (awakening of the conflicts or aggressive situations) and an emotional process. This approach to traumatic experiences under hypnosis was used by Breuer in the 19th century, and was strongly criticized by Freud because it sometimes causes long-lasting regression in the patient. Mostly abandoned by therapists, this practice has been revived by numerous cults. These sessions often create or increase feelings of guilt in the subject and greatly dramatize earlier traumas, and to reinterpret them to the benefit of the cult and to the detriment of previous emotional ties that could have helped the initiate resist indoctrination.

Every hypnotic technique results in the same thing, depending on the receptivity of the subject. Davis and Husband[15] analyzed this relationship in precise detail, by comparing the degrees reached in hypnotic trance and the following clinical signs:

RECEPTIVITY	DEGREE	SIGNS AND SYMPTOMS
Refractory	0	
Hypnoid	1	
	2	Relaxation
	3	Blinking eyelids
	4	Closing eyes
	5	Complete physical Relaxation
Light trance	6	Ocular catalepsy
	7	Catalepsy of the limbs
	10	Rigid catalepsy
	11	Anesthesia
Medium trance	13	Partial amnesia
	15	Post-hypnotic anesthesia
	17	Personality Changes
	18	Simple post-hypnotic suggestions
	20	Coenesthetic illusions, amnesia
	21	Possibility of eyes opening due to fright
	23	Complex post-hypnotic suggestions
	25	Complete somnambulism
	26	Post-hypnotic visual hallucinations
	27	Post-hypnotic auditory hallucinations
	28	Systematized post-hypnotic amnesia
	29	Negative auditory hallucinations
	30	Negative visual hallucinations

According to Vogt, approximately 3% to 15% of the population can reach the level of deep trance.

According to the testimony of former members, Scientology asserts its power on approximately 3% to 5% of subjects that agree to participate in "auditings."

The correlation of the two sets of percentages above shows that the cult members who persevere are subjects accessible to hypnosis, without necessarily having former psychic disorders. Nevertheless, being predisposed to certain disorders, such as hysteria or psychotic hallucinations, may make one more susceptible to a hypnotist. Approval by the hypnotist and the realization of these pre-existing disorders allows for a state of pseudo-comprehension and complicity between hypnotist and hypnotized, which facilitates dependence.

By studying the development of followers of cults that use hypnosis, we noticed that the subjects of group 0 broke off after two or three sessions, that groups 1 to 11 persisted in their attempts but that, experiencing doubt, criticized the cult only to receive the full battery of cult practices of conversion. The subjects reaching degree 13 to 27 represent the average of those members who stayed with the cult, with the degree of responsibility and the ranks obtained belonging to degrees 13 to 20 approximately. The more malleable subjects are the exploited individuals or the noncritical mental patients (degrees 26 to 30). These results show that hypnosis is an element determining the process of indoctrination in cults, and that the less-hypnotizable subjects seem more resistant to conversion.

The autogenic "training" of Schultz differs little from the preceding hypnotic techniques. Like those, it supports the introduction of a "magical" climate between the patient and the expert. Based on Vogt's works on self-hypnosis, it somatogenically induces the disconnect that characterizes hypnotic states. It is based on a technique that makes patients feel heaviness and warmth in the extremities and finally throughout the whole body. Magnified, these feelings will be described as supernormal and will be used as ideological vectors.

A specific ambiance is created between the relaxer and the patient. Great importance is placed on eye contact, incantations and the rituality of the sessions.

> The type of language used between the patient and his therapist approaches incantations. This process of "magic" communication can be comparable to shamanistic processes described by Lévi-Strauss.[16]

The language of the autogenic training would allow an integration of personal myth with the collective myth, symbolized by the word of the doctor inside an imaginary relationship. Self-hypnosis is considered a separate technique unto itself, in particular by Bhagwan and the New Acropolis.

> Position: Seated on a chair, the back and the head straight but without tension. The forearms and hands on the thighs, fingers spread so they don't touch each other. Or, on the ground, in the "Padmasana" or Lotus position, sitting comfortably with the wrists resting on the knees; let yourself go and feel that the ground attracts the physical body but not us, forgetting for a moment your physical body; allow yourself to be filled with peace and affected by nothing; concentrate on your perception of yourself.

1. *Concentration on a point of light*
The eyes concentrate on a point of light or an incense rod. The light point must be a little below the horizon of the eyes.

2. *Concentration on a point or a circle*
Draw a circle with a mid-point, marked clearly. Sit back from the point at a distance of about 10 times the radius of the circle. Here the example given is a circle a half-inch in diameter, so the distance from the point of concentration is 5 inches, which obliges the practitioner to squint for a prolonged period and can become a source of eye trouble and give a sense of dizziness

3. *Concentration on simple objects*
Sitting in a circle, the disciples must concentrate on simple objects placed in the center of the circle (a pencil, figurine, etc.). They must lower their heads when they lose concentration.

4. *Imagination*
Imagine forms and colors. When the instructor pronounces the name of an object, the disciple must form a clear and fixed image in his mind, followed by the sounds, taste, smell, and feel of the object. At this stage, the disciple must measure the imaginary object completely

as though it were real, using all five senses. This way, he quickly reaches a stage of suggestibility compatible with hypnosis.[17]

Effects of Hypnosis

In neurophysiology, it is generally known that the conscience covers three principal states: waking, sleep, and an intermediate phase known as hypnagogic.

It is this intermediate phase that represents the passage from the waking state to the sleep state and vice versa. It is characterized by "a state of dissociation"of the conscience and a progressive disappearance of caution. It is accompanied by a "depotentialization," a dissolution of the critical conscience that is necessary for one to be in control of one's environment.[18]

The subject notes the disruption of reality by images that are difficult to control, accompanied by feelings of moderate unreality and impressions of floating in a half-sleep. It is this state of consciousness that makes hypnosis possible. The Anglo-Saxons consider the hypnagogic phase the door to the conscience (*altered states of consciousness,* or ASCs), with changes to the cognitive states of hypnotized and the appearance of dreams.

A change of visual perceptions goes hand in hand with an alteration of time sense, changes in emotional expression and attention, a selective vigilance, an alteration of the sense of the body and finally an increase in suggestibility. These ASCs can be induced by hypnosis but also by procedures as varied as meditation, introspection, autohypnosis, *lying* (see p. 199), sensory deprivation, drugs, or collective phenomena-in short, by all the panoply of the CC. These states can be followed either by a return to normality, or by the appearance of a pathology. Studies undertaken at the University of Upsala by Barmark and Gautnitz show the similarities between the states obtained by transcendental meditation and ASCs.[19]

The stronger the hypnotic or comparable suggestion, the more the distance between ASCs and reality increases, as well as the possible emergence of hallucinations; and the dependence of the subject on the hypnotist increases. The hypnotist entering the field of ASCs is given additional power by his or her access to the subconscious.

Communication between the subject and the outside world changes progressively from of a mode of communication structured in reality to a mode of communication using elements borrowed from the subject's imaginary world. Karl Abraham[20] stressed that the power of suggestion allows for a weakening of criticism and an increase in faith; the majority of cults use meditation to reinforce obedience and support within the group. Under the pretense of helping a subject deal with pain, they develop techniques of conditioning in which every banal element impacts another. An example of this are the councils lavished by Sri Chimnoy on his disciples, while drawing from his own sacred hagiography:[21]

> Sri Chimnoy, after many mystical experiences, and having reached an exceptional state of enlightenment [reaffirmation of the super-human state of the guru], he directed twice-weekly sessions of meditation at the United Nations New York for diplomats and civil servants at the UN. He wrote a great quantity of books on meditation and spirituality and gave conferences in the largest universities of the world and to all the gurus and cults. We owe to him hundreds of spiritual songs and nearly 30,000 works of art-approximately 10 per day for an individual fifty years old in 1981 that had been drawing since the age of 10.... When you contemplate a photograph of the spiritual Master to reaffirm the higher character of the guru, try to identify yourself with the consciousness of this Master. If you want to be identified with his consciousness, first start to concentrate on the photograph as a whole, then bring your attention to focus on a point, slightly above the eyebrows. It is there that resides the true spiritual wealth of the Master [identification and reaffirmation of the Master's status]. It is there that the third eye, the eye of the supernatural Vision, resides. You will obtain the best results as soon as you are able to identify your own interior reality with the Master's. In addition, if it is purity you wish to obtain, imagine that you are breathing simultaneously with the Master for some five minutes before beginning your meditation [in order to participate in the same essence as the Master, which reaffirms one's higher nature and purity]. Feel that the photograph is ready to offer to you everything that you seek [adoration of transitional objects]. If seek peace, try to look at it with the feeling that it contains infinite

Peace. If you seek Light, Bliss or any other divine quality, feel that the photograph contains it, which absolutely does. It is the incarnation of the fundamental virtues but especially, like God, it is able to present its gifts through prayer and the images pictured....When you meditate on my photograph, do not think about anything. Just try to match your body and your thoughts with mine. If a thought occurs, whether it is good or bad, simply throw it at my photograph, and each time that a thought occurs, consider it as an attack and let me receive it in your place [reaffirmation of the omniscient and omnipotent character of the guru].

Most cult texts use this method of attributing divine "powers" (purity, wisdom) to the guru. The technique of meditating on the Master, his image or his thought aims to strengthen the desire for identification, meanwhile overlooking the fact that this identification is impossible, for it would mean admitting the divine nature of the disciples and consequently affirming their autonomy.

Directed Daydreams and Mental Imagery

Very similar to one another and often accompanied by conditions close to sensory isolation, these techniques are used to recreate in the subject a set of fantasies, a sub-delusional or delusional rebuilding of the subject that is under the control of the cult. Accent is placed on past lives, the fetal existence, reincarnation or "animal reincorporation."

Directed daydreams consist of using topics suggested or induced during an oneiric experience [editor's note: a session of dream interpretation]. This technique is normally supplemented by an interpretation of data collected by the therapist. In the CC, the imaginary baggage that surfaces during dreams is not interpreted symbolically but, on the contrary, is presented as reality from a subject's present, past, or future. These dreams become a manifestation from the beyond, the supernatural world or the divine world. However, the typical nature of these dreams authorizes the cult to propose the most absurd interpretations by covering them with the seal of mysticism. Thus, it was suggested to one follower that his feeling of being burnt, after receiving a sunburn after of a pseudo-medical cure from the cult, was a sign that he was the reincarnation of Joan of Arc!

These experiences, often distressing for the subject, must immediately be controlled and de-dramatized by the therapist. The CC, conversely, allow the subject's anguish develop for their own manipulative purposes. In Scientology, the listener should never intervene, while the most psychologically dangerous situations must be left intact for the follower to suffer through, according to Ron Hubbard.

The technique of using mental imagery techniques to unearth and manipulate past distress in subjects by cults has gone by a variety of names. It was known as the:
- process of image substitution by Janet;
- fantastical method by Pierce Clark;
- higher cycle of autogenic training by Schultz;
- imagination activities by Jung;
- oneirotherapy of integration by Virel.

All use conditioning techniques close to sensory deprivation, favorable to the spontaneous appearance of mental images with an experience of off-centering, which we will discuss further.

Transactional Analysis

This practice is based on the theories of Bern and is used extensively by cults. But it is especially important in its aspect of behavior reconditioning and rehabilitation. The technique is based on the theory that the personality consists of "distinct states of ego" able to co-exist simultaneously in the conscience. These various states of ego correspond to experiences, which can be attached to a parent-ego, a child-ego or to an adult-ego. These three states borrow from three different sources of necessary information in their development. The child-ego is created in the archeo-psyche, which expresses all the affection of an individual since his or her childhood; the parent-ego borrows from the extra-psyche the information that comes from external factors and mainly from the family unit; finally, the adult-ego is the integrator of the data, it is also the "director-producer," for only it is confronted with the actual environment. The emergence of any of these characteristics can be manipulated and distorted by cults.

Therapeutic transactional analysis studies the relations between the various states of ego and verifies their coherence. However, the cult does not take account of these balances and allows the rupture between the egos to develop by getting information that comes from the archeo-psyche or the extra-psyche, and negating them or affirming them according to their interest. Delusions are reinforced and developed while, at the same time, the adult-ego of the follower is dissuaded from processing the new information. Certain cult groups know to use these dynamic processes of analysis empirically, such as Otto Mühl's group AAO, and Scientology.

The Primal Scream

Primal therapy, which was invented by Arthur Janov,[22] has been all but abandoned, especially due to lack of evidence that it actually works, and also due to the disappearance of its creator.

According to Janov, we all carry from birth certain elementary needs: to be kept warm, to be nourished, to be cherished. The way we structure our personality stems from these needs. Either these needs are met and the personality blossoms, or they are opposed and the personality closes down out of frustration. The continuation of these needs contributes to the creation of neuroses. The distance between the real needs of the child and his environment decides the "principal primal scene." This primal scene represents the disparity between the reality the subject wishes to have and the unreality to which he or she is subjected; this creates the neurosis. Primal therapy attempts to revive one of the traumatic scenes that made the subject give up reality and created the neurosis. Janov called this technique "doing a primal." Reliving the experiences is accompanied by a massive emotional discharge that usually results in outcries or sounds evocative of the situation. These sounds, which can range from simple whimpers and tears to outright howling, gave their to name this therapy.

In a remarkable article published in *Science and Life*,[23] Michel Rouzé underscored the astonishing similarities between the techniques used by Scientology and primal scream therapy.

Techniques from Reverse Psychiatry

Techniques based on the theories of those who are against psychiatrists (Laing, Cooper and Rosen), or those resulting from Moreno's psychodrama, result in meetings of group catharsis (in the Aristotelian sense) colored by directed interpretations. The goal of such groups is creating "communities" of people with similar problems, set up and run like a cult. These techniques are particularly effective because the only way the "community" can fail is if a participant behaves particularly immaturely or rebels unacceptably around the other members of the group.

Techniques Derived from Behaviorism

Flooding and *rebirthing* are especially used by cults to reinforce the cult's rule and to underscore conflicts with the external world. Inhibition is always reinterpreted in a way that reinforces the break with reality.

Flooding (immersion) means "to immerse" the subject in an environment saturated with meaning. Therapeutically, it aims to cause a stress reaction that must be controlled by the subject in order to control his or her phobias or anguishes. For example, one will lock up a subject with a phobia of the color yellow in a room painted yellow and furnished in yellow, make him eat lemons, and have him or her dress in yellow. The aggressive aspect of the immersion is moderated by the therapist's presence and assessment of when to stop the experiment. The CC will not take these precautions. They will push the test to its conclusion, i.e. to the emotional breakdown of the subject. The tests will be selected according to their symbolic value and with the goal of perverting perception.

Rebirthing attempts to reinvent a subject. It is not actually a specific technique, but a variety of different techniques combined to reach a similar goal. The phenomenon of regression can be initiated by any of these techniques: hypnosis, sophrology, directed daydreams, etc. The danger of regression therapy, if unchecked, is that it may create psychosis in the subject. However, it is very often this type of psychosis that is sought by the cult, which it presents as the expression of a fetal or womb memory.

The Electrometer

This technique is not widespread and, to our knowledge, Scientology is the only one among the CC known to use it (in the form of the "E-meter"). Other cults derived from Scientology call it the "electro-psychometer."

The electrometer was introduced into Dianetics in 1951 by Volney G. Matthison, shortly before Ron Hubbard created his own movement: "Concept Therapy." The E-meter is composed of a single dial with switches, liquid crystals and potentiometers, all connected by two wires, themselves connected by alligator clips to a set of cylindrical electrodes that look like vegetable cans. Inside is a standard Wheatstone bridge electronic circuit. The whole thing looks like a molded plastic apparatus from the 1950's. The operation of the apparatus can be summarized as follows: a micro-current (milliampere, microvolt) circulates between the two electrodes. The current reading is displayed on the dials. The subject holds an electrode in each hand. The degree of his or her resistance, which is displayed on the dial, is related to several physiological or physical parameters: the body surface in contact with the electrodes, how moist the hands are, body weight, hand pressure on the electrodes. Resistance varies with these parameters, changing the displayed values, oscillating around an average value that corresponds with the starting calibration.

Since the discovery of electrophysiological signals, much thought has been given to the uses that police and other information services could gain from it. The signals have been used as a reflection of the relative equilibrium of a person, as the equilibrium has been shown to be upset when the subject feels threatened. On the basis of this principle, research has been carried out to highlight the relationship between electro-encephalographic readings of a person telling the truth and those of a person telling a lie. However, since installing electrodes along a person's scalp is a complicated process, the electroencephalographic signal was, little by little, abandoned in favor of the psychogalvanic signal.

The Galvanic Skin Response

We know that aggression and stress modify human physiology. Under aggression, the heart accelerates, the breathing rate increases, and there is a rise of cortisol, adrenalin and noradrenalin in the bloodstream.

If the resistance between two points of the human body is recorded, this resistance falls during a time of stress. Due to hormonal secretions related to aggression, discharges of cortisol and adrenalin cause the subject to sweat. Moreover, dilation of the blood vessels and the acceleration of the heartbeat decreases the body's overall resistance. These variations in electrical resistance increase the intensity of the current measured between the points in the body. If two electrodes are attached to the subject's skin (generally, to each wrist), stress results in an electric discharge, thus giving rise to the name 'galvanic reflex.'

Interest in galvanic skin response and its police applications fell out of favor because of an obvious lack of reliability (external factors, subject conditioning, variability of responses). Now it is only recalled in anecdotes. This is why, based on the more or less reliable apparatuses used to record PSR, Ron Hubbard created the electrometer, an instrument giving about the same results as the more sophisticated apparatuses that were used by the American police force from 1950 to 1970.

Biofeedback

Biofeedback, or biological feedback, makes it possible to record a physiological phenomenon, to amplify it and to transform it into a visual or sound signal perceptible by the subject. The subject then becomes conscious of the changes in his or her involuntary physiological operation and gradually learns how to control it.

Initially, one is taught to control the physiological phenomena that become apparent through amplification; later, the equipment takes the place of voluntary control and the mere appearance of an "abnormal" signal is enough to cause, via biofeedback, a regulation of the physiological phenomenon that caused it.

This technique takes account of all physiological functions: dilation of the blood vessels, skin temperature, heartbeat, renal function, brain waves, blood pressure, muscle tone, gastric and sphincter spasms. Used in psychotherapy for a number of psychosomatic symptoms, biofeedback facilitates relaxation and the appearance of alpha brain waves, classic evidence of advanced believed states of well-being. However, this technique, with which we personally worked for several years, has very limited applications. Currently, it is mostly used in sphincter rehabilitation.

An examination of the electrometer reveals a striking similarity to apparatuses used to measure PSRs (psychogalvanic skin response). The equipment used in PSR is almost identical to that used by the Scientologists, equipment declared obsolete by the scientific community due to its unreliability. The equipment used in biofeedback is more sophisticated and records body functions with much higher precision. Moreover, having the machine run by an "auditer" removes the reflex character of the biofeedback, thus relieving it of any possible interest.

E-meters are identical to lie detectors, and both are founded on the principle of PSRs. Scientology denies this and accuses psychiatrists of collaborating with the police force and the secret service in order to torture individuals psychologically. However, Ron Hubbard himself affirms:

> Although this text principally deals with the use of the electrometer — an instrument especially designed for use in Dianetics — the data it contains are also applicable to any lie detector, such as those used by the police force and psychiatrists. Using instruments to measure thoughts is not new [sic]. It is the comprehension and the manner of measuring which are new.

This apparatus, which could be used as a teaching aide to assist in relaxation, is totally useless for the purpose proposed by Hubbard. Furthermore, using it under the guidance of a Scientologist reinforces the constraining nature of the technique of auditing.

The Experimental Basis of these Techniques: Behaviorism

Since Skinner, experiments have shown that animal and human behavior is governed by contingencies known as "reinforcements." Placed in a given environment, a subject will emit information which acts on the environment and which elicits a response from the environment. If the information conforms with the environment, it will give responses that reinforce the initial behavior (positive reinforcement). If they are in opposition to the environment, the responses will tend to reduce them (aversion) and to remove them (extinction). From then on, the subject will tend to avoid those responses from the environment (negative reinforcement). If behaviorism explains human behavior in relation to information that comes from the environment, then it is possible to put it to use for psychotherapeutical practices of behavioral conditioning or therapy (for example, to treat alcoholism). But it also allows for the possibility of using it for conditioning or deconditioning for military purposes (special forces, marine commandos, etc.).

One can only imagine what a cult could do with such information, even if it is acknowledged that "bad" behaviors are never corrected by electroshock therapy, no matter what may be claimed in fiction works inspired by "re-education camps" or in films like *Clockwork Orange*.

In Scientology, the question posed by the auditer contains a potentially repressive message. The "pre-clear" must progress on "the bridge,"[24] and his or her answers must conform to those required by Scientology and its worldwide plan. Any answer that results in a fall of "tone-arm"[25] is considered by the system to be bad. The follower must give the answers the cult wants to hear; he thus adopts very constraining avoidance behaviors. Liberty and personal judgment are relegated to second place.

The electrometer thus acts as a repressive therapy of conditioning, far from the alleged search for freedom that was used to lure in the subject. When questioned about the technical value of the electrometer, Scientology ended up with a retraction:

> The Hubbard electrometer, intended for pastoral advice, is an instrument that is sometimes used in Dianetic spiritual healing and in the religious philosophy applied in Scientology. By itself, the electrometer does not achieve anything. It has neither the intention nor the effect of diagnosing, treating nor preventing any disease, nor to improve health or any bodily function.[26]

The Court of Appeals in Paris, in its judgment of February 29, 1980, said that Scientology "employs under conditions that do not conform to science the apparatus called an electrometer, using the phenomenon long known in psychophysiology under the name of electro-dermal reaction, or galvanic skin response.... This apparatus confers a scientific prestige likely to impress the new members, whereas its employment from the psychotherapy point of view is not accompanied by controls essential for recording and interpreting these extremely delicate phenomena."

The preceding lines were written in 1980. At that time, however recent, galvanic skin response still held some credit with physiologists; today, it seems to be defended only in extremely credulous or ill-informed circles.

Mantras and Chants

The use of mantras is one of the most widespread techniques in cults. While it lends itself to caricature, its widespread popularity very often masks real dangers.

The word "mantra" comes from the Sanskrit for "sacred formula." In cults, it is used as "an instrument of thought." In the Vedic tradition, the mantra is raised to a divine dimension: it is the word of God, but it also God revealed and God's capacity to create. The principle is simple: the repetition of a sound, a syllable or a sentence at a variable rhythm. This repetition makes it possible to reach a dreamlike state that can lead to hypnotic sleep.

The most well-known mantra is the famous *om,* whose origins reach back as far as the third millennium BC. It is used today by all those who are of Buddhist or Hinduist tradition. This sound can be used alone, or accompanied by another complex formulation, invocation or prayer, such as *"Om hum vajrange mama raksa phat svaha,"* which means: *"Vharanja,* protect me."

The sound *om* or *oum* is also found in Christian liturgies celebrated in Latin, such as *"Pater Noster, sanctificetur nomen tuum, adveniat regnum tuum..."* The important thing is not the significance of the pronounced sentence, but the ritual pronunciation of mantra, whose effectiveness results from the rhythmic repetition of the sound either loudly, sotto voce or even mentally, as is acknowledged by Transcendental Meditation. A similar effect is obtained by the recitation of repeated prayers, rosaries or various litanies, as long as it is done automatically and for a long period of time.

Glossolalia [*speaking in tongues*] play an identical role but, moreover, they aim to create the impression that the guru holds a supernatural gift of languages. In the Bible, the Acts of the Apostles report that on the day of the Pentecost Saint Peter, who spoke Aramaic, was understood not only by his compatriots, but by all the foreigners who attended his sermon. Glossolalia are seen as being the expressed sign of a conversion taking place, or of divinity. (Acts, 2, 4: "They were filled by the Holy Spirit, and began to speak in other tongues, according to the directives of the Spirit.")

In cults, glossolalia are considered to be a language of the beyond, of cosmic or extraterrestrial beings; the guru and his officiants are the messengers. Group hypnosis is often involved in the obligatory chanting which is widespread in the pentecostalist Churches and several Christian groups that are part of the charismatic revival within the Roman Catholic, Anglican and Lutheran churches.

Less direct, but still potent in symbolism and meaning, chants, too, encourage the feeling of group bonding, and their repetition represents the reaffirmation of commitments of those within the group.

Friend, the time is coming for different songs.
You must leave, leave your house,
and give up everything for one name alone:
Acropolis, Acropolis!
Take the path that we have taken,
Soldier of the shadows, child of the night,
All your friends will know this name:
Acropolis, Acropolis!
On the path to truth,
You will discover eternity,
And you will understand why is
The Acropolis, the Acropolis.

Sometimes, the messages take a more pragmatic tone, with hints of a Nuremberg gathering:

The street belongs to the ones who walk it,
The street belongs to our commandos' flags,
We are surrounded by hatred.
We are surrounded by a hail of dogmas,
Trampling the dark mud;
The banners wave.
How many are struck down on a bright fair morning —
Our proud friends who smiled at fate!
We will fall on the way,
We will fall in combat, we will fall,
Trampling the dark mud.
The banners wave,
Since we must live and fight in suffering.
The day will come when we will impose in France
The force of our weapons,
The force of our arms and our hearts,
Trampling the dark mud.
The banners wave,

And the day will come when we hold up our torch.
All the youth of France will unite around our flags.
We will remake France,
We will build the kingdom of tomorrow,
Trampling the dark mud.
Our banners wave.[27]

Prayer, too, has a not inconsiderable hypnotic effect, well-known among cults who promote it not as a dialectic means of supporting moral development but as a practice of rhythmic repetition:

> Listening attentively to what we say helps maintain the mental focus necessary to isolate us from external distractions. The whole body, helped by certain positions of prayer, is predisposed to be used as a flexible instrument, while the lips modulate the words in such a way, by accentuating and lengthening, for example, certain vowels, which are the occult engines that project the prayer in subtle directions.[28]

Techniques for Group Conditioning

Group conditioning is based on the principles of group dynamics. The CC use a combination of techniques. Thus, collective trance is obtained by manipulating sensory stimulation and group dynamics. Every technique of individual conditioning can be used to condition a whole group and, at the same time, intensifies its effects due to the reaction of a number of participants and the charisma of the father-guru.

The techniques of group conditioning are not easily applicable just as they are: the rules that define these therapies are not particularly compatible with cults. Only the practices of T-groups are easily applicable; they were used largely by AAO, under the leadership of Otto Mühl. They allow the individuals who take part in it to freely express themselves. It's difficult for the cults that use this technique to create hierarchies within the group, since that is a far cry from the goal of group therapy. Cults use them to encourage emulation, which is far from the goal usually pursued in therapy and education groups. Rituals, with their aspect of incarnating certain figures, partly play the role of psychodramas controlled by the cult. The goal is to awaken the primitive impulses of the individuals and use them to cement the members of the group together by manipulating their empathy.

Rituals

By giving each individual a precise role in the group, rituals reinforces the feeling of membership and the process of identification. Achieving a new status or symbolic role publicly proclaims the change in the subject's state. Grades conferred are compensation that create a spirit of competition within the group and increase the "productivity" of the symbolic structure.

The goal of ritual ceremonies is to bind the group together. They exploit both the emotions and symbolism. They are permanent psychodramas where each participant is "recreated" within the group structure, and his prestige is enhanced both in his own eyes and in the eyes of the other members of the group. As in all the psychodramas, they take advantage of the baser emotions, and place the subject in a state of dependence on the group and the guru, and especially on the myths that animate the cult. Participating in rituals gives each participant the feeling of belonging to something supra-human, divine and cosmic. Baptism, professions of faith, public confessions and marriages have no other goal but the re-affirmation of submission, while reinforcing certain behavior patterns in followers. Baptism is a tacit expression of the interdiction of betrayal and escape. Public confessions (Friends of Man, groups stemming from the evangelical church) focus on guilt and place members in a position of waiting for forgiveness and desiring redemption. Intra-cult marriages (Moon) underscore the couple's subservience to the cult and allow the cult to intrude into marital life. The psychology of these groups is underlain by a collective pathology that is used as a tool for conditioning (which we shall study further).

Very often, rituals begin with a series of calls and responses, whose hypnotic function is obvious. Here is an example:

The assistant invites all the people present to stand, then claps his hands and says, allegorically:

> Assistant: The door is closed [gestures for the people present to sit back down].
> Officiant: My mind is anxious.
> Together: My mind is anxious.
> O: My heart is agitated.
> E: My heart is agitated.
> O: My body is tense.
> E: My body is tense.
> O: I relax my body, my heart and my mind.
> E: I relax my body, my heart and my mind.
> O: Relax your body and calm your mind.
> Now imagine a transparent and luminous sphere, descending towards you and landing in your heart. You feel the sphere transform into an expansive feeling inside your chest.
> Assistant: With this force that we have received, let us concentrate our minds on what we need to achieve.
> O: Peace, Love and Joy.
> E: Peace, Love and Joy for you, as well.

One can see that most rituals are inspired by each other and that the most recent gibberish copies the rituals of ancient initiatory societies. That certainly is the case in the preceding example from The Movement, which is largely inspired by Masonic traditions in their repetitive nature while extending their general symbolism:

> Officiant: Where do you come from?
> Participant: From the great mountains of the Orient.
> O: What did you seek there?
> P: I sought the greatest of the poets, but I was informed that he had died and his corpse was dismembered.
> O: And tell me, bright one, who carried out such a misdeed?
> P: A black bull, some drunk women, a brother or a traitor.
> O: What do you want now?
> P: I seek the greatest of the poets.
> O: Who told you that he was here?
> P: The guard of the great mountains of the Orient said: "The Master is to be found in the great mountains of the Orient."

O: Whoever dies before dying will never die. Now that you have died and have descended to the threshold of the shadows, at the sound of the scales you will tell yourself: "My internal organs are being weighed," and it is certain, for to weigh your internal organs is to weigh your actions."[29]

The ritual cements the group and creates a hierarchy in the relationships, by implanting a new way of thinking that will persist long after the ceremony is over.   Disturbed by the statement of an unconventional "truth," the cult member tries to decipher the sermons, which is an indispensable factor leading to his conditioning.

Subliminal perception

Subliminal perception is frequently mentioned in the study of supposed methods of conditioning. This technique caused a huge uproar and claims of "mental rape" around the time of the 1988 presidential elections when French television channel A2 was accused of having used it while displaying the credits for a newscast. Further study showed that, indeed, a portrait of François Mitterrand had appeared inside the station logo for a microsecond.

For neurophysiologists (and the publicity agents, interested chiefly in the marketing potential of this supposed technique), there are three levels of stimulation that modify an individual's reactions towards a stimulus:

- the physiological threshold of feeling;
- the conscious threshold of feeling;
- the absolute threshold of conscious perception.

The physiological threshold of feeling is where the stimulus is too weak to involve a sensory response.

The conscious threshold of feeling corresponds to a stimulus sufficient to involve a sensory response and allow conscious analysis of this response by the subject.

The absolute threshold of conscious perception corresponds to the lowest level of perception; stimulation starts a sensory response but requires the subject's sustained attention to perceive the stimulus and its significance. One example is that of the bird song masked by the noise of the city, but perceptible if one concentrates and listens.

Subliminal perception is the perception of a stimulus at a level between the physiological threshold and the absolute threshold of conscious perception. In this zone, the subject is not conscious of the stimulus, but is supposed to react in its presence.

A number of laboratory studies have been conducted that validate this phenomenon. Successful application of these findings to the field of mental conditioning remains, however, a matter of speculation. Certain studies seem to show that subliminal visual or aural conditioning in movie theaters can increase sales of refreshments. However, the results are not significant enough to be regarded as evidence of a real effect.

Additionally, experiments have shown that any changes in behavior occur only immediately after the subliminal message is given and they disappear just as quickly. It is only a temporary modification of the subject's reactions, and not durable conditioning.

The thresholds of physiological and absolute conscious perception vary from one individual to another; the technique entails insurmountable technical risks. Much simpler and more effective is the use of supraliminal messages, or conscious messages, where the symbolic contents gradually distance the subject from his habits and encourage him to break his taboos.

For the CC, the cathartic techniques are noticeably more effective. But establishing them requires conditions that are physically and psychologically difficult to create.

9.

PHYSICAL CONDITIONING

In order to control people, the CC often resort to methods of physical coercion usually reserved for other ends.

Isolation

Indoctrination works best when the cult member has minimal or no contact with the outside world. The cult member receives only a summary of carefully-sorted information about the goings-on of the outside world. In addition, saturated with activities, deprived of leisure, he is not in control of his time.

Financial restrictions are also placed on the cult member in conjunction with this. The obligation to consume certain products, to read certain works, and to venerate certain objects, leads the individual to place the cult's considerations before his own needs. This financial dependence is a prelude to a change in the cult member's social interactions, which are soon reduced (or eliminated). The cult member becomes aware of the irreversible character of the situation only when the rupture from society is complete.

The cult begins this process by cutting the parental bonds, which are dangerous for two reasons. On the one hand, only the parents are generally aware of the personality change in their child; secondly, interference from family could block the process of assimilation. This dynamics of rejection seldom results in explicit orders: rather, the cult uses dialectical or ideological masks that aim to portray the family as a potential danger. Here is how the Scientology considers the question:

> Life in the womb seems far from ideal, and is often painted more poetically than scientifically. Reality shows that three men and a horse in a phone booth would be hardly less comfortable than an unborn child. The uterus is wet, uncomfortable and vulnerable. Mom sneezes and baby is knocked out. Mom bangs into a table and baby has a damaged head. Mom is constipated and baby is crushed. Dad gets excited and baby feels like he is in a washing machine. Mom has a hysterical crisis, baby catches an engram. Dad hits Mom, baby carries the bad memory. . . . Abortion attempts are very frequent. . . . Morning sickness is completely psychosomatic. The mother is often sick only because she tried to get rid of the child, by injections or by means of knitting needles or something similar. Morning sickness was introduced to society only because of these attempted abortions.[1]

In "closed" cults, the second stage of isolation consists of stopping contact between the cult member and his friends and close relations. Finally, the last stage: removing the subject from his place of employment, unless the job is somehow financially beneficial to the cult or it presents no obstacle to total assimilation.

Food Deprivation

Under the traditional alibi of "purification," "elimination of toxins" or respect for animals, most cults preach low-calorie diets, and even malnutrition.

This strategy is seldom sufficient to make an individual malleable to the sects' wishes, but is rather one of the foundation stones that leads to assimilation. Adopting abnormal dietetic practices accentuates the break with the outside world. While stopping short of true marginalization, food choices alone can lead to the formation of micro-movements equipped with rites and doctrines, as in the case of monovegetarianism and macrobiotics.

Moreover, certain food regimens can be used to weaken resistance because of vitamin or protein deficiency. A glucose deficiency can cause headaches and a loss of energy. A deficiency of lipids or protein, or a prolonged hypocaloric diet, by decreasing the physical threshold of resistance, make it easier for the cult to apply indoctrination protocols. A hypocalcemic diet, combined with hyperventilation through voluntary hyperpnea (during ritual breathing), cause a tingling feeling on the lips and hands. The onset of these feelings, close to the symptoms of spasmophilia, may be interpreted by the cult as a demonstration of shared energy waves or the presence of a spirit.

Systems of food deprivation, such as macrobiotics, instinctivotherapy or vegetarianism, are likely to be used as technical conditioning by the sect. We will see further how other cults use such systems to cultivate initiates.

Sleep Deprivation

Systematic studies on sleep deprivation clearly show that it has a strong effect on one's psychic balance. Totalitarian conditioning generally uses this method, more or less empirically.

Sleep deprivation is never presented as such: it is integrated into rites. Pretexts include religious offices, fixed hours of meditation, prayer, and the position of the moon and the stars. In the end, the member is encouraged to sleep on the floor, or in a "prayer" cell, or in strange positions. It's well-known that sleep deprivation lasting longer than seventy-two hours leads to hallucinations or delirious disorders. These hallucinations will be used by the CC as evidence of mystical experiences or divine visitations.

More subtle is the repetitive deprivation of sleep, for short periods, disturbing the cult member's sleep several times during the night in order to participate in ritual prayers or to keep him from achieving REM sleep. Deprivation of REM sleep, even if it gives the impression of allowing physical and psychic recovery, causes a variety of psychic disorders, of which the most benign are depression and irritability, and the most serious are dissociative states that evolve over time [*editor's note*: in dissociative states, certain mental faculties split off from the central consciousness and function separately, eventually evolving into a split personality].

A third technique is that of repetitive, long-lasting night rituals. Even if the CC allows the cult member to sleep during the day "to recover," it has been established that this practice can also cause psychological disorders by changing the bio-rhythms.

The insidious nature of this treatment is reinforced by the cult member's certainty that the disorders don't stem from the practice, because he is convinced that the few hours of sleep he gets are enough. In reality, while awake, the brain synthesizes natural sleeping pills which, under the influence of the biological clock, cause a person to feel sleepy at the end of the day.

Sleep deprivation causes an accumulation of these natural sleeping pills, which can metabolize into toxic products.[2] It causes, in order of appearance, mood disorders that alternate between euphoria and depression, and feelings of permanent excitation with involuntary contractions of the eyelids. Then come eye troubles, hallucinations (luminous, bright rings surrounding objects or people), flickering lights, moving shapes. A more advanced stage mixes complex visual hallucinations and bodily sensations. The last phase of the disorders is the disorganization of thoughts, which is spontaneously reversible if the sleep deprivation ends; but it is likely to cause major psychotic disorders. It should not be forgotten that dreams are one of the factors of building and stabilizing the personality. By depriving a member of sleep, the CC hold a powerful tool that enables them to act as much on the intellectual abilities of a cult member as on the personality.

With Mandarom, the time schedule is monastic:

3:30 AM, Wake-up and a quick wash with cold water.

4:00 to 4:30 first communal prayer in the temple.

4:30 - 6:00 individual prayer in cell.

6:00 - 7:00 meditation.

7:00 - 8:00 hatha yoga session.

8:00 - 12:00 breakfast, then a specific task within the community.

12:00 - 12:30 prayer.

12:30 - vegetarian meal.

13:00 - 15:00 personal tasks, prayer, meditation, personal study.

15:00 - 20:00 communal activities.

20:00 - 21:00 meditation.

21:00 - a meal, vegetarian and frugal.

21:30 - communal prayer.

22:00 - sleep.

Compulsory Labor

Physical exhaustion is a mighty weapon. A good many cults use it, and some have been indicted for this reason. Not only is forced labor a source of income for the sect, its systematic application, coupled with malnutrition, reduces resistance to indoctrination. The triad of labor/ sleep deprivation/malnutrition is an ideal instrument for breaking the physical and mental resistance of an individual.

A judgment returned on March 3, 1993, by the County Court of Paris against Mr. and Mrs. Mihaies, the leaders of the Citadel — also known as the Biblical Christian Church, or Charity, or the Gabriel Fauré Musical Association, or House of Artists — clearly shows the importance of physical mistreatment in conditioning cult members, especially in the case of children. Here is an extract from Claire S's testimony:

> It is a sad truth, I was taught by Mrs. Mihaies, who was in charge of the cult, how to beat children with a belt to hurt them as much as possible. Mrs. Mihaies would say, "Was your child bad? Punish him. Your child has evil in him. Make the evil leave. Strike the child to get the evil out." It was the law. The children are beaten, they are separated from their parents and the parents do it for the good of their children, persuaded that they are unable to raise their own children

properly, since there is this Mihaies couple there, and they know better than you do, about everything; they know better than the parents how to raise children, and so the parents are paralyzed.

Anticipated results:

Due to their parents' participation in the religious movement known as the Citadel, the children in the cult knew a life of restriction and were subjected to an overly severe regimen of physical discipline likely to seriously compromise their future upbringing; the aim was to make these young children withdraw from any family life or social life other than that of this religious group....[The court] convicted the Mihaieses.

Most of the time, these techniques lead to the complete exhaustion of the individual's physical and mental resources.

Young recruits, snatched up by the militant Moonies, are subjected to a to regimen intended to reduce their resistance and their personality: Very little sleep, excessive work — up to 15 or 18 hours per day — long prayer meetings, little food and frequent fasts make up their schedule. This rhythm of life is intended to break them of their former behavior, to condition the recruits, cut them off from their current life and associations.[3]

Chemical Use

The use of drugs in indoctrination is rare. Certain CC use hallucinogens: hashish, psilocybes, cocaine. However, the CC generally discourage the use of illegal substances to avoid confrontations with the law. More complicated but more widespread are the techniques of overdosing on vitamins, which cause liver and kidney complications as well as delirium and complete dependence of the individual on the cult.

The cults are not reluctant to use traditional hallucinogenic poisons. One survivor of the Solar Temple massacres is currently under medical supervision, as his blood analysis revealed massive levels of lysergic acid. It seems that he injected rye mold into his body regularly, either in its natural form, or in the form of LSD, during ritual "services." The product was probably dissolved in the wine served in the ritual chalice. This is, anyway, what the survivor claimed while in our custody. Using poisonous hallucinogens during initiatory rituals has been commonplace for a long time. The rites evoked by Carlos Castaneda in his works were much influenced by peyote, as well as datura and mescaline.[4]

Less known is the use of products that induce deathlike states. In *The Serpent in the Rainbow*, an American ethnobotanist, Davis Lagging, tried to show that the Haitian voodoo shamans used a toxic substance, tetradotoxin. This can cause a cataleptic state, simulating death. This state was also observed in zombies — supposedly, the Haitian living dead. The victims would return to normal due to some unknown antidote. Datura, found in potions that have been analyzed, was responsible for keeping the zombies in a state of dependence. His conclusion is that most of these catalepsies are caused by suggestion, hypnosis, and by the ingestion of natural and synthesized chemicals.

One of the better-known episodes of supposed sorcery was that of people who were "possessed" in Pont-Saint-Esprit. Their hallucinations and "visions" were caused by rye mold, or ergot (from which LSD can be synthesized), which had been extracted from bread flour.

Sensory Deprivation

In the 1980's, certain New Age cults experimented with *tanking,* with relative success. This consisted of isolating the subject in a closed box, immersed in a solution of Epsom salts (or magnesium sulfates) warmed to body temperature. A high concentration of Epsom salt was used — approximately 850 grams per liter of water — because of its reduced cutaneous aggressiveness. This practice of creating as near-total sensory deprivation as possible was gradually abandoned because of the dangers, the results being contrary to the desired effect: auditory and visual hallucinations, and pre-psychotic delirium.

The first systematic experiments on sensory deprivations were carried out in Great Britain, while interrogating members of the IRA. These experiments were made the focus of an Amnesty International report in

1973, during a conference on the abolition of torture. On this occasion, Doctor T. Shallice gave a theoretical explanation of the disorders related to sensory deprivation:

> A very weak excitation of the cortex in an entirely neutral environment causes nightmares, a deformation of self-image and hallucinations, which in their turn can cause anxiety. Without external stimuli to distract the subject from these visions, it becomes very difficult for the subject to combat anxiety. This anxiety becomes, itself, the source of subjectively unpleasant events and physical disorders. A retrospective tension develops, which ends only when the subject decides to end the experiment.[5]

Sensory isolation is difficult to accomplish. You have to remove stimuli of all five senses and to maintain constant temperature and pressure in a confined area. Contrary to what one might think, an easy way to get around these difficulties is to saturate the senses with insignificant information. This technique was apparently applied in German prisons to the members of Baader-Meinhof. The principle consists of keeping the lights in the room permanently lit and creating a sound environment that erases all other noises, or a repetitive sound which, little by little, disturbs the thought processes (water dripping onto a metal surface).

German researchers refined the process in the Eppendorf research center, where it first used its famous "white noise,"[6] an atonal sound system that blocks out not only external sounds but also sounds produced by the subject himself. Of course, few CC have such equipment; however, sensory isolation is practiced in a lesser way, through a combination of rudimentary techniques:

- soundproofed cells, broadcasting of mantras or songs that facilitate the hypnotic process and mask unwanted noises from the outside world;

- permanent lighting: as used in meditation (candles, oil lamps);

- reduced living space: daytime is spent in the cell, while nighttime is spent in bed or in praying;

- saturation of olfactory senses with burning incense;

- loss of appetite due to repetitive diet (bran, for example).

Paradoxically, pain protects against this type of conditioning, for it provides internal information that compensates for the deficiency of external perception. Studies on outmoded sanitariums showed that isolation actually supported the appearance of paranoid disorders and delirium. These disorders come from the subject finding it impossible to apply real ideas to situations that may come up. Isolation and prison constraint prevent the individual from expressing himself because of the deprivation of space-time references. With the isolated subject's sense of time disrupted, his reference points are made all the more meaningful since they are rarer (mealtime, prayer, etc.) and they become substitutes for the natural interior rhythm.[7]

The rhythms imposed by the CC are harder to adapt to because the cult member does not have time to adjust his internal clock to them. The return to normal life proves even more difficult. Isolation causes, if not sensory alienation, at least a poor understanding of personal space and the passage of time:

- space is limited to movements within the CC, within the enclosure of its buildings or its temples;

- temporal, for time is measured only by rites, without a coherent external reference.

All other dimensions of time lose their meaning.

Studies on prisoners undertaken by J. Porta[8] showed that 25% of people subjected to similar sensory deprivation present psychiatric disorders after four months of captivity. 14% of the prisoners were prone to severe delirium and hallucinations, and their personality had been reduced significantly.

It is interesting to note that the topics of these psychotic delusions were primarily cosmic or religious, with alternatives including desiring power, of being persecuted, hypochondria, and sometimes a loss of identity. The various experiments on sensory deprivation underscored general disorders that were independent of the technique employed. The subjects have no focal point to concentrate on, and gradually lose their sense of time. In its place, feelings of anxiety arise, generally revolving around a specific concern: the sound of the heart beating, breathing, contractions of the muscles or internal organs. Little by little, hallucinations appear, increasing until the subject has completely replaced his or her external reality with an internal one.

Ending the isolation does not erase all the disorders. Sometimes hallucinations and delirium remain; sometimes, more simply, residual damage consists of trouble perceiving and comprehending the passage of time.

It is easy to see how the CC can draw religious or cosmic interpretations from their cult members' hallucinations.

"Lying"

Buddhism, Hinduism, and the cults that claim to descend from these two religions use a particular technique of "centering" called "lying." This technique consists of remaining stretched out on a surface and corresponds to *cittha shuddhi* of the Vedic tradition. The subject must also empty his mind, in order to reach a state identical to the practice of the *asanas* (yogi postures) or the *zazen*. Presented as therapy by some[9] it can lead to states of total dissociation, as we observed in a young Buddhist — and was, in fact, reported to us by another disciple of Buddhism.

Stretched out in a comfortable position for one or several hours, the cult member allows all internal information to come into conscious focus: thoughts (fantasies, memories), feelings (impressions), and emotions (sadness, anxiety, joy). In practice, the subject should not oppose any perception, it must all be released, as though the subject was an empty bottle that has let himself be filled with thoughts that were usually repressed. The techniques of self-hypnosis and autogenic training are similar, even if the passive character of *lying* sets it somewhat apart. They all facilitate infantile regression, encouraging the "fear of the unknown," which we will discuss further.

This technique also supposedly unearths memories from past lives. The absence of critical thinking and control of information "released" by the subject allows for any interpretation.

Sound and Music

We have seen that the repeated use of mantras, songs and glossolalia constitute a referred means of conditioning, especially practiced in mystical or religious groups. Music and song have the same function, when composed in certain ways. Anyone who has participated in, or listened to, liturgical songs has noticed the emotional effects. Nothing gives the impression of belonging to a spiritual community more than the invigorating chants of *Te Deum*, a sad and exalting requiem, or a Gloria sung by the Cistercians.

Rhythmic music serves to modify the state of consciousness and can lead into a trance. Ethnologists have studied this phenomenon in groups that manipulate via trance, such as voodoo groups and shamanism. With the fall of Communism coinciding with a resurgence of shamanism in Siberia, in Yakutia and Mongolia, this has become a new and prominent field of study.

> Féodor [the Shaman] refuses to speak. He refuses to look up. He steps outside to collect himself in the Taïga. When he returns, he takes a drum out of his bag. "I am at the limit of what I can do with the spirits." His drum bears two white lines, signs of a Shaman of white magic. He goes into his hut and starts a fire. The ritual begins. Sitting in front of the hearth, he sings and plays the drum. The rhythm is regular and soft. He sings, adding bird calls and animal sounds, accompanied by the crackling of the fire. No gesticulations, a slow dance. For the first ten minutes, nothing happens. Then the hut begins to vibrate, and it seems as if the bench is being raised — as if by waves. It began at the center beam of the roof, moving on the left and then on the right, a kind of internal vibration. It seemed like nothing could be done to stop its undulating movement.[10]

Such is the account of a shamanistic experience in Siberia brought back by two journalists, accompanied by a Sinologist, Olga Rödel. When consulted about this phenomenon, Dr. Jean-François Jal, a researcher in the CNRS Department of Physics in Lyon, provided this explanation:

These phenomena can be explained simply by the propagation of sound waves. The first condition is to produce sounds whose frequency is as near as possible to the fundamental sounds of the human body. These are the low frequencies. Night clubs use this, in the repetitive rhythms of modern music. For the Shaman, the hut made out of wood gives the resonance. There is no trance without music. The skin of the drum sends vibrations through the air, which are sent to the ear, to the tympanum. The tympanic pressure (by means of the inner ear) influences equilibrium. Thus, the sounds that collect on the line of resonance can give the impression of traveling through space.

A few years ago, André Neher established that the forms of music most likely to induce a trance bore similar characteristics. Low frequencies are the most effective, and the rate must be between four and twelve beats a second. This rhythmic pattern matches the alpha rhythms of the brain. The change in emotional state is due to the matching of rhythms. This simple physical, explicable phenomenon governed by the natural laws of sound waves traveling through various materials are interpreted by cults as a supernatural cosmic demonstration.

Ritual Greetings

Genuflections, greetings and prostrations have a psychic effect on cult members. All ritual greetings have symbolic equivalences, a visible demonstration of the allegiance the cult member has for the guru, like a knight to his lord. By answering with a sign of forgiveness, the guru downplays the subject's allegiance by acknowledging the subject's faults and lower station. Between these two gestures is the symbolism of one party's permanent subservience to the other. These acts bring the body into harmony with the mind through a visible display of the respect the cult member owes the cult and the guru, and over time become automatic, as in the rituals of the yogi asanas or the practicing Buddhist.

Practices at the meditation centers are more demanding and more severe, so that one could scarcely get started without an instructor. The yogis wake up around three a.m. and immediately begin the four exercises of the day, namely 1) one hundred prostrations; 2) one hundred recitations of mantras for Vajrasattva; 3) one hundred prayers to the yoga-guru; 4) one hundred offerings of mandalas. Two hours of quiet meditation follow.[11]

Deprivation of Personal Clothing

Seemingly innocuous, this technique is extremely hard for most cult members. Its effects were underscored in Amnesty International's reports in connection with the prisoners from Northern Ireland, who referred to have isolation tactics applied. This was also the reason for the IRA hunger strikes in 1980 and 1981, which led to the death of Bobby Sands and eight other prisoners — which actually attracted little attention from the English government, who only changed their attitude because of international pressure.[12]

This technique helps wear down an individual's personal identity. Clothing confers individuality to a person. It is a second skin and, at the same time, a mask and a protection. A great many abusive interrogations carried out by various police forces start with stripping a subject naked. In the same way, several CC impose on their disciples a particular type of clothing that makes them all the same. In parallel, although upon entering the group a cult member may be given an outfit that levels him with everyone else, a hierarchy soon emerges. Clothing thus becomes a sign of membership in the group, a pledge to observe the rules, a means of identification and a permanent demonstration of devotion to the guru. The cult member is no longer an individual, but a part of the group.

The Body

Having adopted the dress code, the cult member is naturally led to accept other rules of personal appearance. One cult will preach that hair must be long or braided, while another will recommend it be short or shaven. Then comes the body itself, the last means of asserting group membership. CC are interested in the skin: make-up, tattooing, mutilation. Asserting membership in a group by ritualistic changes in physical appearance is an ancient practice.

Although not common, mutilation exists in certain sectarian groups and certain CC. For example, the Yakusa cut off their left ear to announce their loyalty. When the Russian *Skoptsy* cult was officially disbanded in 1871, its descendants took flight and, until WWI could be found in Romania. However, the ritual of castration characteristic of this movement (*skopets* means "eunuch") holds little favor among the new *skopetisti*, whose main frame of reference maintains that only terrestrial mortification can offer eternal security. It appears that this cult has once again gained favor in Russia and Romania since the fall of Communism, as did shamanism.

Sexuality is another mode of intra-cult expression, whether between cult members or the cult member and the guru, representing a will to intrude even within the body. Sex is an ideal means of breaking in, an obvious sign of the sect's domination. The principles set up by AAO and Kommune speak much of this transgression of individual taboos:

1. Free sexuality, dissolving relationships between couples;

2. Collective ownership, abolishing private property;

3. Close-cropped hair, abandoning hairstyles common to "the little family" [the external world];

4. No personal clothing, overalls for all;

5. No sexual relations outside of AAO;

6. No external socializing with groups (bars, restaurants, cinemas);

7. Communication is limited to the sect;

8. No exchanges with the outside world, no visits to the outside world or with people from the outside world;

9. The practice of SD within the group, higher than that of any other communication, makes any other type of exchange useless;

10. No individual rooms;

11. The outside world is regarded as evil;

12. The group is structured hierarchically according to the level of the cult member's consciousness [level of involvement];

13. Work is conducted under the control of a chief of communica-

tions.[13]

Totems

Since cult members cannot be absolutely controlled at every moment of the day and night, the CC often recommend carrying objects that remind the cult member of his or her membership to the sect. The transitional object has a double purpose:
- assertion of membership in the group;
- a protective role (amulets, talismans, grigris).

Wearing an emblem of the guru, a symbol or an object maintains the continuity of the bond with the cult, while creating a form of remote control. Belief in the object and the recognition of its potential power establishes a symbolic tie. At the same time that it affirms to others the subservience of the cult member, the object acts according to the principle of magic by adjacency, as described by Freud in *Totem and Taboo.* It becomes an object of substitution, replacing the distant Master.

In the New Age movement, for example in Iso-Zen, wearing certain crystals is recommended. Each crystal is supposed to carry a vibration of the Master in agreement with that of the disciple. Certain cults rationalize carrying this totem or fetish by developing it to a such a degree that it becomes an essential part of the conditioning. Mahikari is a case in point; it allots so important a role to the "Omitama" that it occupies a preeminent place in the disciple's life and constrains him or her to stupefying levels of discipline.

This is how Chapter 27 of the elementary introductory course to Mahikari presents the *grigri* Omitama:

> By receiving Omitama, one is connected to God by an intermediary of the divine spirit, just as by installing a radio or television receiver at home, one is connected to a transmitter. Omitama is completely different from other talismans or various amulets. Not only does it enable us to benefit from God's protection at every moment, but moreover, it gives us the power to save others. Oshienushi Sama devotes all his strength to the realization of Omitama in a holy place, filled

with pure vibrations; she prays that all people, in spite of the accumu-
lated impurities, be seen as worthy in the eyes of God. This is why it is
important to not open the case of Omitama, in order to protect its contents from the impure vibrations.

Follow the guidelines for respecting the Omitama, be careful when
carrying, removing, or putting it down, and when changing the chain you
wear it on, when going to the public baths, showering, being X-rayed,
etc.

All of the powers allotted to the thing are completely irrational;
opening the case to study the contents is a divine prohibition, which prevents, from the outset, any disciple questioning the effectiveness of the
talisman.

10.

PROVEN METHODS:
SCIENTOLOGY

The study of Scientology's methods of manipulation uncovers a particularly interesting model of conditioning. This CC uses a panoply of diverse physical and psychic techniques.

These techniques are described in the various brochures and publications that the cult passes out, but it is difficult to establish the precise links between them and the various "stages" of conditioning. Only by reading all of the texts and comparing the conditioning techniques with those already studied by science can we understand how they fit together with the overall plan of Scientology. To do this requires reading many nebulous writings whose hidden meaning really only becomes clear to someone willing to be completely immersed in the cult and its ideologies. The wide circulation of the many different texts without presenting any immediate threat allows Scientologists to appear to be open-minded and to deny any charges of hypocrisy.

Recruitment

At first, a simplistic, easy-to-digest philosophy is offered to new recruits. It uses traditional topics: human rights, the fight against discrimination, increased freedom, attaining a level of calm and wellbeing, self-realization, social success. These philosophies are reinforced through the cult's philanthropic associations (Association for Human Rights, Against Discrimination, School of the Awakening, School of Rhythm, National Commission for the Implementation of Laws and Social Justice, Action Committee for the Respect of the Rights of Defense, League for Honest Justice, Support for a Healthy Environment).[1]

The second "bait" of recruitment consists of a personality test (Oxford capacity test[2]), supposed to highlight the subject's weak points. In actuality, it makes it possible to found a beginning dialogue between Scientologists and recruitables. Offered free on the street or in Scientologist offices, it is seen by the potential recruit as a gift from the cult, proving their lack of self-interest. If the subject's conviction is not completely won over, the next step is to try to attract him or her with the presentation of real or supposed important people that already belong to the cult. After having convinced the candidates that international stars like Julia Migenes, John Travolta and Chick Corea were into Dianetics, arguments that strike closer to the recruit's own interests are brought up. In France, Scientology claims support from many well-known figures. It is supposed to be studied by high medical and religious authorities[3] and is supposedly the subject of many high-profile studies and theses.[4] After the phase of intellectual "persuasion," Scientology proposes to the future follower that the Church will pass along techniques that will bring him wisdom and truth.

The mental manipulation used by Scientology relies on two key elements: auditing and *the purification rundown*[5] which we will study separately.

Degrees of Manipulation

Manipulation applies to both CC staff members (i.e. in the missions or at a local meeting place of the CC) and cult members who live outside the mission. Being a staff member puts additional mental and physical pressure on the subject by allowing him or her no free time or space. After having exhausted their financial resources to pay for the introductory courses that lay the foundations for conditioning, new recruits are often tempted to break free from the cult.

To counteract this, the CC proposes that the new recruit becomes a staff member. The offer, while appearing generous, is deceptive: the "wages," which are ridiculously low, are mostly returned to the cult to pay the recruit's "debts." Moreover, the CC enforces the bonds with the follower by writing a pseudo-contract that leaves the applicant completely at the beck and call of the group. This unconscionable bargain is disguised as the cult taking mercy on the recruit. Thereafter, the hierarchy will "sell" the advantages that come with community life to the follower, which will lure him in as an escape from the degradation that has already begun of his previous life, with broken social ties and increasing financial debts. And the trap is sprung.

Sometimes the contracts, in addition to their obvious antisocial character, cross the boundaries of the ridiculous when they ask the follower to subscribe for a billion years:

> I, the undersigned... am currently employed in the Sea Organization. And being healthy of spirit, I agree to carry out and follow through with the wishes and aims of the Organization, which is to help make this planet and the universe a more ethical place, and I subscribe fully and without reservation to the discipline, the morals and the conditions of this group and promise to obey them. Consequently, I pledge allegiance to the Sea Organization for the next billion years.

The above is the contract of the Sea Org of Scientology, signed in front of two witnesses. To avoid criticism, the cult, for some time, worked out a "politically correct" answer: it claims that it asks members to sign the contract as a symbolic bond; whereas the contract is indeed an act of subservience.

Neo Languages

Training and use of a vocabulary specific to the cult have two principal functions. The first, once more, is to cut the subject off from his natural environment and to immerse him within a community that has its own language. The second is the progressive distortion of the meaning of words which, through progressive stages, redirect the subject's thinking and speaking patterns.

English is the elected language of work and exchange. Implemented in non-English-speaking populations, this rule tends to make them lose their identity even more. As for the English-speaking populations, they are made to learn new words (for example, *wog* means "non-Scientologist"), sometimes derived from slang. This supposed initiatory language serves an additional function for the initiates: it enables them to recognize themselves and other Scientologists safely when separated from the cult. Lastly, the development of the "parallel language" goes hand in hand with ascension in the group. The higher the station, the more complicated and elaborate the language.

There is a propaganda technique that was used for a long time by the Socialists, the Communists and the Nazis that is of interest for public relations specialists. This methods circulate in spy rings and are used fairly regularly. Here, the trick is that words are redefined in order to mean something different, something that supports the propaganda being spread. It is not a question of the natural evolution of a language. These are changes made for the sole purpose of supporting the propaganda, carefully conceived and with campaigns that are designed to sit well with public opinion. When one repeats a new definition often enough, opinions can be amended by shifting the significance of the word. The technique can be either good or bad, depending on the objectives of the propagandist.

"Psychiatry" and "psychiatrist" can be easily redefined to mean "antisocial enemy of the public." Words can be redefined by associating various emotions and symbols to a target word. Scientologists thus redefine "doctor," "psychiatry" and "psychology" so that they mean "undesirable antisocial elements." Redefining a word should be done so that the new definition is repeated as often as possible. This, in regard to the words to be redefined, means battling public opinion to make *your* definitions credible and not those of the opposition. A coherent and repeated effort is the key to success with this propaganda technique.[6]

Guilt

The paramilitary nature of CC organizations means the regulations are strictly enforced, with nonconformity leading to being designated an "enemy" of the cult, or a "suppressive" (any person whose acts are considered prejudiced against the organization). Any attitude considered as suppressive results in forced a rehabilitation based on self-criticism, confession or auditing. The following lines are extracts from *The Questionnaire of Confession* from Johannesburg, or Joburg:

> A confessional is not a procedure to be implemented mechanically. Your job is to obtain data. Sometimes someone will give up information freely, while another may try to implicate you during the questioning. This is a sure sign that the subject is hiding information.[7]

Sometimes the crime is too serious to be solved by means of "handling" by an "officer of ethics," and the subject must be completely silenced. There are no less than 36 levels of disciplinary action, which range from blame to exclusion. In addition, public denouncement and the denunciation are the rule in Community life. This denouncement is strictly to demand accountability for the subject's actions, and not a question of pointing out his or her faults to the others. It is used to bring to light any suppressed attitudes within the organization, thus preserving the organization itself. Only acts prejudicial to Scientology are likely to be judged; all others are tolerated.

Denouncements and self-accusations are well-documented. This way, they take on a final and public importance. Accessible to all members, they are the final proof of the subject's conformity to the organization. Displayed in a public setting, they place these documents in full light, deprive them of any secrecy and, consequently, of any identity.

Self-accusation makes it possible for the Scientologists to take immediate control. By the techniques of auditing and detailed documentation, a mental patrimony common to groups is created, replacing the personal memories of the individual.

Scotomization

Rules serve to repress the followers of the cult. Scientology designates by the initials PTS a person that is likely to start trouble by being, for example, critical of the cult. This can lead to the person's being thrown out. Once the danger is gone, the rest of the followers are given places in the organization that will be in relation to their knowledge, as well as their individual's malleability and credulity. According to each individual's recognized talents, he or she will become a leader, an employee subordinate — or a slave.

Auditing

The centerpiece of the constraints exerted by Scientology on its members is the technique of co-auditing, or auditing. An instrument of manipulation, it is also an invaluable vehicle of information by means of the testimonies collected by and about the followers. Auditing allows, at the same time, internal and external control. Having files on each subject (containing letters of success as well as confessions) sheds light on a subject's weaknesses, while being a means of pressure and blackmail if the subject tries to leave the organization.

Getting all the names of friends and family, dates, addresses, telephone numbers and anything else about the subject is part of the agenda in any investigation the CC conducts.[8]

The Technique

Dianetic "Auditing" is credited with quasi-magical virtues:

Dianetic auditing helps to relieve and eliminate the pains and unpleasant feelings that come from mental stimulation.[9] Dianetics operates at the level of the human being and addresses both the body and the mind. The result of Dianetics is a human being in good health with an elevated IQ.[10]

Dianetic auditing can cure disease quicker than traditional treatments. The rate of disease and death in a Dianetic group is insignificant, compared to a group that is not involved in Dianetics. . . . Dianetic auditing also increases the IQ, with an average of one point per hour of processing. Atrophied limbs, liver spots, cutaneous eruptions, and even blindness and deafness can be cured by Dianetics.[11]

Co-auditing is a dual relationship between the subject (a "pre-clear" or PC) and the Scientologist who manages the technique (coach or listener). Although auditing can be practiced in any room, the following conditions were prescribed by Ron Hubbard:

The place must be calm, without intrusive noise or odor, the lighting must be neither too harsh, nor inadequate.[12]

It is not necessary to set up specific conditions to begin a co-auditing procedure. According to Hubbard, progress along "the bridge of total freedom" can be achieved either by receiving auditing, or by delivering it. The roles are thus interchangeable, each one might be, in turn, the auditor or the pre-clear. The possibility of an audited member delivering auditings is of double interest: the subject that delivers the auditing uses his or her own anguishes and doubts to feed the dynamics of auditing. The dynamics of power that is established between audited and listener strengthens all the directing components of the listener and allows him to impose his power on the other. This creates a special relationship, by designating the listener as witness of all the internal conflict of the audited. Whatever the prior relationship of the two protagonists, they become dependent on each other by the mutual knowledge of facts that the law or moral code rejects.

Imagine this scenario. The student and the coach sit apart from each other at a comfortable distance (HCO of May 24, 1988). The listener gives the student a series of instructions or poses a series of questions defined for each session according to a pre-established program. The process is considered a matter of "delivering methods." Each one of these "methods" corresponds to the study of a specific sector of the individual or his social life, or with "discovering" unknown abilities. The name of the technique varies with the progression and depends on the methods implemented. The questions or instructions are repeated several times to the student to put him into a state of hypnosis:

> Look at the ceiling. I will count from one to seven and your eyes will be closed. You will remain perfectly conscious of what occurs. You will be able to remember everything that happens here. If you get into something that you do not like, you can pull back from it easily. One, two, three, four... [13]

In this hypnotic state, the subject refers to situations that trouble him and tries to revive them. Certain methods call upon the reading of specific sentences (extracted in particular from *Alice in Wonderland*); others focus on morals or physical feelings. This last technique is connected with hypnosis and sets the scene for strong suggestibility:

> All suggestions I make to you during the session will be cancelled when I say the word, and will not hold any power over you. If I made suggestions, they will be without influence on you as soon as I say this word to you. [14]

> Any process of auditing done on an authoritative basis is an effort to control and dominate the subject. It can succeed in driving out physical episodes, but it inevitably lowers the capacity for the subject to reason on his own. Even good co-auditing results in some reduction in self-determination. [15]

One patient frequently suffered from faintness after sessions, with nausea, giddiness and anxiety. These disorders are related to dehypnotization, a post-hypnotic phase of re-confronting reality after dealing with an imaginary world or the dreamy world of hypnosis. Dehypnotization, which normally must be slow and accompanied by a progressive return to normality is, in Dianetics, brutal and immediate, with consequences to both the body and the mind.

Auditing with the Electrometer

The method of co-auditing can be supplemented by the use of an electrometer. This practice strengthens the symbolic power of the listener and increases psychological dependence by depriving the subject of the rest of his or her free will and ability to feign cooperation. The subject being audited is completely convinced of the infallibility of this technique of detection and his or her inability to deceive the cult.

According to Hubbard, human beings are composed of three parts: the spiritual, the mental and the physical. The spiritual and mental aspects are located outside of the human body. The spiritual aspect comes from a cosmic form of energy that is expressed through the mental aspect (via physical support of the body). Any variation of this body energy results in a mental radial force that is great enough to be recorded for all to see: this is the purpose of the electrometer.

For Hubbard, the electrometer's function was to highlight the variations of these "mental effects," which correspond to the evocation of painful memories (engrams) or to the connection of the subject with elements of the cosmic memory bank *(sic)*. Consequently, according to Hubbard, any variation of the needle corresponds to a mental radial force and is the reflection of a painful memory unearthed. A needle in balance indicates, on the contrary, indifference to an evocation and the neutrality of the memories or images being invoked.

Compared to normal Dianetic auditing, auditing with the electrometer brings a dimension of pseudo-science to this practice.

Solo Auditing

A third mode of auditing is solo auditing, where the subject himself handles the session. This is true autosuggestion, an autohypnosis that one sees only when the subject is completely won over by Scientology, and there is no longer any reason to try to take control of his or her thoughts.

The personal life of the follower is brought back to the supervisor, who determines the contents of the following session. These documents constitute a centerpiece of Scientologic constraint, for they are confessions that could be used against a subject who might try to escape the influence of the cult. While the sessions themselves take on a serious and highly technical air, they contain a mass of information that binds the subject to the organization. The moral influence that they hold is nothing compared to the power the subject gives them through these sessions, both consciously and unconsciously. Instruments of permanent denouncement within the cult, they can become tools of blackmail in the outside world, for they contain the individual's past, his fantasies and phobias, his errors, his bad habits, criminal background involving himself and his associates inside or outside of the cult.

These reports can be also turned against their superiors. During an investigation of one Scientologist's residence, the police discovered a letter from a member, addressed to the leaders, in which he admitted to having obeyed their orders.[16] [Author's note: He acknowledged having conducted surveillance on *me*, and having sent numerous pieces of mail to me.]

The techniques used in co-auditing use methods copied from hypnosis and related techniques like hypnocatharsis. Hypnocatharsis was much used by the Americans to treat "shell shock," and Hubbard even admitted to having used it as a model after seeing it practiced in military hospitals (after being hospitalized during the war). These techniques call upon free mental imagery, without a starting topic nor induction. They require conditions close to the state of sensory isolation, which are favorable to the sudden appearance of mental images. "The objective processes" are directly copied from these techniques, which were developed since 1950 by André Virel.

There are also elements that refer to transactional analysis. The concepts of the parent-ego, the adult-ego and the child-ego are replaced by the concepts of MEST[17] and of the thetan (very similar to the archeopsyche of transactional analysis). If transactional analysis has a therapeutic aim, in allowing analysis of "the transactions" (i.e. interrelationships between various egos, different from the Freudian ego), the subject is made to want to have "normal" behaviors by eliminating deviant attitudes and approaches.

Scientology uses, to the fullest extent, this attitude of behavioral rehabilitation, while suggesting and imposing on the hypnotized subject the idea that he is much safer inside the program designed by Hubbard, an idea that stays with the subject even after emerging from hypnosis.

Induced delirium is also used. In therapy, one may agree with a delirious subject in order to establish a bridge of communication and to gradually extract the subject from his or her delirium. On the contrary, Scientology will take advantage of the subject's state by feeding him or her Hubbard literature.

Scientology also applies techniques derived from conditioning therapies, standard *flooding,* or immersion in a stressful situation. The subject is put in a situation loaded with things that cause high anxiety or that will bring out aggressive memories that cause the subject to react emotionally and forcefully which, in theory, is intended to separate him or her from the repressed or overwhelming anguish. In fact, repetitive positive reinforcement leads to the installation of fixed ideas acceptable only to Scientology. The method of co-auditing is an amalgam of known methods in psychiatry, psychotherapy and psychoanalysis, but major differences appear between the practices of Scientologists and those of psychotherapists. The psychiatrist's function is to discuss pain, psychic anguish; he is expected to show attention, interest and benevolence. On the other hand, Hubbard requires Scientology listeners to not express any compassion towards the patients, whatever the degree of their suffering.

In any real therapy, the indispensable condition is the existence of a patient-doctor relationship controlled by the therapist and based on the control of transference and counter-transference. An unwritten but obvious rule of psychiatry, like medicine in general, is to not voluntarily worsen the symptoms and to not engender a new pathology or a relapse of old illnesses. This is not the case with co-auditing: several patients whom we have treated attest that the Auditing actually caused delirious incidents (that were not controlled, but encouraged throughout the sessions, and finally required the subject to be cared for in a specialized group).

Co-auditing is interested, in fact, only in releasing emotional outbursts, without repairing the imbalance that follows. No real therapeutic process is put to work in order to control the anguishes resulting from co-auditing. After the phase of destabilization, no reconstructive therapy or support is offered.

At the time of Auditing, the subject can enter a hypnotic state of trance. Depending on the degree of this "trance," the effects will be greater or lesser, with emotional consequences that are difficult to control, likely to set off depressive processes, and even to make the subject suicidal.

> The pre-clear may be prone to many effects. He may feel a considerable emotional liberation. He may be angered by memories, or cry when recalling some loss, to the point of near-hysteria.[18]

Any hallucinatory phenomena will be magnified and presented as proof of a good procedure. The cult will talk about:

- "the circuit of demons": hallucinatory delirium will be explained as part of an existing ideology, or a mixture of magic and extraterrestial references;

- "pre-birth memories": delirium that stems from supposed experiences as a fetus, forming the basis of Hubbard's view of "engrams" (experiences) received prenatally, resulting from supposed attempts at abortion by the mother (!)

- "exteriorization": psychotic episodes of depersonalization are interpreted as astral projection;

- "former lives": delirious figmentations reinterpreted as karmic memories (a contribution of Hinduism to Scientology doctrines).

Auditing, which is apparently a banal interview between two people, actually constitutes the instrument of Scientology's domination of malleable or gullible people. Auditing can be the catalyst in the subject of, at best, emotional disorders and more or less reversible emotional crises and, even worse, hallucinatory disorders, delirious "memories" that sometimes lead to death either because of mystical conviction ("I am a pure spirit"), or because of the subject's desire to escape a distressing life, leading to depression and suicide. Fortunately, this technique meets with failure in subjects who oppose manipulation. The rest of the subjects most often become full-fledged disciples of Hubbard.

Purification Processes

This is the second keystone of mental manipulation. It follows a protocol based on pharmaco-dependence and physiology. It leads to physical exhaustion of the individual, who has been physically strained in order to make him more susceptible to psychic manipulation. Scientology justifies it by pseudo-medical, religious or initiatory reasons:

> A healthy spirit in a healthy body is a principle that is found in the majority of religions. Developed in 1980, this program has already been used by more than forty thousand people, helping them to feel better in their body and freer spiritually. Because of its effectiveness, this activity is also part of the procedure used by certain drug rehabilitation centers.[19]

> The theories and processes of purification assist the spiritual improvement of people who have known mental and spiritual anguish, as testified by those who were addicted to drugs and exposed to toxic substances. This book [in discussing the procedures of purification] represents a report on research and results noted by the author. It is not to be interpreted as a prescription for medical treatment or drugs, nor does it claim to heal the body and makes no such claim....The author does not offer any guarantee nor commitment concerning the effectiveness of the program of purification.[20]

The first justification of *"the rundown"* in purification rituals is officially spiritualistic and is integrated in a step that is supposed initiatory. [*Editor's note*: "rundown" is defined in the Scientology glossary as "a series of steps which are auditing actions and processes designed to handle a specific aspect of a case and which have known end phenomena (indicators in the PC and the meter which show that a chain or a process is ended)."]

> It is imperative that in public places they display visual evidence that Scientology is a religion. . . . Printed texts have to reflect the fact that the organizations are Churches.[21]

However, although he warned against it, Hubbard himself ascribed a medical value to the Church, since he recommended it to help cure drug addicts, in order to obtain "liberation from the restimulating effects of drugs and toxic residues."

> To date, more than one hundred thousand people have been freed from drug addiction by resorting to this technology, and each month, the thousands more are added to this long list . . . .

> Purification must allow for the full spiritual blossoming of the person by removing drugs, toxins and other residues that remain in the body after the absorption of dyes and artificial preservatives, pesticides, and drugs. These toxic residues affect the emotions, intelligence, behavior and the spiritual life of any individual living in the twentieth century. Scientology responds to this modern pollution with a modern and effective purification: running, intensive saunas, and carefully measured doses of vitamins and minerals.[22]

Here we see more evidence of the continual ambivalence of Scientology, which, according to circumstances, is presented either as a religion, or as a scientific community. It was while following failures met during the implementation of the auditings that Hubbard introduced purification, asserting the need to purify the subject of any harmful influence resulting from society, by detaching the thetan from his paramount state and by accentuating all the negative effects of MEST.

This is an initiatory-religious explanation that combines ritual purification with initiation ceremonies of the great religions (baptism, fasting, ordination, etc.). This kind of talk was integrated into Dianetics at a time when Hubbard preferred dialectical religion to the Scientism formerly preached.

> I must face up to the fact that we have arrived at a place where science
> and religion no longer meet, and we must from now on stop pretend-
> ing to have only material aims. We cannot discuss the fields of the
> human soul while closing our eyes to this fact.[23]

Purification is supposed to remedy a variety of pathologies such as
myopia, cellulitis, hygroma, colitis, dermatitis, acne, dysmenorrhoea,
cephalgias, hypoglycemia, edemas, hemorrhoids, hypertension, psoriasis,
paraplegia, and Peyronie and Basedow diseases.

> Hubbard's program of purification constitutes the first means ever
> used that claims to remove environmental toxins from the body, toxins
> absorbed during a normal life in this extremely polluted world.[24]

While we acknowledge that aggressive "therapeutic" acts sometimes
result favorably against psychosomatic pathologies, it is at the very least
doubtful that "carriers" of such varied diseases see themselves as relieved
and cured by this technique. If that were proven (and surely, the scientific community would have caught wind of it if it had), then purification
would truly have to be considered a "Fountain of Youth," as Scientologists ensure it is. This assumption enables them to join the myths of eternal youth and universal panacea which, from time immemorial, have
been proclaimed by charlatans everywhere.

> It is possible that a person can cure skin cancer with Niacin. In case
> skin cancer reoccurs, it will disappear completely if one continues
> using Niacin.[25]

Scientology literature mentions many "medical" works that tend to
prove the effectiveness of purification. These reports are found in magazine financed by special interest groups founded exclusively to promote
these doctrines. This way, it's possible to create a pseudo-bibliography
whose exact sources will be forgotten in a few years, replaced later by a
more complete item to be published in a more well-known magazine.[26]

Purification interests Scientology for two reasons. On the one hand, it creates effects in the subject that can be interpreted in a way that benefits Scientology. In addition, it exhausts the subject by changing his or her physiology, making the subject more fragile and dependent with regard to verbal techniques of manipulation.

Scientology's purification relies on four techniques simultaneously:[27]

- the sauna: for up to 6 hours at a temperature of 60 to 80 degrees;
- physical effort: daily jogging for 20 to 30 minutes;
- a diet rich in raw vegetable fibers, accompanied by a food ration of polyunsaturated oils and rock salt;
- megavitamin therapy, by absorption of vitamins marketed by the cult or its parallel networks: vitamins A, B, C, D, E, B1 and PP with amounts largely exceeding the practices of French and British/ American nutritionists.

Once started, the program must be carried through to its term, for sometimes people come down from the therapy and do not finish *the rundown*. This is not in the best interest of the CC.[28]

The Sauna

If one analyzes *rundown* purification point-by-point, one notes that the way the sauna is used by Scientology presents considerable dangers.

Scientology recommends durations of dry "sauna" for several hours at high temperature, using Swedish and Finnish practices to show it as harmless. However, the Finnish Society of Sauna recommends approximately a temperature of 80o but with a humidity varying from 50 to 60 grams of steam per cubic meter of air. It limits the time to three 10-minute consecutive periods, each one followed by a shower or bath. In the case of more prolonged stays, it is important to take account of the relative humidity in the sauna. Saunas can involve tachycardia (100 to 160 beats per minute), peripheral vasodilatation, diastolic voltage drop and variations of systolic pressure. Water loss (sweat) reaches approximately 500 grams. There is also an increase in the secretion of vasopressine, renin and aldosterone. While cardiac traumas resulting from sauna are not significant and are generally reversible, some deaths have occurred among people who were weakened by too long an exposure to the sauna. [Author's note].

While the Finns use the sauna for approximately one hour per week, Scientology advises six hours for twenty-eight consecutive days.

The well-being felt by the cult member is related to the increased secretion of endorphines as a result of early hyperthermia. It is on this pleasant feeling that Scientology founds its "selling points."

Running

Scientology suggests that the muscular effort required for running is necessary for the hyperoxygenation of the body.

Jogging for less than 15 minutes involves an anaerobic muscular operation (muscles consume the food and glycogen in the body, without oxygen), and it is only after this "suffocating" period that the muscles finally adapt to work in the presence of oxygen. The effort is accompanied by pulmonary hyperventilation (100 to 120 liters against 6 to 8 liters per minute of rest) and by tachycardia (150 to 200 beats per minute). This acceleration of the body's rhythms is not even close to being synonymous with hyperoxygenation, since the muscle then produce greater quantities of waste, CO_2 and lactic acid. Jogging involves extracellular dehydration during the first minutes, intracellular during the following ones. One can see secondary disorders if the dehydration is too intense [*Author's note:* increases in the central body temperature, cardiovascular collapse, delirium].

The practice of physical exertion together with the sauna leads to additional intracellular dehydration — which initially affects fragile cells like the nerve cells and increases the likelihood of metabolic disorders at the cerebral level. Sleep disorders are all the more frequent, since they go hand in hand with the hypoglycemic imbalances born from a food regimen low in sugars.

Hyper-Vitaminization

Taking high amounts of vitamins that act in synergy can cause psychotonic episodes [emotional stimulation], accompanied by mood swings, muscular excitation, and delirious fits as well as toxicity in the liver and kidney, leading to heart failure. These pathogenic consequences were known to Hubbard:

> Its effects can be quite dramatic. Doctors who have devoted themselves to study megavitamins employed enormous amounts, 5000 Mg for example. Personally, I know that such amounts are not necessary. . . . The manifestations caused by Niacin[29] can be terrifying.[30]

Among the side effects of a massive dose of Niacin are cutaneous eruptions with pruritus, which has been presented to the patients as evidence of its effectiveness. "Taking Niacin removes radiation, and the proof is that the outlines of the bathing suits appear on the body of the subject." The occurrence of abdominal pains then their disappearance; ear inflammations and their healing are interpreted as the body "reliving" illnesses or traumas undergone earlier in life.

At higher doses, Niacin toxicity can result in the decay of liver cells or fibrosis, in a process identical to that of cirrhosis. Disorders characterized by hematosis (vomiting of blood) may be observed when the amounts taken are as high as those prescribed by Scientology (higher than 3 grams per day). The first side effects (redness, pruritus, feelings of heat) appear with far smaller amounts. These disorders may be accompanied by states of confusion and agitation. As for consuming massive amounts of calcium and vitamin D, they can cause a hepato-renal insufficiency and a reduction of the body's natural waste disposal operations. The all-over drop in the excretion of toxins brings about an auto-intoxication of the body, resulting in hyperuremic crises. This hyperuremia causes a loss of vigilance and signs of mental confusion. Clearly, reduced vigilance facilitates the dependence of the subject and makes him more susceptible to mental manipulation; and hyperuremia may cause hallucinations, episodes of delirium or coenesthetic experiences, all of which are reinterpreted as a "paranormal" experience.

The disorders described by members of Scientology, whom we have had to treat after "purification," are typical pre-confusional states: vertigo, bright visual images, giddiness, tachycardia, etc. The *rundown* of purification can be lethal because of its direct toxic effects (by aggravating pathology, inducing cardiac disturbance and renal or hepatic insufficiency), or by its indirect effects (creating a psychiatric pathology characterized by dangerous or suicidal behavior).

With auditing and the *rundown* of purification, Scientology has put together a coercive system that uses all the technical and medical resources that support an effective and permanent mental conditioning.

One must wonder about the general indifference that surrounds these practices, an indifference that conflicts with the systematic and justified denunciation that every human rights institution promotes for the least coercive practice. Perhaps this is proof that these cults have successfully infiltrated society and the State and that these cults represent powerful financing and useful special interest groups.

11.

MENTAL PATHOLOGIES
PRE-DATING THE CULT

On the Part of the Guru

Paranoia

We've seen that invention is the essential characteristic of a guru, and that the fable of his life story is centerpiece of the cult's founding myths. The creation of a guru is both mythification and mystification. Concurrent with the fiction inherent in the mythomania, gurus exhibit other telling behaviors that point to underlying mental disorders, both in their actions and their words.

No guru is without paranoia. It is this psychosis that gives him the feeling of being different than the rest of humanity; and it gives him the conviction that he has the role of leader and guide to play. It is a personality disorder that is characterized by four criteria, well-known in psychiatry: inflation of the ego, warped judgment, mistrust and psycho-rigidity. One only needs to read a guru's writings, to listen to him speak, or observe his actions to see these four elements at work in him.

Hypertrophy of the Ego

The hypertrophy of ego has to do with the traditional "I" ego. The entire world must be in agreement with the mounting desires of the guru, who becomes an expression of divine will, and of his thoughts, which become a reflection of the absolute truth. This is the makeup of an egocentric person, one who disparages everything outside of himself. "Without me, there is no health." In all modesty, Moon introduces himself to his disciples as "the greatest man in the universe, a giant, the prince of God sent to Earth." This is the characteristic that gives the guru's disciples the impression that he actually is a para-divine being, for he defies death and denies the limits of space and time. This conviction allows for the creation of ritual sacrifices and explains part of the disciples' devotion — a devotion that can lead them to death.

> Even when dead, the guru's body must retain the majesty that befits royalty, whom only the worms will return to vulgar material, as if the two had something in common.

This is how Livraga, founder of the New Acropolis, affirms to his disciples his divine essence and a supposed infallibility, as do most gurus.

> Just like Jesus, at his feet, following his example, we lay before our worthy brothers the gift of our science so that, as in the Scriptures, they will grow and multiply. In other words, our disciples are conceived by the cosmos with the sole purpose of training other disciples, for the future will need this cosmic food.[1]

Warped Judgment

To the casual observer, the laughable speeches of the gurus are so full of inconsistencies and nonsense, they could not possibly lead to such dramatic events as suicide or murder. Warped judgment feeds off superstitions, paralogical reasoning, denial of reality and improper interpretations. It tends to replace the coherent elements of society by the inconsistent nature of sectarian speech. The guru is the basis of the cult.

To prove the inconsistency of the guru's judgment would entail questioning the very idea of the cult, for he is the backbone of the system, and the credibility of the leader and his ideas are what cement the group.

These aberrations of judgment are found throughout the ideology of the cult, and it is around them that the cult's paralogical reasoning is built; it is they that mix contradictory ideas with the most elementary logic.

> I do not know exactly why the Lord created mosquitoes. They are probably just a type of demon or devil sent by the Lord of the flies [*sic*]. Since mosquitoes, flies, cockroaches and termites fly, then I suppose that the devil is also their lord. Demons like darkness, they like to attack you when you are spiritually asleep.... The demons poison your thoughts, ... the mosquitoes prick you.... Thank you, Lord, that they cannot harm you... You are vaccinated by the Spirit of God.[2]

Mistrust

Being tried for crimes by the outside world makes the guru distrust everyone, feelings that will be reinforced by the fact that his disciples are convinced that he is persecuted because of his knowledge and power. There is a resulting exchange of mistrust, a phenomenon of feedback between the disciples and the guru.

The subservience of the first persuades the second that he is in the right; in return, he entreats them with deranged conviction that the outside world is persecuting them. This mistrust can be directed toward a given community or the whole of a population or, better still, towards the cosmic neighborhood in which the cult is immersed, for example,

> "The black Forces that invade the world invented or recreated in man antagonism, the class struggle, political parties, feminism, machismo." These are the body of the tail [*sic*] of the same dragon, of the same obscure energy that comes down to us at the threshold of the age of Aquarius.

This dynamic of generalized mistrust is the basis of a Manichean system on which rests the psychodynamics of the group and its leader, and which culminate in hysterical paranoia.

Psychorigidity

Whatever the arguments developed against his thought, the guru is convinced that only his reasoning is reliable, and that only he holds the truth. Nothing and nobody will make him change his mind.

To him, his opponents are only weak and silly humans. Not only are the arguments against him ridiculous but, on the contrary, they feed his conviction and work their way into his speeches; the opposition he encounters seems only to prove the world's lack of comprehension and incapability of serene analysis.

Here is how Solazareff describes "the aggressions" that he feels come from democracy, which is, in his opinion, an enemy of his theocratic essence:

> There is not the shadow of a doubt that a bunch of thugs have donned the trappings of power. It falls to the divine power [Solazareff himself], to diffuse the color of the responsibilities. Through the artifice of democratic law, the people have become very grand, the majority in natural voting, tending toward the left, which is composed of a bunch of schoolchildren and licentious psychologists who base their theses on middle-class values that have been the downfall of the West. We must understand that it will never be possible to get out of this vicious circle until the power of a divine nature once again takes up the reins of history.

Delirium

Often, the guru takes up cult evangelism when he has experienced a primary delirious experience. It is almost impossible to draw a line between real and imaginary incidents in gurus' presentations. Only their biographies can provide elements, without, even then, being decisive. These biographies, as we have seen, depict lives more confabulated than lived, richer in lies than in experiences of delirium

Since the 19th century, psychiatric literature swarms with false stigmata created mostly by patients. However, beside the stigmata of hysterical origin, and therefore sincerely experienced, one may observe adulterated stigmata as well, whose only aim was to create a divine character, likely to draw attention and attract study. The same applies to many allegedly mystical, cosmic and extraterrestrial experiences, created entirely by their authors.

It is striking that in spite of evidence of fabrication, in spite of criticism and proof that they are made up, these latter "experiences" stand up to commentary and analysis. The collective imagination has a need for the magical and the unreal, and the incredible is far more powerful than logic and common sense. Studies on cults' founding myths show that the more fantastic and marvelous the storytelling, the better the cult endures and resists external criticism. Conversely, the more the guru's ideology rests on logic, the shorter life the cult will have.

Besides his pseudo-experiences, a guru may actually have had an episode of delirium, a fit of primary delirium or *spaltung*, i.e. disorganization of the thought process with a breakdown of the usual systems of reference. This type of symptom poses the fundamental problem of the mystical experience.

The Mystical Experience

For a psychiatrist, to accept the concept of a mystical experience is to authenticate a psychic phenomenon that is outside the field of psychiatry and to release it from any hint of esotericism, secrecy, hoax or mythomania.

We have already stressed the difficulty in discerning between fantasy and reality in a guru's accounts. How can we determine with certainty the border between mental disease and fraud? The same applies to the mystical experience. Faith intervenes when knowledge ceases; knowledge is often perceived as the enemy, as demonstrated by fundamentalists of every stripe, who believe man can be only the creation of God, and who exclude in fact any thought of evolution, going as far as ransacking museums where skeletons of prehistoric man prove the incongruity of their beliefs.

Mysticism is defined by the dictionary as "a religious viewpoint that supposes the possibility of an intimate communication of man with divinity, communication that proceeds by gaining knowledge intuitively and spontaneously through contemplation and rapture."

The Churches themselves are wary of the mystical experience. Not long ago, the prior of a Cistercian abbey told us that one of the brothers had discovered that his breakfast had been transformed into the blood and body of Christ. The prior sent the monk to work in the abbey's garden, which quickly calmed his mystical flight.

By claiming an original mystical experience, gurus fit into the current trend of assimilating mystical experience to those, apparently corresponding, that one finds in neo-Platonism and religions like Islam, Hinduism, Buddhism[3] and, to a lesser degree, Christianity.

Gurus' tales and their "ineffable and intransmissible" character stand in favor of their psychiatric origin. However, authors such as H. Baruk consider these interpretations as reductive and isolate these tales from the field of pathology. Others, like W. James, are quick to compare the mystical experience with the psychedelic experience. He stresses that certain drugs create different states of consciousness and that there exists in man a true mystical sense that causes and develops certain spiritual abilities. He is joined in that position by (the late) Timothy Leary, advocate of the use of LSD, and Carlos Castaneda.

How to assess the validity of a mystical experience? Is it reality or mental illness? Each side has a different answer, according to his or her convictions. One can, however, see the profit that can be gained by the gurus from this indecision, and all the extrapolations that can be made of it. A mental patient will believe he is the Master of his disciples; a swindler will claim to have had a mystical pseudo-experience; a manipulator will use all the techniques of hypnotism, drugs and chemicals and conditioning to lead his followers to a psychiatric state interpreted as an initiatory phase.

For Roure, Barte and Carbonnel, the mystical experience seems to be one stage in the breakdown of the field of consciousness. It is accompanied by a distortion of the perception of reality, depersonalization, and a wide range of feelings of happiness and elevation. Sometimes, it is supplemented by profuse imagery related to oneiric (dream-like) connotations.

The mystical consciousness draws heavily on various aspects, from the simplest to the most complex, from this distortion of reality. It may be satisfied with a simple oneiric vision, without changing the person's basic personality, or it can overwhelm him with hallucinations and delirious perceptions. Changing, evolving — it can only be described reductively.

If there is a true mystical experience, it is embedded into a personal or group history which makes it possible to describe it as a religious or initiatory vision, and thereby to give it meaning. If, by contrast, it is psychotic in nature, it won't be integrated into the group's story — it will evolve of its own account, leading its "author" towards depersonalization, hallucination, delirium and permanent psychosis –except when recovered and used by a cult as testimony of a pseudo-revelation or a pseudo-supernatural power.

Worrisome Strangeness

Occultism and what is still called parapsychology were first addressed by Freud in 1919, in *Imago,* under the name "anxiety."[4] Parapsychology studies the literature of demonology and seeks explanations for phenomena as varied as possession, spirits, phantoms, and specters and poltergeists. While these studies have managed to show that cases of possession are hysterical and neurotic in nature, they have nevertheless had difficulty in theorizing on a common cause or feature as a whole. Using Freud's expression, "worrisome strangeness," modern parapsychologists have tried to initiate psychic experiences which, being far from the field of true scientific study, have produced studies and results sufficiently ambiguous to keep them out of legitimate newspapers.

In addition to full-blown psychosis, there seems to be a wide range of experience of intermittent psychosis, momentary or episodic, grafted onto behavior that in general appears well-adapted and normal, in people who are able to answer for themselves as convincingly as normal people do. . . . Just consider how facilely normal people answer for everything. Among these beliefs in supernatural forces, not very striking since they are so banal, we will state that they include what one could call delusions that have come to seem banal.[5]

Just consider the many branches of paralogic and the parasciences that abound today, such as astrology, numerology, chiromancy, and other disciplines that delight fans of clairvoyance. However, to accept pseudo-rationalizations of this type is to allow that some lives are paranormal — lives that are connected to pathology, at the very least. A patient who believes in these things signals to the psychiatrist that he is living in a private universe, that this private universe was created due to an episode that would be termed a fit of delirium if it led to a cohesive delirium that is obvious to everyone, but which, in many cases, is limited to a bout of "worrisome strangeness."

This brutal interruption of an ordinary state of consciousness by unconscious elements that a subject can't possibly understand or control gives him the feeling of being witness to supernatural events. It convinces him that he holds a power or a knowledge superior to those around him — and seems to herald a new era for him. For Freud, this represented "the return of repressed memories, revived by external events."[6] The worrisome strangeness appears when the hero changes register, reaches a new stage of personal identity, or when an element of knowledge, progress or access to the world of adults appears; in other words, when he goes through an initiation.

Pondering the character of epilepsy and madness, Freud wrote:

The layman sees the demonstration of forces that he did not think were there, but of which he may have had an obscure premonition in the recesses of his personality. The Middle Ages, with sound logic and almost correctly from a psychological perspective, attributed all these morbid manifestations to the influence of demons.[7]

Esoteric and initiatory literature abounds in accounts attesting that this worrying strangeness, which they call "satori," is a break of the silver cord, astral projection, etc.. This experience of strangeness is situated at the boundary between what is "normal" and what is a pathology, and it can slide into either mental illness, or wisdom. But, even more so than with mystical experiences, it is difficult to tell the difference between someone who believes the illusions and someone who is trying to con others into believing in "visions."

Pre-Psychotic Off-Centering

Using techniques such as mental imagery to search for hidden abilities of the body and mind leads to a change in the usual "perception" of the body. Conditioning a subject to fix his or her attention on a specific body part, or on a specific physiological function, involves blocking out most of the field of awareness by amplifying perception of the specified part of the body. Thus, the field of awareness is invaded, for example, by breathing or by concentrating on the feeling in a finger or an ear. Through this phenomenon, the body is not perceived in its unity but, on the contrary, is divided into segments, piece by piece, with one distinct piece next to the other (psychotic body segmentation).

An anarchistic perception ensues which, when it happens within the therapeutic context, must be followed by a synarchical and unitary rehabilitation — but this rehabilitation is refused or opposed by the cults. Off-centering, combined with disaffection and sensory deprivation, is often used in aerospace medicine but also as a form of conditioning within the realm of torture.

In a article published into 1984,[8] the psychologist Philippe Grosbois defines the technique of off-centering thus:

> Off-centering leads to a disintegrated perception of the physical body, while leaving the subject's awareness intact. Little by little, initially corporalized images will emerge, then discontinuous mental images and, finally, coherent landscapes in which the subject will imagine he is moving, inhabiting an imaginary body as in hypnosis-induced dreams. The subject imagines his physical body to be a costume that

he can cast off, along with his physical limitations. The subject projects onto a visual world the psychic difficulties he had previously embodied in a coenesthesic way. He goes through a series of critical phases that are no other than different stages of fear. Distorting self-image inevitably leads to fear and anguish. The loss of the body and space-time reference marks corresponds to a release-capture, a giddiness, a kind of fright. Where there is dissociation from the body, bodily death, there is also an alteration of space and the sense of the passage of time. After leaving this adventure of off-centering, where communication between the oneiric consciousness and an imaginary universe is established, a restructuring takes place to confirm to this new perception, regardless of any logical analysis or rational interpretation. The phase of off-centering refers to a rite of passage which involves an interruption of real time; upon return, this rite gives the moment new meaning. It is the symbolic death of the body and is followed by a "rebirth."

This off-centering therefore requires either therapy in order to recover, or a "serious" socialization process that involves culturally integrating the initiatory practices by the whole of a society (for example, shamanism).

Systematized Delirium

From the initial bout of delirium, a mystical ecstasy, or from experiencing a worrisome strangeness or off-centering, the guru will develop an irrational thesis that he then systematizes and builds, before spreading it to contaminate his immediate entourage and bring in new converts.

Each guru has his own agenda, which he polishes according to his tastes and aspirations. For some, hysterical and mystical megalomania becomes obvious. "The Christ of Montfavet," George Roux, is a good example. In his eyes, his divine nature was beyond doubt, since he believed he was God himself, embodying the elements of life. "I am God," he affirmed, "for I am the elements of life. I am the air (R), I am the water (O), and I am light (UX)..." [*Translator's note*: in French, "aire" rhymes with the letter "R," water is "eau" — pronounced "O," and "the UX," or "L'UX," recalls Latin, "lux".]

With Guru Maharaj-Ji, the divine essence asserts itself only in relation to others: "They think that I came to rule, and they are right. I will control the world, so listen to me, act accordingly, and bow down."[9] With other gurus, this type of delirium manifests only overtime, developed and maintained by cult dynamics and the permanent game with which the guru deceives his followers — like Ron Hubbard.

In all cases, the guru's delusion is systemic, and is diluted little by little through the phenomenon of conviction fusing with dogma. To the follower, this delusion seems clear, orderly, and coherent, and there is little to criticize. It is a delusional conviction that contaminates the people close to the guru, but it is based on hallucinatory models interpreted by megalomaniacs.

Sometimes, the delusion reaches the level of paraphrenia, with fantastic mythical elements and tinged with religious, cosmic or apocalyptic themes. This is delirium is based on the megalomaniac character of the guru and an wealth of captivating topics. Among the models currently in use, the Master of Mandarom is outstanding:

> That night, I saved the Earth, for I fought against a billion lemurs, which I cut down with my laser.[10]

Psychopathy

To be psychopathic, according to Anglo-Saxon psychiatry, is to be antisocial. This disease is primarily characterized by a pervasive amorality that can lead the guru to commit harmful, even criminal, acts, contrary to the rules of society. This is generally the last step a guru takes to ensure that his followers stay in his exclusive control.

This type of personality is built on mythomania, and is frequently accompanied by "uninhibited" sexuality that takes the form of polygamy or ritual sex within the cult, as with the Raëliens (sensual meditation).

Mythomania brings out a character that replaces the mediocrity of reality with a seductive game intended to attract followers by giving them something new to identify with. The personal myth comes together with the concept of the "ideal self" for the guru, which means that he becomes the ideal to strive for. Thus, it is obviously easy to "sell" a guru such as Claude Vorilhon, alias Raël, accustomed to space voyages, the frequent guest of extraterrestrial beings, while it would not be so easy to "promote" a failed recording artist like Claude Celler, who tried his hand at singing and race car driving before building his cult.

The difficulty for the therapist is to convince the cult members of the mythomaniac character of their guru's presentation, for any comparison with reality turns to the advantage of their idol. Examples of past mediocrity are viewed as initiatory experiences necessary to the realization of the Master's mission. Thus Raël can compare his prior years to the time Christ spent wandering in the desert.[11]

Describing Guru Vorilhon's adventures, François Cornuault puts together his biography, drawing on stories that recall those of Baron de Münchhausen.

> Claude left our planet for the first time for an unforeseeable destination, wearing a sweater and a nonpressurized pair of jeans.... Upon his arrival on an unknown planet, our traveler was accepted by the President of the Eternal Council, a large but extremely civil character who held his hand out to him and, without bragging, announced that by an amusing coincidence he was named Yahweh. Together, they ate a banquet of vegetables and fruits that were tasty, though of a perfectly unusual flavor. Claude recognized the Buddha among the guests — he recognized him by his large belly — and he recognized Shiva. . . by his six arms, which helped him eat faster. The lymphatic young man with perforated hands was Jesus. . . . Claude was invited to six days of continuous feasting, with the anointed officials. He discussed with them the problems of our modern world and learned that we were in great danger because of our immorality and corruption.[12]

Unbalanced personalities also demonstrate an impulsiveness that comes from an inability to tolerate frustration. Before joining a cult, this tendency results in social instability and the incapacity to assume the role of a responsible adult. Inside the cult, it strengthens the bonds between the followers and, at the same time, the authority of the Master. This partly explains some of the psychological and physical violence that come from the guru.

> Convinced that too many errors had occurred in auditing, Hubbard announced one evening [while on his yacht], that the responsible parties would be thrown into the water. The following day, in a general gathering, two names were called. The two disciples advanced trustingly and were made hang off the rail as their punishment, under the horrified glances of their comrades.... Afterwards, near suffocation and bleeding, they came back up the ladder and were obliged to give a military salute and request permission to return aboard. Among the disciples was Julia Salmon, who was fifty-six years old and of fragile health. She was thrown into the water like the others, bleeding and screaming with fright. Ron Hubbard took an obvious pleasure in this, and I even heard him joking about it.[13]

Perversions

Many cults develop deviant sexual conducts. This attitude is readily explained by two elements. First of all, by tolerating conduct usually condemned by society, by morality, or more simply by common practice, the guru encourages his followers to transgress taboos that they feel bound by and which are, to some extent, at the foundation of their existential discomfort. The second explanation is that the cult allows the guru to breach any standard and to live out any fantasy that is condemned by the outside world.

These perversions cover the full range of "atypical" sexual behavior. These practices give the illusion of expressing one's individuality and paving the way to new knowledge. In fact, gurus often suffer from disorders of sexual identity, and are often impotent, unable to obtain satisfaction within a traditional "framework."

The practices of Ron Hubbard, described by his son, are particularly revealing. Whereas Scientology encourages "the impulse to survive through sex (2D)," its creator resorted to excesses symptomatic of sadism and, simultaneously, impotence.

Once, a girl was made to rub her hand from the top to the bottom of the inside of my thigh, while talking about anal sex and other sexual activities, on me and with me, in the crudest language. Every time that I laughed or reacted, she acted as though she was a failure.... Another time, the boy who supervised the classes took my hand and rubbed it back and forth on my groin in an imitation of masturbation, then he used my hand to hold my sex against his, above his groin. While he made me move my hand, he described varied types of masturbation, such as, for example, "the Italian whore's fist." He assured me that this was necessary to help me to communicate well, with anybody, about anything.[14]

Sadism, incest, pedophilia: there are no limits to the guru's perversion when he is ensured of his followers' approval.

The niece of the guru of a small cult, the Friends of Man, testified against her uncle:

He threatened to rape me to teach me a lesson, if I showed too much emotion. As I was not yet twenty years old, I had to be set straight before it was too late. My mother nearly electrocuted herself. She found a live electrical cord hanging in the room where she did the laundry.[15]

Moïse David cultivated family ties in a quite specific way, as his daughter, Deborah, testified:

As I had refused his advances, I was not worthy of being called Reine (Queen) anymore. He said that it was actually my little sister Faith who was the legitimate queen, for she never refused her father. For the first time, it was revealed to me that, since her earliest childhood, she and my father had been practicing incest.[16]

For his part, David gave this account of his experience, not only without denying the incest, but asserting its cultural and educational aspect. He belongs to the lineage of major pedophilic perverts.

I could write a whole book on the way in which we played "flirty fishing" with Small-Joy (Faith). But it is a complete subject by itself, and it is an extraordinary way to involve our most skillful children in witnessing, and in winning young people's hearts. Believe me or not, flirty fishing can be used with children as well, because the sub-plot is to catch men with bait. Children are a very specific type of bait, and they can help us catch a certain type of "fish."[17]

This is how, little by little, the guru communicates his madness to the cult.

ON THE PART OF THE FOLLOWERS

Certain individuals who are not pathological know how to encourage mental illness by using it to make a sales point of their doctrines or to strengthen the bonds that link them to the "sick."

A few years ago, a young schizophrenic was grabbed by a cult in the South of France. This teenager professed to have the mystical power to communicate with the beyond. Her refusal of any treatment created ongoing conflicts with her mother, the father being deceased. The mother, powerless, thought she saw a warm reception, a listening ear, in the pseudo-benevolent attention of the cult's disciples. In fact, having access to the young girl's "mystical powers" was a true god-send for the CC which, by enhancing them and by presenting them as mystical experiences was better able to enroll the child in the cult. A few months later, the mother joined, too.

Most studies done on cult members describe borderline personality pathologies, i.e. attitudes that allow a minimal social interaction, but which are prone to decompensation when traumatized. The entry into the cult represents, in fact, *an acting out,* an act that allows the social expression of a repressed conflict or a previously hidden deficiency.

Several studies stress the existence of intense narcissistic wounds, which entail even greater vulnerability when the family ties are weak.[18]

The cult population is extremely disparate. The percentage of subjects having mental disorders before entering the cult varies according to the study. It is questionable which of the disorders were pre-existing, and which were induced by manipulation within the cult. Analysis is all the more difficult since a preexistent pathology can be worsened significantly by the treatment inflicted.

It would be impossible and unreliable to generalize by giving a standard pre-or post-cult model of pathologies. Only systematic research conducted on specific groups would make it possible to unravel the pints of convergence inside of each group.

Disciples of Scientology

The Dericquebourg study[19] emphasizes the profile of recruits of the Church of Scientology. The cult itself provided the documents used to develop the required profile. The 180 files we refer to represent a population of candidates being considered for "preliminary interviews," prior to actual recruitment.

Only the weaker fringe of these "canvassed" will remain in the cult — at most, 5% to 10%. Thus we cannot conclude, based on these incomplete elements, a standard profile of a follower of Scientology. We do have the advantage of studying an "entire population," covering all levels of entering and development within this CC. Although providing a better reflection of reality, our study only gives an account of the French Scientology phenomenon from 1980 to 1990. One could not — without cheating — extrapolate the results.

Studying the cases of the victims and the consenting followers led us to several observations. The average age of recruitment ranges between 18 and 35 years, but those who continue in the cult are mostly 18 to 25 years old. Some older people have responsibilities, but they are rare and were recruited as young people. The cultural level is generally low, even if one finds some college or graduate students, as well as some professional economists. The majority have elementary education, while some are nearly illiterate.

A recruit's social level is usually low: the unemployed, welfare clients... This has to do with the recruiting methods, which promise socio-professional success without a college diploma.

A minority consists of people from a liberal background or professions that are attracted by the philosophical or metaphysical aspect of the doctrines. In his study, Dericquebourg concluded: "The average recruit is far from being a young, fragile, immature person who seeks to solve his or her psychological problems."[20] However, it is that type of personality that forms the basis of the majority of the CCs.

Children of God

Although still active in France, this CC has hardly added any recruits since its prohibition in 1978. Information about the group relates primarily to the 1970's. Today, there is a core of 40- to 50-year-old followers whose profile starts with the beginning of the utopian and generous spirit of 1968, that believed in an ideal life and only wished to help create a society based on equality and brotherhood. However, over the years, this core underwent a psychological mutation that led its members to a change of tack toward Fascism and Aryanism. This change of course took place due to a radical desocialization of the cult and a gradual reduction of the members' cultural level.

The earlier phase of recruitment had focused on students and people of an elevated cultural level, mainly in nontechnical disciplines (literature, history, languages), plus some computer specialists and accountants. The second population, recruited later, includes manual laborers and those who found shelter within the system but who, little by little, became the "servants" of the preceding population. Lastly, a third population is represented by the children of the preceding generation: children born within the cult, raised by it, whose cultural level is definitely lower than those of their parents' background. The cult plays a role of destroyer of culture, and parents who enjoyed a high level of education are not able to criticize this aspect of the CC and do not try to modify its policy, even to benefit their own children. Clearly, the community nature of the cult and the dilution of the parental bond contribute to this loss of responsibility.

Faith Healing and Prayer Groups

We have treated several members of so-called healing groups, prayer groups, and channeling groups, most of them relatively small. Currently, it appears that the majority of their gurus are female, even if recent history retains the name of famous gurus like the Melchior brothers (the Three Sacred Hearts) or the Christ of Montfavet. Women seem to do better in this type of cult, which values emotion over doctrine.

These individuals show a boundless faith in their guru's powers, they believe with all their hearts, and they would do anything to receive the benefits of their guru's ministrations. All categories of age and background are represented in these cults. They reproduce the structures of primitive churches, open to all, with no real doctrine but with a powerful empathic force.

The Omega Group

A few years ago, while they were being investigated for charges of embezzlement, we had the occasion to examine the member of the Omega group. They consisted of approximately fifty people waiting for a millennial cataclysm or an extraterrestrial event. Part of the group was highly cultivated; they gravitated around a leader who was a doctor, and membership seemed to have more to do with financial interests than with a shared faith. Along with the well-educated, and below them, we found socially dependent members of society as well, obviously manipulated by the upper echelon of the cult. The group was structured according to the usual relationships of the outside world, reconstituted inside the cult. Thus the ones who were manipulated were the usual clients of manipulators, with whom they had forged professional or friendly ties in the past. Patients had been attracted to the cult by doctors and paramedics, the others by salesmen and the ad men of whom they were already customers.

Omega was thus the perfect reproduction of traditional society, if one ignores the credulity and the delusion maintained by its leaders.

Moonies

A study by Galanter[21] in 1978 showed that, out of 237 followers of the Church of the Unification, 91% felt their initial existential confusion (prior to recruitment) fall significantly after the first month of conversion, at the same time as the degree of sectarian conviction increased. However, in the following months, relational pathologies reappeared: 19% said they felt attacked, 22% presented sleep disorders, 21% had eating disorders and 12% had hysterical episodes. 41% claimed to have had, during the conversion period, transcendental experiences (feelings of body change); 35% had sensed near them the presence of "important people" or "an indefinable entity;" 39% had felt changes in the rate of the passage of time. These are similar to prepsychotic episodes experienced by people outside of the cults.

Galanter noted that these delirious or pre-delirious episodes are used by the cults, which present them as mystical proof of conversion to further the process of manipulation.

12.
PATHOLOGIES INDUCED BY CULT MANIPULATION

GROUP PATHOLOGIES

The phenomenon of alienation within a CC is accompanied by semiological signs for which we will retain the definitions used in *The Diagnostic and Statistical Handbook of the American Association of Psychiatry,* fourth edition.[1]

In fact, group pathologies often alert the outside world to the presence of the cult: they are the visible expression of the mental damage caused by the cult, chiefly collective delirium.

Group Catharsis

This is the first stage experienced by a group. It amounts to a "purging" of prohibitions, by means of rituals. A feel of community is created and is fostered by the leaders of the group, generally built on a series of call and response sermons that lead to a cathartic release of collective energy that is both therapeutic and a method of conditioning.

This catharsis can be a factor of group cohesion as well, which freemasonry describes as gregarian, from *gregus*, "the flock" — hopefully not so much as in the "flock of Panurge" following the leader to jump off a cliff as, on the contrary, a flock gathered under the crook of a protective and benevolent Shepherd. It can also mean to obey a negative dynamic leading to mass hysteria. Known since antiquity in its forms resembling epilepsy, hysteria was integrated in the religious corpus of Saint Augustine, who saw it as a sign of satanic possession of the body, or the Devil struggling to stay put during an exorcism. From the Middle Ages to the 18th century, those who were "possessed" were often hauled before the courts of the Inquisition and often were beheaded.

Clearly, one may take advantage of psychodynamic hysteria today. Gurus present themselves to groups as privileged interlocutors from beyond. The guru supposedly carries messages between the cult and his supernatural "contacts." Any hysterical crisis is a "sign" that only the hysterical person can decipher. Because of this "gift," the guru transcends his nature and that of the group and rises to a higher level in terms of ultimate knowledge and revelation.

The perception of these "messages" sets the group ablaze in regards to the dynamics of communion with the "contact," and, in turn, the group perceives itself as undergoing a change. This soon leads to mass hysteria, which shows up in various cult members as going into a trance, or less dramatic forms of pathology. To use the language of alchemy favored by certain cults, the hysteric "transmutes himself" in the crucible of the group, heated by the fire of mass hysteria, causing the transmutation of the system galvanized by the spectacle of his "aureole" of glory.

Shamanism is an expression of this phenomenon, which one also finds in voodoo ceremonies. It is not entirely foreign in the faith healing groups that preach the use of mediums or, to use New Age terminology, *channeling*. In fact, the hysterical crisis is, to cults, proof that communication has been established with the beyond, with the cosmos, the angels or the spirits.

Mass Hysteria

Mass hysteria is an uncontrolled explosion of libido impulses. Episodes of possession constitute the most typical example of this phenomenon. The hysteria of an individual can be reproduced within an entire group when the crisis of "possession" is considered a manifestation of the beyond; consequently, the supernormal becomes accessible to all, and all the members consider themselves able to establish a union with "the transmitter of messages," the medium, the *channeler*. In short, the hysterical person is promoted to role model.

Collective Trance

Collective trance differs little from mass hysteria in its instinctual dynamics. It is the manifestation of libido impulses, uncontrolled by any restraint or taboo, simply because of the "ambiance" created within the group.

In contrast to mass hysteria, trances are more organized. This borrows from shamanism and enjoys a symbolic prestige in which hysteria is revered. It is modeled around a culture. Generally, a certain dispersonalization of the shaman takes place, making him simply the voice for the guardian spirits of the community. Hypnosis aims to divert the libido energy into symbolic meaning that will, *a posteriori*, enrich the group's discourse. Among the topics developed by the groups built around the phenomenon of trance is that of reincarnation; trances symbolize the passage of the old person into death, then from death into the new person. Used since the beginning of time, reincarnation has found a new strength in utopian societies striving for the development of human potential, copying the Esalen communities of California. These groups mix the empirical knowledge of the Shamans with the contributions with Gestalt-therapy and bio-energy. As trances can affect any individual, even one untouched by neurosis, this phenomenon seduces more converts than mass hysteria (which is considered dangerous). Trances not only leave more room for critical analysis, but equally reassuring, they do not change the subject in any material way once the experience is over.

Collective Delirium

These cults are driven by a constant, low-grade delirium, which mirror the delirium of the guru. These irrational whispers establish a harmony between individual pathology and collective pathology. The topics and the organization of these delusions must be identical to those of the guru's, or they will result in criticism and harsher punishment. Along with *sub rosa* delusions, the group shares a history of experiences that bind them together. The cult will redefine these paroxystic delirious phases when discussing supernatural events: how many delirious episodes are ascribed as divine manifestations, communication with the beyond or with God? The collective delirious experience strengthens the cohesion of the group by making them feel as though they belong to an elitist community as well as by reinforcing the individual delusions within the collective delusion.

Mass Suicide

The tragedy of what happened to the members of the Order of the Solar Temple is still fresh in our minds. Murders and suicides are woven throughout this story, according to the rituals thoroughly established and registered in the cult's myth. These are not like the traditional suicides that were the result of a collective depression. On the contrary, these dramas have two different meanings, one sacrificial, the other redeeming. First, there is the murder of the Antichrist, of the apocalyptic beast embodied here in the form of a crucified new-born baby. Secondly, there is a question of redemption for part of humanity. With all their horror, these suicides are attached to the example of Abraham sacrificing his son. They are also rites of passage: death is seen as an accession to the divine, to the initiatory mutual birth, through a symbolic solar ritual. In 1978, the collective suicide of the Temple of the People had already warned the media about the risk represented by cult structures, especially after their guru was exposed with denunciations by renegade members.

Suicide is a taboo more powerful than all others. The instinct of survival and the desire of self-protection are considerable obstacles to the guru's will. Thus there is a confrontation between the suicidal tendencies of the cult and its guru and the survival instincts of the individuals in the cult. The result of this combat is a mixture of murder and more or less voluntary suicides that have been witnessed in Guyana, Waco, and the Solar Temple in France, Canada and Switzerland.

In addition, whereas the ritual deaths are meticulously planned over some length of time, their actual implementation differs largely from the initial plan. At the final moment, it is rare that the followers maintain their cold determination. The example of the Solar Temple is revealing. While the crucifixion and the sacrifice of a baby may have fitted nicely into the holocaust plan of Luc Jouret, the cult's leader, use of asphyxiation, cyanide poisoning, strangulation and explosives proves *a contrario* that these deaths fitted not within the framework of symbolism but were, in fact, premeditated murder: the objective was simply to destroy any trace of cult activity.

INDIVIDUAL PATHOLOGIES

Whether they use exclusively psychic practices or both mental and physical techniques, mental handling generates or reveals many psychiatric pathologies that often require long term treatment. The observation of these disorders makes it possible to define several types of pathologies covering the range of psychiatric diseases. Within each one of these nosological entities, one can encounter symptoms of variable degrees of gravity, from people who can carry on a normal life to those who find normal life impossible. One thus finds the three main psychiatric portraits: depressive phenomena, neurosis, and the loss of personality structure with psychotic disorders.[2]

Depressive Phenomena

Depression has two origins. On the one hand, it is related to the cult member's incapacity to meet the cult's demands, and his inability to satisfy this bond complicates social integration within the cult. In addition, it may be, for the ex-follower, the result of emotional deficiencies induced by being removed by the cult from his or her former life, and the absence of a system of reference after being abandoned by the cult. These disorders take on all the traditional aspects of anxiety-depressive pathology. They stretch from minor anxiety-depressive syndromes to extreme melancholy and suicide attempts. They can take various forms, from panic attacks to abnormal feelings of anxiety.

Generalized Anxiety and Atypical Anxiety Disorders

Upon leaving a CC, the ex-follower suffers from a general feeling of tension. He is in a state of suspense, expecting some sort of repercussions from his act of "treason." He lives in a state of permanent imbalance between his old world and the new one. He notes with concern that his stay in the CC revealed that he had previously-unknown problems with his family, society, and himself, and he feels responsibility for that. The return to reality is accompanied by a relinquishing of all "truths" he had thought he had acquired during the long months, even years, within the cult.

His new condition is complicated by an unwillingness to admit that the time spent within the cult was entirely wasted and that any elements perceived as positive would have been possible acquire in the outside world without the accompanying suffering experienced within the cult. This constant psychic pain causes a permanent state of hyper-vigilance. The subject is permanently apprehensive, waiting for new misfortunes, and his vigilance makes him doubt any proposed new system of reference, as he doubts his capacity to reinstate reality. His concern feeds off the fear of being punished by the followers that remain in the CC, at the same time as of the fear of having the leaders of the CC expose all the real and imagined crimes confessed and often recorded, as in the questionnaires kept in the famous "religious files" of Scientology. It is the threat of repression, the fear of being dis-owned, that is the umbilical cord between the cult and the subject, a cord that can not be cut definitively for its significance is not easily recognized. At this stage, the subject is still a fish caught in the net of the cult. The anxiety is persistent in the follower, and sometimes emerges from being mere background noise to manifest in acute episodes.

Panic Attacks[4]

The persistent memory of life within the cult and the brutal perception of reality can cause true crises of panic, the subject completely convinced of his impotence to combat the after-effects of his experience. Sometimes, memories of cult life rise to the surface, invading the field of consciousness and confusing the subject's sense of reality. These panic attacks sometimes lead to the cult member re-entering cult Utopia — in the outside world, the former cult member fears he will go insane, be attacked, or not be able to deal with reality. These feelings are sometimes strengthened by neuro-vegetative body disorders: sweat, palpitations, and feeling of oppression.

Chronic or Acute Permanent Stress[5]

Although it merges with anxiety, the state of chronic stress is directly dependent on how aggressively the cult marked the subject in body and spirit. Therefore, it is deeper and more durable. The fear of retaliation from an aggressive cult persists until the subject is asleep, where it returns in the form of repetitive dreams.

Next comes a reduction in interest in the external world and other people, a restriction of affections, the feeling that one must always be on the alert. Another side effect are memory disorders, parasitized by reminiscences of the cult experience. This type of pathology is present in the subject long after he leaves the cult. The difficult task of managing systems of contradictory thought and reference (subservience to the cult and the need to preserve its society) is the most frequent cause of this particular pathology. Difficulties resulting from family, social and professional conflicts are added to this sense of ambiguity. Physical and psychic exhaustion make up the rest.

Most of the time, cults do not try to ease the depressive states of their new followers. Quite to the contrary, they support the depression, as it makes it easier to cut the cult member off from his past life and makes him amenable to further conditioning. In addition, each traumatic or aggressive episode that happens during the subject's life within the cult can induce a corresponding depression identical to those seen in the event of physical or psychic trauma. The subject settles into an acute or chronic post-traumatic state of stress.

Another type of depression is the pathology caused by leaving a cult. The return to the outside world is accompanied by a rediscovery of the "damage" caused by the original breaking away from society, and the confrontation with this reality creates a phenomenon of anguish, made all the more profound since the systems of reference have disappeared.

Neurotic Behaviors

These deal primarily with obsessive rites or phobic behavior resulting directly from the precepts followed by the cult. Depending on the degree of these disorders, the cult member can develop handicaps that prohibit social reintegration. The practices of ritual diet, ceremonial dress, prayer and meditation are drastic. When the subject decides his former cult existence and the former conduct of the cults are considered shameful, "dirty," or likely to slow down his progress in rejoining the outside world, he tends to isolate himself from society or to develop phobias.[6]

Phobias

Cult ideology is based on the internal-external dichotomy and a Manichean view of good and evil, leaving the cult member with a permanent fear of the world.[7] All CC speech feeds and supports social fears. The cult acts as though it is a rampart against the evil that reigns outside. Confrontation between the cult member and real society causes episodes of anxiety[8] that can reach the level of great panic attacks with physical manifestations. For example, the doctors treating the children who were let go in the days preceding the destruction of Waco observed massive somatic disorders, in particular cardiac disorders (tachycardia, arrhythmia, palpitations, syncopes) and intestinal disorders (diarrhea and colitis). These disorders developed directly following the traumatic events, therefore proving to be the psychosomatic origin.[9]

To a lesser degree, we have seen these disorders in the children of the Family of Love, when they were confronted with normal society, which had been described to them since birth as the Kingdom of the Devil. These disorders were reinforced by the "obligatory" contact with a select few "representatives" of the outside world. The obligations that come from belonging to society are often denied by the cult, and they are the cause of a wide range of more or less complex phobias. This is often the first obstacle to surmount when trying to begin a psychiatric dialogue with the member or ex-member of a cult.

Doctors and family are invested with a malevolent power by the cult, for they embody the hated society, of which they are the symbolic instruments and, at the same time, the defenders. The unconscious persistence of the conduct and rituals taught by the cult places the subject within a framework where he finds himself hemmed in between the old constraints of the cult and the new requirements of society. Stubborn obsessing over ideas, stereotyped behaviors and absurd impulses is typical of a obsessive compulsive disorder. The subject, conscious of his own bad judgment, has almost insurmountable difficulties in controlling his thoughts and is involved in a multitude of behaviors, which he rejects intellectually but can withdraw from only with painful effort.[10]

At a more advanced stage of the disorders, the subject is caught "between two worlds," the unreal cult world and that of social reality. He sees himself as being the product of "a mutation," which places him apart from other humans while still being human. This is especially true of followers who had mystical experiences or intense pseudo-mystical experiences, and those who "talked" with supernatural beings or with aliens. His perception of reality degrades even further, as well as his perception of himself. Feelings of strangeness and unreality, characteristic of depersonalization disorders, increase.[11] The subject sees himself as a "robot," believing himself to being in a daydream, while still feeling as though he's taking an active part in the real world. These conducts seldom remain isolated: they are gradually integrated into paranoid interpretations to become psychotic delusions.[12]

Sometimes the disorders manifest only in intermediate states, involving just one psychic sector. The cult member thus may be unable to dredge up memories of one element or one isolated episode of his life, creating a partial amnesia that generally corresponds to a denial of past reality because the anguish of recalling that episode is too great for the subject to handle.[13] This can lead to the subject feeling pains that have no real somatic support, but which correspond to a somatization at the time of a crisis of acute anxiety started by the unconscious recollection of distressing or guilt-ridden past experience.[14]

Psychotic Disorders

These form a great part of cult and post-cult disorders. They are generally built on a former personality weakened and replaced by a structure known as schizoid.[15] These disorders follow a steep curve that can be summarized as follows:

Stage 1: Moderate withdrawal, loss of contact with society, schizotypal personality. Superstitious, believes himself to have gifts of clairvoyance, telepathy, or a sixth sense. Social isolation with limited contacts and recombining of an exclusively cult system of references. Recurring illusions (feeling the presence or influence of a person usually absent, or deceased).

Stage 2: Problems discerning between reality and delirious thought. Absurd approach to reality. Integration of the cult fantasy with the subject's logic. Odd, religious delirious ideas or nihilism. Inconsistency, with increased illogical thought. Problems with speaking — blunt, abrasive, inappropriate language.

Stage 3: Adamant defense of delirious topics. Complete belief in the ideology presented by the cult. Appearance of living a "mystical" existence while maintaining minimal contact with ambient society. Deterioration of job performance, social relationships and personal care.

Stage 4: Complete loss of all sense of reality. Complete immersion in the ideal of the cult. Absence of criticism of illusions. Total replacement of logic with delirious interpretation.

Stage 5: Total loss of structure. Life becomes a state of paranoid delirium. Pseudo-mystical experiences. Sensory and coenesthetic hallucinations. Paraphrenia. Aggravated, inconsistent. Expresses delirious ideas, disorganized behavior.

Stage 6: Heboidphrenia. Total loss of the original personality. "Spaltung" or fission. Catatonic stupor. Catatonic negativism. Catatonic position (fetal). Catatonic rigidity.

Among the followers and ex-followers with whom we have talked, we have observed all the previously-described stages of psychosis. Here are some cases, classified according to the thresholds of manipulation reached.

Stage 1

- Young lady, 24 years old, single, university drop-out, in conflict with family. Moderate follower of the Golden Lotus three years prior to entering therapy. Therapy failed. Progressive subservience until totally subservient to the cult (faithful disciple for ten years).

Stage 2

- Unmarried woman, 35 years. One child, civil servant. Disciple of Vital Momentum for six years. Believed herself to be telepathic as a result of their influence. Recovery under treatment ;

- Man, 54 years old, craftsman, single, small physical handicap. Belonged to the Rosicrucian Brotherhood for eight years. Believed he had telepathy and the gift of healing. Treatment failed;

- Couple, 34-36 years, two children. Members of groups studying UFO's and extraterrestrials. Wife became critical of the group and managed to leave the cult. Divorce. Subservience of the husband to the groups concerned. The children need psychotherapy.

Stage 3

- Married man, 50 years, in trade. Church of Scientology for two years. Somewhat critical of delirious episodes. Left cult, but still is minimally influenced by the cult.

Stage 4

- Unmarried man, 35 years old, childless. Practiced Buddhism in ashram for four years. Extraterrestrial delusions requiring treatment. Therapy failed; suicide.

Stage 5

- Married woman, 40 years old, nurse, two divorces, childless. Intensive participation in Church of Scientology for two years. Mystical delusions, auditory and coenesthetic hallucinations. Total recovery under treatment.

- Single man, 31 years old, no profession. Belonged to the Rosicrucian Brotherhood for four years. Mystical delusions. Recovery under treatment, but retained paralogical thought processes.

- Married Man, 42 years old, kinesitherapist, two children. Disciple of Vital Momentum for five years. Mystical delusions. Divorce, no therapy undertaken, total subservience to the cult.

Stage 6

- Married woman, 34 years old, sterile, abandoned by husband. Member of Church of Scientology for three years. Fetal stage, sucks thumb, enuresis and encopresy (bed-wetting and fecal incontinence) Total recovery under treatment.

Cults accept subjects without restriction until Stage 4 — the levels at which they remain perfectly usable. The appearance of Stage 5 is alarming. Stage 6 represents too-advanced a degree of pathology to be tolerated by the cult. It must result in expulsion; the subject becomes a nonproductive burden.

The inventory of these pathologies is not exhaustive — they interpenetrate and change throughout cult and post-cult life. The cults also shelter a number of silent psychotic pathologies. They reinforce the paranoid tendencies of the subjects and deprive them of real analysis. They interpret, incoherently, primary delirious experiences and claim them to be signs of mystical revelation. They feed badly structured delusions, and build them up inside the paranoid group dynamics. They reinforce feelings of isolation, incomprehension, loneliness.

The major problem confronting the therapist of an ex-cult member is to differentiate between the pathological elements resulting from leaving the cult and any former pathologies. But it should be noted that the existence of intense spiritual or religious doubt appears to experts more and more to be a major factor in people's decision to join a cult.[16]

13.

TREATING THE PATHOLOGIES

Prevention

There are few preventive measures one can take to keep an individual from joining a cult. Of all the preventative measures, however, strong socio-familial and cultural bonds are the best support.

Because it deprives the individual of any freedom of choice, joining a cult could be regarded as an addictive behavior. The concept of addiction comes from an old French word that means "civil imprisonment," according to Jean Adès.[1] While addictive behaviors may be expressed in highly diverse ways, we can identify and define some common points that they all share:

• clinical unity: whatever its object, the addiction implies that a desire has evolved into a need, from use to misuse. It involves the loss of control and a changed attitude towards the circumstances. The behavior is pursued because of the psychophysiological developments of dependence — regardless of all consequences, even the most harmful;

• psychopathological unity, illustrated by certain biopsychological factors, innate or acquired, such as impulsiveness, thrill-seeking, intolerance for boredom, or the pursuit of dangerous, humiliating "games";

• biological factors, certainly dubious, but claimed by several researchers. Addictive behavior could be encouraged by a low level of cortical stimulus, probably genetically influenced and mediated by cerebral systems of compensation, with the majority of cerebral neurotransmitters modulating the activity. In addition, there could be biological factors that immunize a person from falling under the power of a cult, as is the case with hypnosis.

The biological hypothesis is far from proven; but this line of research offers more hope than the one that claims the effects are permanent and that partially absolves society. Bankruptcy of ideologies, loss of guideposts? Isn't this explanation too simplistic?

In thirty years, experts who work with drug addicts have not managed to explain satisfactorily the phenomenon of "drug appeal," much less the "drug culture." The same applies to bulimia, compulsive shopping, sex addiction, or addictions to work and gambling.

Cult addiction is even less explored; yet cult addiction fits all the criteria of addictive behavior, as defined by Goodman,[2] and thus by analogy as defined in *Diagnosis and Statistical Manual of Mental Disorders* in its fourth re-edited edition). The fact that they do not meet popular approval is an additional element of attraction. Lastly, in the two systems, as illustrated in the table below, the hierarchy of dependence and exchange is completely similar.

The convergence of several elements in this portrait results in our thinking that cult dependence is a new addictive phenomenon. This report should lead to the establishment of a plan of prevention, designed to avoid calling forth equal and opposite measures, and designed to combat those already in existence.

Analysis of these elements shows that the psychological effects of the cult addiction fall into two groups:

- on the one hand, psychological elements dominated by an anxiety phenomenon;

- in addition, social elements that correspond to the progressive social breakdown.

General therapy aims to reduce the anxiety of the subject by all known techniques, but also to reconstruct the social weave destroyed by the cult. Tracking cult-related behavioral pathology is primarily a family

	ADDICTIVE DISORDER	**CULT DEPENDENCE**
(A)	Repeated failure to resist the impulse to undertake a specific behavior	Inability to refuse to perform objectionable duties preached by the cult, acts only as the
(B)	Increasing tension before performing the objectionable behavior	Ongoing anxiety to respond to the requests of the cult and desire to satisfy them
(C)	Feeling of pleasure or relief by engaging in the behavior	Relief at being accepted by the cult, feelings of a duty accomplished via cult activities
(D)	Feeling of loss of control while engaging in the behavior	Loss of autonomy to the cult, abolition of free will
(E)	*At least 5 of the following 9 items:*	
1	Frequent preoccupation linked to the behavior or to related activities	Invasion of the behavioral and social field by cult activities
2	Greater frequency of the behavior, or for longer periods than intended	Progressive immersion in cult activities, which engage the subject for longer and
3	Repeated efforts to reduce, control or stop the behavior	Subject repeatedly fails to withdraw from cult influences
4	Significant time lost in preparing for the behavior, carrying it out or recovering	Social dependence on the cult, abolition of personal temporal space
5	More frequent repetition of the behavior when occupational, domestic or social obligations should be receiving attention	Increasingly frequent conflicts between cult space and personal social space, to the detriment of the latter
6	Significant occupational, social or leisure activities are abandoned or reduced because of the behavior	Progressive abolition of social activities contrary to the interest of the cult or not profitable for it
7	Pursuit of the behavior in spite of knowing that it exacerbates social, psychological or physical problems	Resistance to any critical external analysis aiming to reduce cult activity
8	Tolerance: need to increase the intensity or frequency of the behavior to obtain the desired effect; decreased effect if behavior is continued with the same intensity	Increased physical, psychic and social dependence on the cult. Any maintenance of previous life is felt to be a failure. Need for increasingly powerful commitment
9	Agitation or irritability if the behavior cannot be continued	Irritability and fierce opposition if the cult membership is criticized or opposed, by the cult or by the outside world
(F)	The symptoms of the disorder persist for at least a month, or occur repeatedly over a prolonged period	Psychological dependence lasts even after the link with the cult has been broken

function, but interpreting it often requires the involvement of a health care professional. As for treatment, the weight of responsibility for the anxiety phenomenon cannot be the sole burden of these same professionals, who will undertake to identify the origins of the phenomenon and will aim at solving the causes, after having distinguished what parts of the problem were present before and after cult manipulation. Well-meaning parenting finds its limits here; family and close relations are often at the heart of the dynamics of anxiety, at the same time as they are the participants. They are seldom able to assess their share of responsibility.

Detecting Cult Involvement

As with drug addicts, early diagnosis is a determining prognostic factor. In the beginning, the follower questions the validity of the new concepts proposed to him. At this stage, the parasitic thoughts have not set in, the reconstruction of the personality has not yet calcified. The earlier the intervention, the easier it will be to establish a real exchange, both diagnostic and therapeutic, with the individual.

Contrary to a generally accepted idea, joining a cult is seldom brutal, except in the borderline cases of spontaneous rupture with the former life — particularly in cases of the emergence of mental instability. Easing into a cult is always accompanied by a host of signs which touch on one or more aspects of social life. Changes in behavior and thought are certainly the most difficult to apprehend in the beginning, for a philosophical or mystical crisis, rejectful behavior or a crisis of identity do not inevitably involve joining a cult. The appearance of a paralogical thought in an individual, even if it hits upon one of the traditional topics of cults, can be either the sign of mental illness or a simple questioning of the world — without attaching the subject to a specific cult or community.

Paradoxically, cult life is reassuring to certain families. It makes it possible to pass off, onto the outside world, responsibility for a possible crisis, whereas this crisis, generally, was born inside the socio-familial cell. I, for my part, have been dealing for several months with a family that refuses to admit that the entrance of one of its members in a cult is the direct consequence of a rupture in family dialogue. The parents are only seeking to establish the diagnosis of cult addiction, i.e. "to make other people wear the hat," and to transfer the responsibility to society — the police force, the law, the medical community.

While the psychic elements and the behavioral changes are signs to be heeded, it is still important to know how to read them. It is important to be attentive to any change in the behavior of a close relation. A number of signs are given different social alibis. New food choices, for example, will be excused as the subject wanting to lose weight; a new way of dressing will find a pretext in the guise of fashion or a desire to be original; new topics of reading will be excused as the subject searching for personal or academic answers to questions, while sudden schedule changes can be falsely attributed to new sporting activities! Attention must also be paid to mood changes or changes in judgment calls on prohibited behaviors. In fact, the accession of a man or a woman into a cult generally changes every aspect of life; consequently, it is advisable to consider how much of a subject's life has been affected before worrying about cult activity — still, even simple changes can be revealing, especially when the subject has made changes in his or her financial status. Upon recruitment, the cult seeks to satisfy its own financial needs. The subject is immediately encouraged to purchase products manufactured or promoted by the cult. Unexplained financial difficulties, accumulation of bills, new credit cards, the sudden sale of personal objects (discs, clothing, stereo equipment, mountain bikes, etc.) are signals that should be taken seriously.

A colleague of mine, years ago, had joined a cult at one point. His membership had been completely unnoticed by his wife, until she received a call from a collection agency. The size of the amount claimed and the absence of a logical explanation encouraged her to carry out a discrete inquiry, at the end of which she discovered that her husband had lost his credit rating and had used up his resources securing loans to pay for training courses in the cult, training courses that were masked as professional conferences and seminars. As in the case of addiction, increased debt or financial activity without a corresponding increase in income are often an element of detection that is much more useful than trying to gauge changes in mood or judgment.

"Extracting" a Subject From a Cult

In the 1980s, "de-programming" and its corollary, kidnapping cult members, were well-documented by the media. If families truly had any other option for recovering their children, they were rare cases that are not useful as examples. A paradox: for the close relations of the cult member, it is extremely difficult to choose between respecting the free will of the person and the desire to help a family member in danger. The ideal case, but also the most rare, is that of the cult member who spontaneously becomes aware (or while under the influence of his friends and family) of the counter-productive nature of the cult doctrines and their impact on his social life and his mental stability.

In certain extreme cases, the physical or mental degradation of an individual is such that he is unable to see it. The cult member's friends and family are then naturally obliged to turn to legal and medical assistance. But alas, family alone is generally unsuccessful in halting the progressive degradation. Unable to react, they restrict themselves to respecting a "free will" already partially destroyed. In the same way, the family feels reluctant to resort to force when any attempt at assistance is rejected. In any event, it is essential not to break off ties with the cult member: to do so would mean passing up opportunities when an intervention would be favorable.

Any physical, mental or social disorder has a specific legal correspondent within the body of the law, making it possible to assist a subject. Ignoring someone who is in danger is not an option, especially if any criminal offence may be involved (aggravated assault, violence, deprivation of care, rape, indecent assault, etc.) Too often, we are unaware of the danger. Social withdrawal most frequently has debt as a corollary: one can, in this respect, engage all the civil procedures of trusteeship and supervision while also alerting a medical professional of the subject's mental status. While these procedures do not always achieve their goal, they do show the advantage of bringing to bear an inventory of tools, expertise, and research. They also sow disorder in the cult and devalue the cult member in the eyes of his Masters, which often causes the cult member to be released by the cult, even rejected, if the subject does not represent a commercial value proportional to the nuisance that his presence may create within the cult.

Coercive care must be avoided as much as possible, but one should not ignore the advantages that may attend hospitalization at the request of a third party; they are defined by law (1990). Cults enjoy the game of claiming religious freedom and alleging police repression, which they often do: the risk from this is small, compared to preserving the mental or physical health of the person in question.

However, it is still preferable to obtain the consent of the cult member before asking his family to begin hospitalization. It is important:

- to make the subject aware of the loss of his or her social status and individuality (avoid any subjective analysis in terms of blame, culpability, error, etc., in favor of an objective inventory of the state of affairs);

- to review the situation and to propose a credible and realizable alternative immediately;

- to remove blame from the cult member, making possible his "return";

- not to extract consent by any means that may be criticized in hindsight, leading the person to reject it and return to the cult; it is preferable to begin the process through actual consent, not manipulation;

- to not use double talk and to not make pseudo-concessions, which will be used by the cult as a proof of insincerity;

- to not change an opinion or attitude, giving the impression that there is doubt in regard to the course of action;

- to systematically question the cult member on the significance of the various visible elements of the cult, in order to lead to analysis, or even to criticism;

- to not use topics already attacked by the cult, under the penalty of causing the follower to defend the cult;

- to debate solutions suggested by the cult, refuting them with concrete and unassailable arguments; never fight on ideological ground alone. The cult member's conviction must be obtained by proof and not by counter-indoctrination;

- to entertain and revive all the subject's tendencies of the individualism. Flatter his ego;

- to found the argument against the cult on intellect and proof, and not on the affect: in particular, not to act under the influence of anger, fear, constraint or blame;

- to use the successful experiments of others, but only under the recognition that there is no one solution: each cult member is an individual, and must be treated so;

- to provide evidence in good faith, without trying to cheat. It is better to refuse a proposal than to pretend to accept it. One can deceive one cult member for a little while, but not a whole cult;

- to never give the cult member the impression that the family has differences in opinion on the subject of his membership in the cult, or any other subject likely to throw doubt on the cohesion of the family;

- to fight the cult's "love-bombing" with family "love-bombing," outside the scope of cult interpretation;

- to not mix emotion and intellect: conviction must be fought by intellect, the feeling of membership by *love-bombing*

- to never forget that, for the cult, anyone is an enemy who is not a follower, and that everyone is described as such.

Therapy

As in any form of addiction, the assumption of responsibility by the member of a cult cannot be conceived without the co-operation of the subject. Even if the urgency imposed by a crisis sometimes requires hospitalization (such as in the case of delirious episodes or mystical delusions with major social repercussions), "rebuilding" the cult member's personality cannot be done without his or her consent.

The role of family and close relations is fundamental here. Maintaining emotional ties, which are always abused by the cult, is the only bridge that connects the cult member to reality. It is through the gifts of emotional and intellectual exchanges that the cult member's close relations and therapist can help the subject to undertake his or her behavioral and social reconstruction.

The Emergency Phase and Recovery

Caring for an ex-cult member often requires the services of a multi-disciplinary team. The damage may be as much physical as psychic: we once had to hospitalize a young woman who had lost 80 pounds in two years. She spent thirty days in intensive care before we could consider treating her on an out-patient basis — which was not possible, regrettably, due to the severity of her mental condition.

Sometimes, the assessment is much simpler and requires only a slight re-evaluation. For example, one patient I met little while ago had suffered nothing more than a bungled circumcision from his cult experience.

During the early phase of the follower's recovery, treatment is primarily symptomatic. Psychiatric therapy should be started immediately. With regard to the most glaring pathological elements, often the cult only served to trigger mental disorders that were already lurking in the subject. In any case, first it is advisable to reduce the psychiatric symptoms that make it impossible to deal with reality: delusions, hallucinations, severe depression. Later, a second and more complex stage will try to making the ex-follower aware of the mistake he or she made in joining the cult. The third step will be devoted to analyzing the reason for the subject joining the sect in the first place. Here, one finds the problems inherent in all dependency therapies. Beware of bogus de-programmers, who often use techniques that are just as risky as those used by cults! This type of treatment gives results that are neither valid nor lasting.

The cult's appropriation of all social activities must be countered with behaviorist techniques, and the analysis that must follow — slow and progressive — is absolutely mandatory: without it, relapse is certain. The cult finds a home in people with relational, cultural, or social vacuums. Only when these deficiencies are mitigated can treatment be effective. Social therapy incorporates dialectical and didactic phases of identifying the deficiencies; it precedes the phase where family and social interaction can be re-established, during which we would eliminate any remaining behaviors that do not support the rebuilding of the personality.

Treating the Depressive States

The follower who leaves a cult is immediately haunted by feelings of having committed treason against the group, which is transformed little by little into guilt with regard to family and close relations. At this time, feelings of uselessness and failure may be overwhelming, alternating with dreams of redemption. The prospect of returning to the cult or the temptation of suicide are then omnipresent and must be dealt with as another issue altogether; medication may be necessary to counteract these urges.

The feeling of emptiness that ensues after leaving a cult goes hand in hand with an ever-present symbolism of death, which can be expressed as much in the conscious mind as in the unconscious mind; the will to live may be quite extinguished. Melancholy (a feeling that time is dragging, a lack of goals, loss of idealism) can be fought by proposing new activities with powerful symbolic value. The difficulty lies in the managing the double constraint: urgency of the treatment and respect for the person. How can one reconcile the need for strong intervention with the benevolent neutrality that one owes the patient? On the one hand, an overly directive therapy is likely to make the patient feel like a failure again, with all the thoughts of death and humiliation that go with the death of ideals; on the other hand, not to intervene might easily leave the way open for disaster.

Treating the Psychotic States

The greatest difficulty encountered in treating post-cult delirious and hallucinatory states lies in the confusion between typical cult elements and religious or social myths or stories that may have been a prelude to cult conversion, but which belong to the personal, pre-cult, history of the subject. The second difficulty lies in distinguishing between real pathologies and socially acceptable mythologies. The current recrudescence of parasciences, occultism, extraterrestrial fables and others is a considerable handicap, for the subject uses them to justify his or her attitude. The risk, for the therapist, is to over-emphasize the rational view or, on the contrary, to be too tolerant of these beliefs.

As for psychosis, family archetypes are completely altered; a symbolic Oedipal complex develops, where the guru takes the place of the father and the cult takes the place of the mother. Therapy aims to reconstruct, with the patient, a symbolism that is compatible with that of society at large, while avoiding the hazards of cult parasitism and the earlier pathogenic elements that predated the cult experience. Analysis of family conflicts, in fact, is seriously disturbed by the overlaying of images of the guru and the cult. The Oedipal relationships are doubled, as if the individual had had two childhoods and two adolescences that are intertwined and complicate each other — resulting from belonging both to a family, and to a cult. Analysis must take account of this interaction, complicated by the emotional trauma and guilt that accompanies leaving a cult.

Treating Neurotic States

Cults set up various rituals that are used as tools for mind control, but also as answers to the follower's feelings of psychic emptiness and existential concerns. Society is also invaded by these rituals. An argument prevalent among followers is that one ritual is as good as another, and that the cult's are as good as the outside world's. The ambiguity of therapy (typified in "de-programming") lies in the question, how to *de-condition* without *reconditioning*?

Behavioral therapy cannot do much, here; it is important to reinforce it with analytical therapies that can, initially, be supported by pharmaceutical elements, the only remedy for the depression entailed by the loss of these rituals.

Persistent obsessive ideas are a major obstacle to therapy. Whereas spontaneous ritual conduct (ritualistic phobias) is perceived by the subjects as a real behavioral disorder, the rituals coming from cult training are seen, on the contrary, as legitimate catharsis.

"Flashbacks" are often a problem. Comparable to a drug addict's LSD flashbacks, this is a spontaneous and unforeseeable return of memories of cult life for several minutes or several hours. The subject is then convinced he is back in cult life again. He feels thrown into a nebulous world, then in an unreal universe, before doubting his mental equilibrium. This phenomenon is in fact related to a specific stimulus that releases a system of stored memories; the stimuli and triggers must be identified. Hearing (songs, music) and the sense of smell (various scents) are sometimes responsible. "The odor of roses," stated an ex-member of Elan Vital, "plunges me into a state of dependence: I remember seeing the guru walking along the carpet of roses that we had to make for him." Sight, taste and touch are also responsible, but hearing and the sense of smell are more often the culprit. In any case, the usual treatments for classical phobias are appropriate.

Handling

It is fundamentally important that the therapist take note of the techniques used by the cult to which the patient belonged. This is necessary both in order to appreciate their role in activating the pathologies and to avoid using any therapy that would recall, even vaguely, the cult's handling methods. Information is also required as to the themes expounded upon by the guru, in order to isolate those beliefs that existed prior to enrollment. It is conceivable that a cult might merely reveal existing problems, but more often it provides elements that go into the construction of an original pathology.

Caring for a former cult member means reducing the psychic space occupied by cult philosophy and gradually restoring it to its original in-tegrity. Major technical problems are born from the obligation to break the barricades protecting the member from the outside world (enemy of the psychological space that was taken over by the guru). The risk of "de-programming," as it is conceived and practiced, is that it must bru-tally demolish the pathological stability provided by the cult ideology. The pathological structure can be obliterated only by upsetting the view of reality held in the sacred inner core, to the detriment of the latter. Next comes a phase of "empty thought," accompanied by tremendous anguish born from the loss of standards and landmarks. This period is followed by a phase of major existential doubt, during which the weakening cult thought pattern and the growing sense of reality are consciously con-trasted.

Lastly, once a logical thought system is recovered, the patient usu-ally starts to take stock, which can be very upsetting when the patient be-comes aware of his social folly. All these anxieties can set off serious pathologies (depression, psychosis, suicide, etc.). The necessary shatter-ing and then rebuilding of the inner core that had been taken over by the cult illustrates the weaknesses of "de-programming" and explain its fail-ures and its risks. Applied intensively (16 to 18 hours a day, for a brief period), it completely destroys the cult personality, but the process of re-building the personality is organized according to guidelines that are, for all intents and purposes, imposed by the "therapist" and influenced by those close to the subject. The danger of this method is that it makes sub-sequent analysis useless, and places the subject in a state of total depend-ence. The result is worse than cult alienation.

Post-cult care must, on the contrary, be conceived as a long term process; images can be substituted only gradually. Above all, it is essen-tial that the care fit within a framework of total cooperation between the subject's family and doctors. Much too often, families, upset by such an experience, try to solve on their own the social and medical problems raised by the reintegration of the ex-cult member. Likewise, the experts, psychiatrists and psychologists, far too often refuse to see the former cult member as a patient, and instead of acting in his true best interests they shelter him under the traditional argument of respecting his freedom of thought. Others mask their total ignorance of the phenomenon by behaving with more than a little condescension towards the cult members and their disoriented families.

Gathering Information

This is the basis of all forms of psychotherapy: one can only treat appropriately a case that one knows well. Still, this knowledge is not always enough; it would be illusory to claim to hold the key to all the problems with cults.

Each cult has its doctrines, each group its own practices. Preliminary work consists of collecting the maximum amount of information on the group to which the member belongs. This inquiry must be carried out from the very start of membership. At the same time, it is of utmost importance that those close to the follower do not break off relations with him, for two obvious reasons: the necessary maintenance of emotional ties, through which normal relationships can be born again, and the important information that can thus be collected. For family members, it is not only a matter of collecting newspaper clippings or second-hand testimonies, but of participating, as much as possible, in the cult's public meetings, seminars, and guest days. They should also pick up as many original documents as possible: brochures, letters, mailings. These documents will make it possible to get a good picture of the cult and its members. Admittedly, there will be gaps in the picture, but how can desperate families trying to get help from a doctor or trying to interest the public services in their problem get any help without providing the least bit of coherent information? Their anguish will not strike much of a chord among professionals, if their requests do not come from objective or irrefutable evidence.

One last recommendation: be as circumspect as possible, because when conflicts erupt between the follower and his close relations, the source of information dries up and an adversarial relationship may emerge.

This research is, admittedly, tiresome and trying. It is not easy to infiltrate these often aberrant groups, whose program is more likely to turn people off than to have much appeal. The hard part is to participate without cooperating. And without converting to the cult's way of thinking: there is a real risk of becoming too involved in the cult dynamics. The account of Julia Darcondo,[3] who tried to help her son and ending up converting to Scientology herself, is a good illustration of this danger. Therefore, one must take care not to regularly attend such groups without getting information in advance about the risks, and without making sure someone close to you knows what you are doing.

Synthesizing the Information

Once the information is collected, it must be used. First of all, we must distinguish the dangerous practices from the eccentric and benign activities. Several questions come up after that. Is the cult group part of a larger movement or is it completely autonomous? Is it part of a "federation" or a larger, widespread cult? Is the guru here or far away, does he exert his power directly or by proxy? What are the ideals preached by the cult? Do they reprise traditional themes promoted by recognized Churches or Schools? Are there social, financial, or professional dependencies? What are the rituals like? What non-ritual activities are a regular part of this cult, even if (or especially if) they are not openly specified as such? What contracts, loans, or oaths might the follower have committed to? Are there any agencies or organizations serving as fronts, or screens, for the group? Do they have affiliates or branches far away or in foreign countries to which the cult member might be sent?

Such questions help to determine, roughly, the nature of the cult and what techniques of conditioning are likely used.

Getting information about the cult is essential. More important still are the details of the follower's life. How long has he been a member of the community? How did he find out about the cult? What relationships does he have within and outside of the cult? What changes have been observed, from both the psychic and social point of view? How fast are these changes taking place? What are the subject's new habits (the hours he keeps, meetings, leisure activities, choice of reading material)? What have been the professional, social, family repercussions since he became a disciple?

Interpretation must be preceded by rigorous observation. The biggest problem posed in looking after a cult member is his lack of cooperation. All the information collected directly from him should be studied: decisions must be grounded in verifiable facts. That is what it will take, if the family and close relations want to preserve their credibility with the professionals called to assist them.

Interpreting the Information

The help of mental health professionals, well-informed about the cult phenomenon, is essential in this process. Indeed, too often the appearance of changes in habit and character in an individual who is participating in an unconventional group have been badly misinterpreted by his friends and family.

But diagnosing a psychic change in an individual is difficult to do. As for the causes of such a change, as we have said, it is hard to tell the difference between disorders that pre-existed joining the cult and those induced by the cult. It is even harder to identify any potential causality between practices and a pathology that combines inborn traits with elements that are wholly created or are modified by the cult. In addition, it is painful, even impossible, for a family to admit that it is completely or partly responsible for a pathology that led the follower to seek out and join the cult.

However, in many cases, psychoses worsened or brought out by cults are rooted in the family past. Further analysis of the disorders is difficult, since cults "doctor" the truth while caricaturing and blackening family relations. Interpretation must keep track of elements that are denied or hidden by the protagonists, relevant characteristics that existed prior to the cult and those added or revealed as a result of participating in the cult, and finally the elements voluntarily acknowledged in the cult's presentations, such as an anti-family ideology, for example.

Changes in subject's sense of the meaning of life and of truth, which devolve from the cult influence, further complicate the interpretation of his behavior.

Distinguishing Among Pathologies

After identifying them, the expert has to deal with each of the various pathological sectors. Personality tests are an invaluable diagnostic tool in navigating the intricate web of innate and introduced factors. While conversation is not usually enough to show the relative position of the various elements that make up the subject's new personality, tests such as Rorschach invaluable in determining the various influences to which the subject is, and was, exposed. They make it possible to take a snapshot view at one precise moment, and they make it possible to develop a medical strategy.

While the treatment of conventional pathologies responds reasonably well to more or less well-established forms of treatment, dealing with the pathologies induced by the cult depends on an open dialogue with the patient, and it must take into account the ideology of the cult. It varies from one cult to another. That is why a specialist is needed.

Reinstating Reality

Everything about the cult strives to distance the follower from reality and to envelope him in permanent fantasy. The first task of the therapist is therefore to bring the patient back to reality. To do that, one needs to know what techniques were used to create the rupture in the first place. Frequently, even after leaving the cult, the follower cannot distinguish between cult illusion and reality. The two-fold campaign of equivocation within the cult and the use of techniques of mind control usually preclude any real analysis on the part of the victim. Thus Thierry Huguenin, survivor of the massacre of the Order of the Solar Temple, was not completely convinced of the Oz-like character of the "divine manifestations" that he and his companions had witnessed, even when confronted with evidence of the hoax: a flashing electric sword, holograms simulating mystical appearances of the Holy Grail, etc..

The guru's image serves as a perceptual filter. To admit to being the victim of a hoax is to admit that one let oneself be fooled, sometimes for many years. This analysis is sometimes too painful to face.[4] That makes it all the more important to show the ex-follower all of the tricks, techniques and doctrines that were used by the cult. It is essential for the follower to understand the mechanisms of conditioning that were used against him.

In the same way, it is essential to make the follower understand that the techniques and the ideology are one. Often, the subject refuses to dissociate himself from the guru, the doctrines, and members of the cult, although he might dissociate himself from the techniques of conditioning. Even when he admits to being misled by the other members and acknowledges that the techniques used are a form of thought control, he clings to the idea that the doctrines are nevertheless valid and that the guru is a true master. This genuine sage must have been betrayed by his followers, his thought perverted by the group. . . To admit that the cult's ideology cannot stand up to criticism outside of the practices of conditioning, and that those practices arise inevitably from the will of the guru and his teaching — this is the first sign of the follower's real criticism of the cult, and thus of healing.

The ex-follower should be led to see the total similarity between the guru and the cult. The power of cults lies in their ability to be identified completely with the guru but to be detached when their interest depends on it. Thus, in the course of the lawsuits and the conflicts with its followers, the Church of Scientology variously identified itself completely with Ron Hubbard, or somewhat apart under the leadership of Miscavige,[5] or split up the responsibility among many. That is how all the cults in France operate today, assigning blame for any offence or crime to such and such member of the network, whereas the overall spiritual benefit is credited to the guru or the cult.

As the follower breaks the emotional and symbolic ties that attach him to the cult, he is confronted with a feeling of loneliness all the more painful since all his social functions have been changed and his world view has been destroyed. The follower has a natural tendency to expect an answer for everything during his sessions, which creates quite a problem for the therapist. The cult always gave ideological answers that did not allow for any analysis nor dispute; it drew an extremely rigid model of life and thought. On the other hand, the psychotherapist's goal is to give the ex-follower the capacity of analysis, judgment and free will that must govern his choices, along with the risks that those represent and the doubts that they generate.

The follower originally chose the cult because it offered a model likely to solve his doubts and anguishes. Therapy revives these internal conflicts and cannot offer reassuring models to replace the ones it endeavors to destroy in the subject. For that reason, therapy should give the follower an incentive to find answers to personal questions apart from the certainty and convictions of the cult.

The follower's natural tendency is to try to recreate a special relationship with a structure that holds some elements that are familiar and comfortable. Often, he will go from one cult to another. The subject should, on the contrary, be led to regain autonomy: autonomy of action, and also of thought.

The reintegration into daily life is all the more difficult since the follower has changed many of his basic habits concerning food, sleep, clothing, etc.. It is always difficult to lead the subject to re-think all the sectors of his life, but it is essential to make him admit that reality means accepting the "banality" of a normal life, made "petty" by the rites practiced by "most" people. Maintaining a banal cult practice, even if it appears neutral, is a door that leads to a new cult model or to backsliding toward the cult.

The follower must reintegrate himself in practices and socially adapted rhythms of life, while analyzing the potential danger of his old practices. Meeting with ex-followers is particularly effective, in that comparing the experiences often brings proof that the beautiful cult talk was just a lure.

Regaining Autonomy of Thought and Emotions

While fighting against the feelings of loneliness that accompany leaving the cult, the therapist must lead the subject to autonomy of thought and action, outside the control of any guru, master or spiritual adviser. The major feature of cult dependence is the loss of one's own thought; part of the healing is to re-establish it, to get back in touch with one's emotions and free oneself from the rules of "good behavior" imposed while in the cult. All cults aim at tempering primitive emotions to replace them with conventional behaviors. Once the cult's taboos and rules are gone, there is a vacuum in place of the frame of reference; the follower often has trouble controlling his newfound feelings. The person must be taught how to accept the return of perceptions, impressions, and feelings that were suppressed or erased when he joined the cult.

The paradox is that the return of primitive feelings often generates anguish, all the greater since the cult created simple answers to complex situations confronted by the subject. The final phase is a training for life, like a child going into adolescence or the pre-adult age. Thus every sector of the intellectual, emotional and social life will have to be re-addressed — questions as obvious as those dealing with death or sexuality having lost any resonance.

Primitive behaviors must sometimes be re-established and released, leaving the subject feeling sad or angry. Sometimes the follower has to relearn how to eat and drink when he is hungry and thirsty, to learn regular sleep schedules, to feel love without feeling guilty (since it was banned by the cult). It is especially necessary to re-teach him how to express his desires and to carry them out independently of all the judgments that were imposed on him.

The example of the Jehovah's Witnesses, where individuals with a normal sense of sexuality are condemned, is the standard case of the anathema that the ex-follower will have to face.

Reinstating the Follower in Society

Joining a cult is often accompanied by the loss of social status and professional competence. The longer he was in the cult, the harder is his reintegration. It is not rare to meet followers who, having spent ten years in a cult, have lost any capacity to do real work. However, it is essential that the ex-follower enjoys some social status and real medical care; that is the only way he will be able to take part in career training courses and achieve partial or complete autonomy.

It is necessary to act on two levels: the personal level of renewed motivation, and the social level of reintegrating into society. The ex-follower must be able to project himself towards a future where he has lost all systems of reference, from both the temporal as well as social point of view. For him, time has lost its value. The period spent in the cult changed his perception of the flow of time. He is often confused when confronted with daily schedules, like the duration of a therapy or a training course, even the simple prospect of an arrival time to be adhered to. Faced with the frustration born of the sudden absence of the dazzling answers the cult gave, he often expresses an impulse for the immediate satisfaction of his needs and desires, impulses that suggest infantile regression and his relative inability to work out a long-term plan. The rupture with the world is synonymous with the loss of social rights, employment and status, in the broadest sense. Moreover, frequently, ex-cult members are often not regarded as ill or handicapped and, consequently, do not have access to the benefits generally allotted to the invalid and the handicapped.

In that sense, the proposals made in Vivien's[6] report seem to us to be a vital, minimum set of standards essential to the reintegration of ex-cult followers:

> Social Security should be amended so that, as special cases, and after examination by an ad hoc committee, it allows benefits to be paid to people who voluntarily leave cults and who have neither public assistance nor sufficient incomes to cover the costs of the voluntary treatment (Proposal No 4).

With this intention, the Gest report of January 1996 recommends the creation of an office of governmental support for the assistance of former cult members.

In addition to these difficulties, generally financial, the follower must reacquire all the educational input required in order to rejoin society. Sometimes he needs to be registered for remedial schooling or training courses, which might also serve as social crutches; but they are often unsuited because of the age and the cultural level of the interested party, and especially because of the persistence of ideological aspirations generally incompatible with reality. The care of the ex-follower thus follows a precise chronology:

- emergency phase. Family and therapists make the decision for the follower, for and on his behalf, because of the risk he has incurred and because of his non-cooperation

- phase of psychiatric care. The therapist takes the lead, but requiring the overall collaboration of the subject, acquired gradually

- identification of the disorders and pathological conducts

- analysis of these disorders and interpretation of cult teaching

- combat the disorders by behavioral and analytical techniques

- analysis of the former personality, prior to joining the cult

- search for personal stability and identity

- possible family therapy

- phase of social reintegration: the family and close relations become preeminent.

Difficulties Encountered by the Family

As is the case for a number of mental and psychological disorders, it is difficult for the families to determine which behaviors are pathological and which are "socially acceptable" in the developmental state of a member that has been snatched up by a cult. Several attitudes are to be avoided, each one as serious as the next:

- underestimating the gravity of the process of cult subservience and hoping that the subject taken by the cult will become aware of his error and will have the strength and acumen to leave on his own

- wondering for too long about the validity of interfering, and feeling guilty about wanting to intervene, when in fact a very firm stance is required

- doing nothing, under the pretext of allowing the follower his own free will and free choice

- dramatizing everything from the outset, intervening without understanding, and establishing barriers between oneself and the follower, leading to a total break of relations

- leaving no other recourse than forcible intervention, having failed to take the opportunity to keep up a relationship.

The essential difficulty for the close relations will be to maintain the difficult balance between allowing the follower the autonomy necessary to his personal and social maturation, and maintaining a protective framework that is incompatible with his status as an adult. Forms of legal protection such as trusteeship or guardianship might be considered during the intermediate phase of the return to an autonomous social life. Similarly, French law allowed, in 1990, for the hospitalization of persons upon request by a third party. While these measures are hardly desirable, they must not be completely excluded for they very often represent the only effective tool against cult dependence and the psychic disorders that it entails.

Cult members' families positively must get help from society and not try to do everything themselves. Protecting and caring for cult members is a shared responsibility that calls for the devotion and the daily and everlasting patience of close relations as much as on the technical expertise of specialists.

Even if the technical expertise is not yet fully developed, there is a complete legal arsenal of which the family would be foolish not to avail themselves. Cult practices often infringe the penal code, civil code, labor laws or public health codes. Dependent members can take advantage of protective provisions, depending on the supervising judge; children or family law courts can intervene when couples or children are in danger. Government organizations have a role to play when fraud or negligence is involved. The tax department can be interested in a cult's undeclared sources of income. Every avenue must be explored, every element can be used, but this cannot be done on the word of one person alone. Therefore, families must develop a team of specialists, lawyers, psychologists, psychiatrists and public defenders[7] who have dealt in these matters before and can very often clarify the situation, if only by the information they have collected over the years. As for the ex-followers, their experience is irreplaceable, for they are very often the only ones to hold the keys, both in terms of arguments and behaviors, that give access to the prison of post-cult isolation.

Cults are a serious threat to mental health. It is important to be aware of their contaminating power, and the public must distinguish between religious tolerance and ignoring a person in danger. Even though some might caution against over-reacting or, more serious still, even contribute their skills and their abilities to guru, we must become aware that cult ideologies are totalitarian. Because of this, they must be fought as anathema to human dignity.

FOOTNOTES

Chapter 1

1. Séguy (J.), "Églises et sectes," *Encyclopedia Universalis.*
2. "Amway est-il une secte?," *50 Millions de consommateurs*, April 1983.

Chapter 2

1. Brissaud (A.), *Hitler et l'Ordre noir*, Librairie académique Perrin, 1969.
2. Sainte-Croix (de), *Le Vieux de la montagne*, Promothea, 1995.
3. Wach (J.), *Sociologie de la religion*, 1955.
4. *Hitler et moi*, interview with Otto Strasser, by Victor Alexandrov, *Planète*, no 30, September 1986.
5. Goodrick-Clarke (N.), *The Occult Roots of Nazism*, Aquarian Press, 1985.
6. Bergeron (R.), *Le Cortège des fous de Dieu*, Éditions Pauline, 1982. Vernette (J.), *Les Sectes*, PUF, "Que sais-je?," 1990.
7. Cotta (J.) et Martin (P.), *Dans le secret des sectes*, Flammarion, 1992.
8. Le Cour (P.), *L'Ère du Verseau*, Atlantis, 1937. Blavatsky (H. P.), *La Clef de la théosophie*, ECT, 1946. Bailey (A.), *Le Retour du Christ dans le Nouvel Âge*, 1938.
9. Barbarin (G.), *L'Histoire et ses cycles*, Astra, 1946.
10. Lovelock (J.), *La Terre est un être vivant*, Éditions du Rocher, Monaco, 1986.
11. "And the earth was without form, and void; and darkness was upon the face of the deep; And the Spirit of God moved upon the face of the waters." (Genesis 1:2).
12. See the rock opera *Hair* (1968) with its leitmotiv, *Aquarius*.

13. Ehrlich (P.) and Sagan (C.), *The Cold and the Dark*, Norton & Company, New York, 1984.

14. Ferguson (M.), *Les Enfants du Verseau. Pour un nouveau paradigme*, Calmann-Lévy, 1981.

15. Champion (F.) and Hervieu-Léger (D.), *Vers un nouveau christianisme*, Le Cerf, 1986.

16. Vernette (J.), *Le New Age*, PUF, 1992.

17. *Les Cahiers de Sarah, Survivre à l'an 2,000*. Éditions Atlanta, Canada, 1986 (distributed by the Order of the Solar Temple).

18. Hutin (S.), *Gouvernants et sociétés secrètes*, Flammarion, 1972. Ossendowski (F.), *Bêtes, hommes et dieux. L'énigme du roi du monde*, Plon, 1924. Gerson (W.), *Nazisme, société secrète*, NDE, 1969.

19. Nietzsche (F.), *Ainsi parlait Zarathoustra*, Gallimard, 1947.

20. Guattari (F.), *Les Trois Écologies*, Galilée, 1989.

21. Alphandéry (P.), Bitoun (P.), Dupont (Y.), *L'Équivoque écologique*, La Découverte, 1991.

22. Ehrlich (P.) and Sagan (C.), *The Cold and the Dark, op. cit.*

23. Mac Kibben (B.), *La Nature assassinée*, Fixot, 1990.

24. Barbarin (G.), *Les Destins occultes de l'humanité*, Astra, 1946.

25. Porquet (J.-L.), *La France des mutants*, Flammarion, 1994.

26. Riddel (C.), *Findhorn, 30 ans d'expérience*, Souffle d'or, 1992.

27. Huntzinger (J.), *Mieux vaut cru et en bonne santé ou les Quatre Vérités d'un naturopathe*, Éditions du Rhin, 1988. "Le grand bazar du bizarre," special report in *Le Canard enchaîné*, no 36, July 1990.

28. Bonewitz (R.), *Cristal de vie*, Le Souffle d'or, 1992 (or how to use crystals, which have lent mankind energy and "purification" from the big-bang to today).

29. Reichel (P.), *La Fascination du nazisme*, Odile Jacob, 1993.

30. Ferguson (M.), *Les Enfants du Verseau..., op. cit.*

31. *Rapport parlementaire sur les sectes*, Assemblée nationale, January 1996.

32. Finger (S.), "La secte qui piège les beaux quartiers," *Marie-Claire*, July 1992.

33. *L'Union*, 25 July 1995.

34. Dupuis (J.), "Les possédés de Beauvallon," *Le Point*, 29 April 1991.

35. See Darcondo (J.), *Voyage au centre de la secte...* , Éd. du Trident, 1987.

36. Marion (G.), *Le Monde*, 25 October 1994.

37. Faubert (S.), *Une secte au cœur de la république*, Calmann-Lévy, 1993.

38. Le Bé (P.), "Ces étranges conseillers d'entreprise," *Bilan*, no 6, June 1994.

39. "Le Groupement, une affaire au parfum de secte," *Le Revenu français*, 21 October 1991.

Chapter 3

1. Woodrow (A.), *Les Nouvelles Sectes*, Le Seuil, 1981. Darcondo (J.), *Voyage au centre de la secte...*, *op. cit.* Cotta (J.) et Martin (P.), *Dans le secret des sectes*, *op. cit.*
2. Le Cabellec (P.), *Moon ou Jésus*, BIP, 1972.
3. Taisen Teshimaru propagated the Zen doctrine in the West, without forming any movement except for traditional dojos that were entirely autonomous.
4. Chinmoy Kumar Ghose (born in 1931), founded the Sri Chimnoy Church Center in 1971. It obtained NGO status with the UN, which helped it to develop in its early years. He was a former disciple of Sri Aurobindo, who conferred upon him an evangelical mission for the countries of the West.
5. Mahesh Prasad Warna, born 1911, rebaptized Maharishi Mahesh Yogi, degree in physics 1940. Spiritual studies with Guru Dev starting in 1953, in 1958 he created a movement in the US that became Transcendantal Meditation.
6. Omraam Michaël Ivanov (1899-1986) in 1947 created the Universal White Fraternity, which replaced the Divine School (created in 1937), and claimed an affiliation with Tibet. The UWF purports to be a worldwide religion of sun-worshippers.
7. Cited in Renaud (P.C.), *Un nouveau ciel et une nouvelle Terre*, Provesta, 1981.
8. Miller (R.), *Ron Hubbard, le Gourou démasqué*, Plon, 1993.
9. Ron Hubbard (1911-1986), science-fiction writer, founder of the Church of Scientology, whose leaders were convicted many times over for fraud, violence crimes, theft, and espionage.
10. Miller (R.), *op. cit.*
11. Cited by Lasalmonie (A.) in *Dynamique de l'aliénation sectaire*, a medical thesis, Nancy, 1987.
12. Born in 1957, in 1965 Guru Maharaj-Ji took over from his father as head of the Divine Light Mission, founded a few years earlier in India. The *Mission de la lumière divine*, created in France in 1973, was succeeded by the *Centre élan vital* in 1987.
13. Abhay Charan Dee (1896-1977), an adept of the Gandiya Vaisnava Society, created his own movement in 1966 and took the title of Swami Prabhupada ("The Master before whom others bow down"). The International Society for the Krishna is directed today by 11 gurus. For twenty years, the sect has been convicted many times, especially for tax evasion and labor law infringements.
14. Sun Myung Mun, or Moon, born in 1920, founded the Association for the Unification of World Christianity in 1968. This "association" descends from other structures which he led jointly with Bo Hi Pak, a Korean lieutenant-colonel, military attaché in Washington. The political character of the former structures, in particular Radio Free Asia, and their obsessively anti-Communist doctrines give the impression that the development of the AUWC was largely supported by the CIA. Moon has been convicted on several occasions, mostly for sexual perversions.
15. Georges Roux (1903-1981), writer and postal worker, claimed to be the reincarnation of Christ and to have healing abilities. Upon his death, his two daughters created

The Universal Alliance to perpetuate their father's work.

16. Claude Vorilhon, born 1946, created the Movement to Gather the Elohim in 1974; this became in 1977 the Movement for World Geniocracy, then the Raëlian Movement. The essence of the ideology is to create an embassy to accommodate extraterrestrials (the Elohim) that Raël met in 1973 when he was "taken away" by a flying saucer.

17. Éditions raëliennes, 1983.

18. Founded in 1930 by Tsunesabura Makiguchi(1871-1944), it aims to apply the principles of the reformist Buddhist monk Nichire Shoshu. It has NGO status with the UN; it plays an openly political role.

19. The Brahma Kumari World Spiritual University was founded in 1937 in Karachi by Brahma Baba Lekk raj, deceased in 1969. Its main topics are those of a millenarianism based on salvation through a nuclear holocaust that would regenerate the planet. The BKWSU has NGO status with the UN and is an advisory member of UNICEF.

20. Rajneesh Chandra Mohar (1931-1990) took the name of Bhagwan Shree Rajneesh after being declared the reincarnated Buddha, then that of Osho Rajneesh (expanded consciousness) since 1989. After a period of success, Bhagwan's organization started to decline in 1985, after several lawsuits were lodged against the cult and it had been convicted of sterilizing several hundred women followers.

21. *Iso-Zen - Espace Futura - Résonances nouvelles* (tract).

22. *Qu'est-ce que la scientologie? (What is Scientolgy?)*, a propaganda piece distributed by the Church of Scientology, New Era Editions, 1995.

23. Extract from a consultation with Prof. Gallé on the procedure of purification (personal document).

24. CEA consultation (personal document).

25. Lasalmonie (A.) *Dynamique de l'aliénation sectaire, op. cit.*

26. Otto Mühl (born 1925) founded *AAO* (Aktion Analystische Organization) in 1976. He changed it into *Kommune* in 1979, then into *AAO-PVC* ("for conscious living") in 1980; he was condemned to seven years in prison in 1985.

27. Picard (G.), *L'Enfer des sectes*, Le Carrousel, 1984.

28. Lasalmonie (A.), *op. cit.*

29. Jorge Angel Livraga Rizzi (1930-1991) founded the International Organization of the New Acropolis in 1971, which came to France in 1973. New Acropolis borrows ideas from all the traditional doctrines and initiatory schools, especially for recruiting. The doctrines promoted by the cult preach the crushing of the follower's personality and his rebuilding in a élitist vision, and the purpose of saving the West from its degeneration. NA functions on a paramilitary model that strongly recalls the demons of the 1940's.

30. Livraga (J. A.), *Le Labyrinthe de Lapis Lazuli* , La Hache d'or.

31. Hanussen, *Pour vous aider à mieux vivre*, Vienna, no date, distributed by the Hanussen groups.

32. *Ibid.*

33. Lasalmonie (A.), *op. cit.*

34. Cited in Lasalmonie (A.), *op. cit.*

35. Raël, *Le livre qui dit la vérité*, Éditions raëliennes, 1972.

36. Harry Palmer, author of "Cours de magiciens avatars" (costing 40,000 francs for 10 days), is a defector from the Church of Scientology, which pursued him for illegal use of Scientology materials. He claims to have as unusual a background as his famous predecessor Ron Hubbard; he is supposed to have studied psychology, yoga, taoism, applied religious philosophy, TM, PNL, Ruani Satsang, Zen, sophism, etc. (*cf.* the leaflet on "the Basic Course for Avatars").

Chapter 4

1. Lambert (F.), *Étude psychopathologique d'une secte* , medical thesis, Nantes, 1985.

2. Livraga (J. A.), *Le Labyrinthe de Lapis Lazuli, op. cit.*

3. Morin (J.-P.), *Le Viol psychique*, Éd. Roger Garry, 1978.

4. Anzieu (D.), *Le Groupe et l'inconscient: l'imaginaire groupal*, Dunod, 1984.

5. *Ibid.*

6. *The Auditor*, no 168, according to Ron Hubbard, quoted in CCMM, *Les sectes. États d'urgence*, Albin Michel, 1995.

7. A speech by Moon, Pasadena, 1977.

8. Poinsot (M.-C.), *La Magie des campagnes*, Diffusion scientifique, 1957.

9. Freud (S.), *Totem and taboo...*, Payot, PBP, 1989.

10. Anzieu (D.), *op. cit.*

11. Assoun (P.-L.), "Freud et la Mystique," *Nouvelle Revue de psychanalyse*, no. 22, 1980, p. 39 to 67.

12. Remarks on Yvonne Trubert, extracts from IVI brochures. IVI (Invitation à la vie/ "Invitation to Life") was founded in 1980 around Yvonne Trubert (born 1932). Persuaded she had healing abilities, she claimed to be the reincarnation of Christ. She practices "Marian, metal and water" medicine and through her followers benefits from medical and scientist support, which may explain how this group continues to grow despite the public authorities, although the practices of IVI concern charlatanism and the illegal practice of medicine, and even the failure to render assistance to a person in danger.

13. Anzieu (D.) and Martin (J.-Y.), *La Dynamique des groupes restreints*, PUF, 1968, republished. 1990.

14. Ivanov (M.), *L'Amour et la sexualité*, Éditions Provesta, 1979.

15. See *supra*, note 20, Chapter 3.

16. See *infra*, note 18, Chapter 7.

Chapter 5

1. Association for the Unification of World Christianity, created by Moon (see *supra*, note 13, Chapter 3).
2. *L'Esclave d'amour de Dieu*, lettre de MO, DS 537.
3. *Ibid.*
4. *Allez dans les villes*, Lettre de MO, DS 927, 15 July 1980.
5. Bellenger (L.), *La Persuasion*, PUF, 1992.
6. *Stanislas de Guaïta*, Librairie hermétique, 1909.
7. Deutsch (A.), "Tenacity of Attachment to a Cult Leader: a Psychiatric Perspective," *American Journal of Psychiatry* , no. 137, 1980. Galanter (M.), "Charismatic Religious Sects and Psychiatry, *American Journal of Psychiatry*, no 139, 12 December 1982.
8. *Changements dans la personnalité des scientologues. Effets de l'appartenance au mouvement*, Diffusion Église de scientologie.
9. Stoetzel (J.), *Les Valeurs du temps présent: une enquête européenne*, PUF, 1983.
10. Galanter (M.), "The Moonies: A Psychological Study of Conversion and Membership in a Contemporary Religious Sect," *American Journal of Psychiatry*, no. 136, 2 February 1979.
11. Stoetzel (J.), *op. cit.*

Chapter 6

1. Bellenger (L.), *La Persuasion, op. cit* .
2. *Ibid.*
3. Sillamy (N.), *Dictionnaire de psychologie,* Bordas, 1980.
4. Brown (J. A. C.), *Técnicas de persuasion*, Alianza Editorial, Madrid, 1986.
5. Clark (J. G.), Langone (M. D.) *et al., Destructive Cult Conversion Theory, Research and Treatment*, American Family Foundation, 1981.
6. Carballeira (A. R.), *El Lavado de cerebro*, Editorial Boixareu Universitaria, Marcombo, 1992.
7. *Qu'est-ce que la scientologie?*, New Era Editions, 1995.
8. *Ibid.*
9. *Ibid.*
10. *Scientologie, Introduction à l'éthique*, New Era Editions, 1989.

Chapter 7

1. Sillamy (N.), *Dictionnaire de psychologie, op. cit.*
2. *Ibid.*
3. Carballeira (A. R.), *El Lavado de cerebro, op. cit.*
4. Ferrara (J.), "Quand la CIA lavait les cerveaux," *Science et vie,* no 855, December 1988.
5. Gordon (T.), *Enquête sur les manipulations mentales. Les méthodes de la CIA,* Albin Michel, 1989. See also Ferrara (J.), "Quand la CIA lavait les cerveaux," *op. cit.*
6. Gordon (T.), *Enquête sur les manipulations mentales. Les méthodes de la CIA, op. cit.*
7. *Psychiatrie et chasseurs de sectes,* a document distributed by the Church of Scientology.
8. Lasalmonie (A.), *Dynamique de l'aliénation sectaire , op. cit.*
9. *Ibid.*
10. Milgram (S.), *Soumission à l'autorité,* Calmann-Lévy, 1974.
11. *Ibid.*
12. *Ibid.*
13. *Jal nous parle: Liberté et Obéissance,* a New Acropolis document.
14. *Manuel pour l'École du minestère du royaume,* Jehovah's Witnesses, KS 81.
15. Bandura (A.), "Influence of Models' Reinforcement Contingencies on the Acquisition of Imitative Responses," *J. Pers. Soc. Psych.,* 1965, I, p. 589-595. See also, from the same author, *Social Learning Theory,* General Learning Press, 1971.
16. Wheeler (L.), "Toward a Theory of Behavioral Contagion ," *Psychol. Rev.,* no 73, 1966.
17. Festinger (L.), "Informal social communication," *Psychol. Rev.,* no 57, 1950.
18. Shri Mataji Nirmala Devi or the Sacred Mother (Mataji), former disciple of Shree Rajneesh, called Bhagwan, founded Sahaja Yoga in 1970; made headlines following the creation of learning centers in India for young children, who were totally isolated from their parents under the pretext of protecting them from bad in fluences.
19. The quotes are taken from various works distributed by Sahaja Yoga, in particulier *Nirmala Yoga,* a bimonthly published in Delhi, recycling Shri Mataji's writings and speeches, for the use of adepts.
20. Testimony of a Swiss disciple, Grégoire de Kalbermatten.
21. Testimony of a disciple.

Chapter 8

1. Hubbard (L. R.), *Bulletins techniques,* vol. II.
2. CCMM (div.), *Les Sectes. États d'urgence,* Albin Michel, 1995.
3. The thetan is supposed to represent part of a cosmic form of energy that materializes in each individual and carries information necessary to his materialization and his

life. Moreover, the thetan is part of an "extraterrestrial entity" that came from the planet of Xenu; it was frozen when it arrived on Earth, and appeared only after being reheated in the volcanos of the South Seas.

4. Article 11 of the Scientology sermons within the Sea Org.

5. *Dictionnaire de scientologie*, New Era Editions.

6. *Ibid.*

7. Freud (S.), *Totem and taboo..., op. cit.*

8. "Lettre de règlement," HCOB, 30 May 1974.

9. "Lettre de règlement," HCOB, 7 October 1962.

10. "Lettre de règlement," *Volume vert*, no 7, 15 August 1960.

11. Gruzelier (J. H), "Neuropsychophysiological Investigations of Hypnosis: Cerebral Laterality and beyond," in Van Dyck *et al*, *Hypnosis: Theory, Research and Clinical Practice*, Free University Press, 1990.

12. Brenman and Gill, *Hypnosis and Related States*, International Universities Press, New York, 1959.

13. Godin (J.), in *Le Journal de psychologues*, no 105, March1993.

14. Chertok (L.), *Hypnose et suggestion*, PUF, 1989.

15. Quoted in Barber (T. X.), *Hypnosis. A Scientific Approach*, Litton E.P., 1969.

16. Ranty (Y.), "La relaxation de Schultz n'est-elle qu'une thérapeutique magique?," *Psychologie médicale*, no 16, 1984.

17. Bhagwan, *Initiation aux exercices spirituels*, O.I., New Acropolis.

18. Collot (E.), "Hypnose et communication dissociée en thérapie," Cérisy colloquium: "*La Suggestion*," published by "Les Empêcheurs de tourner en rond," 1991.

19. Barmark (S.) et Gaunitz (S.), "Transcendental Meditation and Heterohypnosis as Alterated States of Consciousness," *The International Journal of Clinical and Experimental Hypnosis*, vol. xxvii, no 3, 1979.

20. Abraham (K.), "Développement de la libido. Études cliniques," *Œuvres complètes*, Payot, 1989.

21. Sri Chimnoy, *L'Enseignement du silence*, distributed by Sri Chinmoy, 1981.

22. Janov (A.), *Le Cri primal*, Flammarion, 1975.

23. Rouzé (M.), "Criez et vous serez guéri," *Science et vie*, no 817, October 1985.

24. Scientology term meaning: "the way to becoming 'clear'."

25. Scientology term meaning "electrometer reading," and by extension "level of perception".

26. Flylead from the *Hubbard's Course on the Electrometer*, New Era Editions, 1987.

27. Excerpt from the *Chansonnier acropolitain*, New Acropolis.

28. *Initiation aux exercices spirituels*, New Acropolis.

29. Excerpt from the entry ritual for Mouvement.

Chapter 9

1. Excerpts from *Dianetics*, New Era Editions, 1989.
2. Valatx (J.-L.), "La privation de sommeil," from the " Groupes totalitaires et sectarisme" conference, Barcelona, 1993.
3. Claude Perrotet's testimony, head of the Swiss Unification Church, in *La Tribune de Genève,* 22 May 1981.
4. Castaneda (C.), *L'Herbe du diable et la petite fumée* , 10/18, 1985.
5. Shallice (T.), "Techniques Used in Ulster during Heavy Interrogation and Their Relationship to Research on Sensory Deprivation," *in Cognitive Psychology*, 1973, 1, quoted in Lauret (J.-C.) and Lassiéra (L.), *La Torture propre*, Grasset, 1975.
6. Gross, Burchard et Kempe, "Sensorische Deprivation," in *Psychiatria, Neurologia, Neurochirurgia*, 73, 4, Elsevier, 1970.
7. Lamothe (P.), "Aptitude à l'isolement," 11e Congress of the International Academy of Legal Medicine and Social Medicine, Lyon, August 1979.
8. Porta (J.) and Cacciali (J.-L.), *Actions psychiatriques en milieu carcéral spécial. Droits de l'homme et contraintes de la personne*, Masson, 1980.
9. Massin (C.), *Une expérience du vedanta hindou en psychothérapie*, séminaire du Girad, Euthérapie, 1990.
10. Garanger (M.-C.), "Chamanes," *Actuel*, February 1993.
11. Gard (R.), *Le Bouddhisme*, Cercle du bibliophile.
12. Leaud (A.), *Amnesty International, un combat de l'homme pour l'homme*, Librairie des Libertés, 1983.
13. *Nouvelles de la Kommune*, no 1, 1976.

Chapter 10

1. Drandov (A.), "Scientologie, ceux qui se sont fait avoir," *Politis*, 28 June 1990.
2. A pseudo personality test made up from scratch by Scientology, described as "aberrant" by the National Union of Psychologists.
3. Bornstein Report, re-edited at the demand of Scientology, 27 June 1987; Carbonnier consultation 15 February 1982).
4. See Roubin (M.), *Prophylaxie de la pollution. Une proposition originale. Le programme de purification*, Paris-VI, 1988; Tzanck (I.), *Toxicomanie, désintoxication et réhabilitation*, Paris, 1985.
5. *Qu'est-ce que la scientologie? (What is Scientolgy?)*, New Era Editions, 1995.
6. HCOPL regulations, 5 October 1971.
7. Hubbard (L.R.), *Technical Bulletins*, vol. xii , New Era Editions.
8. *Ibid.*
9. *Ibid.*
10. HCOB verification list, 6 April 1969.

11. HCOB, 24 April 1969.

12. HCOB verification list, 4 December 1977 and 19 August 1987.

13. *Cours Hubbard d'audition,* in *Dianetics,* New Era Editions, 1988.

14. *Cours Hubbard d'auditeur dianétique,* ibid., p. 54.

15. Hubbard (R.), *Technical Bulletins,* vol. I, p. 153.

16. OSA: Office of Special Affairs. Scientology's information office, which the cult uses to gather information on, and to harass, its "opponents."

17. M E S T: The physical universe, a neologism based on M (matter) E (Energy) S (space) T (time). Thetan : an immortal spiritual being, the person him/herself, distinct from the body and mind.

18. *Self-Analysis,* New Era Editions, 1989, p. 62.

19. *Revue de l'Église de scientologie.*

20. Preface to the booklet on purification, New Era Editions, 1987.

21. *Ibid.*

22. *Qu'est-ce que la scientologie?,* New Era Editions, 1995.

23. Hubbard (L. R.), *Nouvelle Optique sur la vie.*

24. *Qu'est-ce que la scientologie?, op. cit.*

25. HCOB, 6 February 1978 R; HCOB, Re-Rev, 21 April 1983.

26. This technique was largely cited in the Bornstein Report, which was an amalgam of articles from various sources, coming from the Scientologic library, therefore open to question as to their impartiality. [Irresponsible] articles were later written, making reference to this report (that was drawn up by an eminent expert), but what is more alarming, medical theses were built around this obligatory reference. In other writings, specific uses of purification were defended; as in Isabelle Tzanck's *Toxicomanie, detoxication and rehabilitation,* which discusses the relevance of Scientology and purification in the treatment of drug-addiction, *via* the Narconon centers.

27. *Qu'est-ce que la scientologie?, op. cit.,* p. 189-195.

28. HCOB, 6 February 1978 RB.

29. Niacin = Vitamin PP.

30. Hubbard (R.), HCOB, 6 February 1978 RB.

Chapter 11

1. Solazareff, *L'Assation philosophique en voie sèche,* Aux amoureux de la science, 1985.

2. Moïse David, Lettre DS 927, 15 July 1980.

3. Roure (L.), Barte (H.N.), Carbonnel, "Rôle du mysticisme dans une approche psychothérapeutique de la maladie mentale ," *Psychiatrie Magazine,* no 5, June 1990.

4. Freud (S.), *Das Umheiliche,* [*L'inquiétante Étrangeté*], in *Essais de psychanalyse appliquée,* Gallimard, 1975.

5. Laxenaire (M.), "Réflexions sur la croyance délirante, *L'Évolution psychiatrique*, no 46-3, Privat, 1981.

6. Freud (S.), *L'Inquiétante Étrangeté, op. cit.*

7. Cité par Moreau (C.), *Freud et l'occultisme*, Privat, 1976.

8. Grosbois (P.), "Initiation et techniques psychothérapiques d'imagerie mentale," *Psychologie médicale*, no 16, 1984, p. 1231-1233.

9. The magazine *Ici et maintenant* from the Mission of the Divine Light, June 1978.

10. Speech by Gilbert Bourdin, from the show *Envoyé spécial*, by Cotta (J.) and Martin (P.), 1994.

11. Blandre (B.), *Mouvement religieux*, Aemir, 1979.

12. Cornuault (F.), *La France des sectes*, Tchou, 1978.

13. Miller (A.), *Ron Hubbard..., op. cit.*

14. Declaration under oath by Larry Wollersheim, trial against Scientology, Los Angeles, 4 February 1980.

15. Lasalmonie (A.), *op. cit.*

16. Testimony by Deborah, *Bulles*, no 4 (bulletin de l'ADFI), 1984.

17. Letter from MO, no 76.

18. Halperin (D.), "Psychiatric Perspectives on Cult Affiliation," *Psychiatric Annals*, vol. XX, no 4, 1990.

19. Dericquebourg (R.), *Les Religions de guérison*, Le Cerf, 1988.

20. *Ibid.*

21. Galanter (M.) *et al.*, "The Moonies: A Psychological Study of Conversion and Membership in a Contemporary Religious Sect," *op. cit.*

Chapter 12

1. *Diagnostic and Statistical Manual of Mental Disorders*, DSM IV, American Psychiatric Association, Washington DC, 1994.

2. The numbers given for each symptom correspond to the international nomenclature of psychiatric troubles established by the American Association of Psychiatry, *cf.* preceding note.

3. Generalized anxiety, DSM IV: 300.02; or atypical anxiety problems, DSM IV: 300.00.

4. Panic attack without agoraphobia, DSM IV: 300.01; with agoraphobia, DSM IV: 300.21.

5. State of permanent chronic stress, DSM IV: 309.81; or acute, DSM IV: 308.3.

6. Agoraphobia with panic attack DSM IV: 300.21; or without, DSM IV: 300.22.

7. Social phobia, DSM IV: 300.23.

8. Simple phobia, DSM IV: 300.29.

9. Psychosomatic troubles, DSM IV: 300.81.

10. Obsessive-Compulsive neurosis, DSM IV: 300.30.

11. Dissociative problems of Identity, DSM IV: 300.14. Depersonnalization troubles, DSM IV: 300.60.

12. Paranoid troubles, DSM IV: 301.00. psychotic troubles, DSM IV: 301.20.

13. Psychogenic amnesia, DSM IV: 300.12.

14. Psychogenic pain, DSM IV: 307.80.

15. Schizoid personality, DSM IV: 301.20.

16. Religious and spiritual problems, DSM IV: V62.89.

Chapter 13

1. Adès (J.), "Le concept d'addiction," *Neuro-Psy*, vol. IX, nos 1 & 2, January 1994.

2. Goodman (A.), "Addiction: Definition and Implication," *British Journal of Addiction*, 85, 11, 1990.

3. Darcondo (J.), *Voyage au centre de la secte..., op. cit.*

4. Huguenin (T.), *Le 54e*, Fixot, 1995.

5. In 1982, L. R. H. became increasingly ill and started to lose his complete control over the cult; conflicts within Sea Org led to the cult being into two, one part under control of David Miscavige, who created the Religious Technology Center, the other under the guidance of David Mayo, who founded the Advanced Ability Center, which was transformed a few years later into the Theta International Movement.

6. *Les Sectes en France*, Report to the Prime Minister, Documentation française, 1983.

7. France has two national organizations dedicated to these efforts: UNADFI, Union nationale des associations de défense de la famille et de l'individu, 10, rue du Père-Julien-Dhuit, 75020 Paris; and CCMM: Centre de documentation et d'action contre les manipulations mentales, 19, rue Turgot, 75019 Paris.

SUMMARY BIBLIOGRAPHY

On cults in France:
- *Les sectes en France. Expression de la liberté morale ou facteurs de manipulation*, Rapport au Premier ministre (rapporteur Alain Vivien), Documentation française, 1985.
- *Les Sectes en France*, Commission d'enquête parlementaire, Rapport au Premier ministre (rapporteur Jacques Guyard), Banon, 1996.
- CCMM, *Les Sectes. États d'urgence*, Albin Michel, 1995.
- Woodrow (Alain), *Les Nouvelles Sectes*, Le Seuil, 1981.
- Fillaire (Bernard), *Les Sectes*, Flammarion, 1994.

On the religious façade of cults:
- Vernette (Jean), *Les Sectes*, PUF, 1991.

On Scientology:
- Darcondo (Julia), *Voyage au centre de la secte : l'étrange impunité des voleurs d'âmes*, Éd. du Trident, 1987.
- Faubert (Serge), *Une secte au cœur de la République : les réseaux français de l'Église de scientologie*, Calmann-Lévy, 1993.
- Miller (Russel), *Ron Hubbard, le gourou démasqué*, Plon, 1993.

On Écoovie:
- Brewaeys (Philippe) and Deliege (Jean-Frédérick), *Écoovie, le mic-mac des services secrets*, EPO, 1990.

On the Solar Temple:
- Marhic (Renaud), *Enquête sur les extrémistes de l'occulte : de la loge P2 à l'Ordre du temple solaire*, Horizon chimérique, 1995.

On children in cults:
- Mountacir (Hayat), *Les Enfants des sectes*, Fayard, 1994.
- Pasquini (Xavier), *Les Sectes*, Grancher, 1993.

On mental conditioning:
- Milgram (Stanley), *Soumission à l'autorité*, Calmann-Lévy, 1990.

On how various cults operate:
- Cotta (Jacques), Martin (Pascal), *Dans le secret des sectes*, Flammarion, 1992.

Also from Algora Publishing:

CLAUDIU A. SECARA
THE NEW COMMONWEALTH –
From Bureaucratic Corporatism to Socialist Capitalism

The notion of an elite-driven worldwide perestroika has gained some credibility lately. The book examines in a historical perspective the most intriguing dialectic in the Soviet Union's "collapse" — from socialism to capitalism and back to socialist capitalism — and speculates on the global implications.

IGNACIO RAMONET
THE GEOPOLITICS OF CHAOS

The author, Director of *Le Monde Diplomatique*, presents an original, discriminating and lucid political matrix for understanding what he calls the "current disorder of the world" in terms of Internationalization, Cyberculture and Political Chaos.

TZVETAN TODOROV
A PASSION FOR DEMOCRACY –
Benjamin Constant

The French Revolution rang the death knell not only for a form of society, but also for a way of feeling and of living; and it is still not clear as yet what did we gain from the changes.

MICHEL PINÇON & MONIQUE PINÇON-CHARLOT
GRAND FORTUNES –
Dynasties of Wealth in France

Going back for generations, the fortunes of great families consist of far more than money — they are also symbols of culture and social interaction. In a nation known for democracy and meritocracy, piercing the secrets of the grand fortunes verges on a crime of lèse-majesté . . . *Grand Fortunes* succeeds at that.

CLAUDIU A. SECARA
TIME & EGO –
Judeo-Christian Egotheism and the Anglo-Saxon Industrial Revolution

The first question of abstract reflection that arouses controversy is the problem of Becoming. Being persists, beings constantly change; they are born and they pass away. How can Being change and yet be eternal? The quest for the logical and experimental answer has just taken off.

(MORE)

JEAN-CLAUDE GUILLEBAUD
THE TYRANNY OF PLEASURE

This provocative book stands our Sixties' liberation on its head, taking an inventory of its unintended side-effects. No, liberty has not made us happy. We have to re-think morality, and the family, and we must not let the Far Right dominate this discussion. No longer knowing very clearly where we stand, our societies painfully seek answers between unacceptable alternatives: bold-faced permissiveness or nostalgic moralism.

SOPHIE COIGNARD AND MARIE-THÉRÈSE GUICHARD
FRENCH CONNECTIONS
The Secret History of Networks of Influence

They were born in the same region, went to the same schools, fought the same fights and made the same mistakes in youth. They share the same morals, the same fantasies of success and the same taste for money. They act behind the scenes to help each other, boosting careers, monopolizing business and information, making money, conspiring and, why not, becoming Presidents!

VLADIMIR PLOUGIN
INTELLIGENCE HAS ALWAYS EXISTED

This collection contains the latest works by historians, investigating the most mysterious episodes from Russia's past. All essays are based on thorough studies of preserved documents. The book discusses the establishment of secret services in Kievan Rus, and describes heroes and systems of intelligence and counterintelligence in the 16th-17th centuries. Semen Maltsev, a diplomat of Ivan the Terrible's times is presented as well as the much publicised story of the abduction of "Princess Tarakanova".

JEAN-JACQUES ROSA
EURO ERROR

The European Superstate makes Jean-Jacques Rosa mad, for two reasons. First, actions taken to relieve unemployment have created inflation, but have not reduced unemployment. His second argument is even more intriguing: the 21st century will see the fragmentation of the U. S., not the unification of Europe.

ANDRÉ GAURON
EUROPEAN MISUNDERSTANDING

Few of the books decrying the European Monetary Union raise the level of the discussion to a higher plane. European Misunderstanding is one of these. Gauron gets it right, observing that the real problem facing Europe is its political future, not its economic future.